Layman's Bible Book Commentary
Luke

LAYMAN'S BIBLE BOOK COMMENTARY

LBBC

LUKE
VOLUME 17

Robert J. Dean

BROADMAN PRESS
Nashville, Tennessee

© Copyright 1983 • Broadman Press.

All rights reserved.

4211-87

ISBN: 0-8054-1187-9

Dewey Decimal Classification: 226.4

Subject Heading: BIBLE. N.T. LUKE

Library of Congress Catalog Card Number: 79-66204

Printed in the United States of America

Dedicated to my parents
Elizabeth and Oliver Dean

Foreword

The *Layman's Bible Book Commentary* in twenty-four volumes was planned as a practical exposition of the whole Bible for lay readers and students. It is based on the conviction that the Bible speaks to every generation of believers but needs occasional reinterpretation in the light of changing language and modern experience. Following the guidance of God's Spirit, the believer finds in it the authoritative word for faith and life.

To meet the needs of lay readers, the *Commentary* is written in a popular style, and each Bible book is clearly outlined to reveal its major emphases. Although the writers are competent scholars and reverent interpreters, they have avoided critical problems and the use of original languages except where they were essential for explaining the text. They recognize the variety of literary forms in the Bible, but they have not followed documentary trails or become preoccupied with literary concerns. Their primary purpose was to show what each Bible book meant for its time and what it says to our own generation.

The Revised Standard Version of the Bible is the basic text of the *Commentary,* but writers were free to use other translations to clarify an occasional passage or sharpen its effect. To provide as much interpretation as possible in such concise books, the Bible text was not printed along with the comment.

Of the twenty-four volumes of the *Commentary,* fourteen deal with Old Testament books and ten with those in the New Testament. The volumes range in pages from 140 to 168. Four major books in the Old Testament and five in the New are treated in one volume each. Others appear in various combinations. Although the allotted space varies, each Bible book is treated as a whole to reveal its basic message with some passages getting special attention. Whatever plan of Bible study the reader may follow, this *Commentary* will be a valuable companion.

Despite the best-seller reputation of the Bible, the average survey of Bible knowledge reveals a good deal of ignorance about it and its primary meaning. Many adult church members seem to think that its study is intended for children and preachers. But some of the newer translations have been making the Bible more readable for all ages. Bible study has branched out from Sunday into other days of the week, and into neighborhoods rather than just in churches. This *Commentary* wants to meet the growing need for insight into all that the Bible has to say about God and his world and about Christ and his fellowship.

BROADMAN PRESS

Contents

LUKE

THE GOSPEL OF LUKE

Introduction

The four Gospels are the heart of the Bible. The Gospels present the good news of God's revelation in Jesus Christ. The Old Testament prepared for this, and the New Testament declares and interprets it.

Each Gospel proclaims the same basic good news, but each has its own way of presenting Jesus Christ. Thus, each Gospel has an appeal all its own. Christians study all the Gospels with profit and enjoyment, but many of us have a personal preference for one Gospel. Luke's Gospel is my preference for reasons I hope you will see as you read this commentary. Basically, I prefer Luke's way of emphasizing God's love for people—for all kinds of people (see further under "Date and Purpose" and "Special Themes").

Author of Luke-Acts

One of the unique characteristics of the Third Gospel is that it has a sequel in the Book of Acts. Both were addressed to the same person (Luke 1:4; Acts 1:1). The conclusion of the Gospel and the beginning of Acts show clearly that they go together (see comments on 24:44-53).

Neither book names the author, but since the second century Luke has been identified as the person who wrote Luke-Acts. We know little about Luke, except that he was a Gentile (Col. 4:11,14), a physician (Col. 4:14), and a loyal associate of Paul's (Philem. 24; 2 Tim. 4:11). This information is consistent with the distinctive emphases in the two biblical books attributed to Luke. Also, the writer of Acts never mentioned Luke, but he included himself at several points in the story. The "we passages" in Acts show that the writer was a companion of Paul's at significant points in his mission to the Gentiles (Acts 16:10-17; 20:5-16; 21:1-18; 27:1 to 28:16).

Thus the evidence favors the theory that Luke the Gentile physician wrote Luke-Acts. By so doing, he made a significant contribution to what has come to be the New Testament. Luke's

Gospel is the longest of the four. Matthew has more chapters, but Luke has more words. In fact, Luke wrote more of the New Testament than any writer, including Paul. The apostle wrote more books, but Luke-Acts is longer than all Paul's letters put together.

Date and Purpose

Luke wrote his own introduction (1:1-4) which indicates that he was not the first to make a written record of God's revelation in Christ. Most biblical scholars believe that Mark's Gospel was written prior to Matthew and Luke (see comments on 1:1-2). The favorite date for Mark is about AD 65. If this analysis is correct, Luke was written after that time.

Luke probably wrote during the decade after AD 70. The events of that period match Luke's distinctive emphases. The Jewish-Roman War ended in AD 70 with the fall of Jerusalem and the destruction of the Temple. This proved to be a decisive date in early Christian history. During the period after Pentecost, all the followers of Christ were Jews. Then Jewish believers like Philip and Paul pioneered in taking the gospel to non-Jews. As a result, increasing numbers of Gentiles were converted. After AD 70 Christianity became predominantly a Gentile movement, and the percentage of Jewish Christians decreased drastically (see comments on 21:5-6,20-24).

How did a Jewish movement become predominantly Gentile?— This was a crucial question during the years immediately after AD 70. A distinctive part of Luke's purpose was to answer this question. The answer is more explicit in Acts, but it is apparent also in the Gospel.

Luke stresses the universal scope of God's love in Christ. The Book of Acts tells how the gospel was carried to the Gentiles under the leadership of God's Spirit. The Gospel of Luke shows that this always has been God's plan. Matthew traced the genealogy of Jesus back through David to Abraham (Matt. 1:1), but Luke went back to Adam (3:38). Simeon prophesied that the child Jesus would be not only a glory to Israel but also "a light . . . to the Gentiles" (2:32). The risen Lord commissioned his followers to preach "to all nations" (24:47).

Luke also stressed Jesus and Christianity as the true fulfillment of God's promises to Israel. Jesus came into the bosom of true Judaism. The people associated with his birth—Zechariah, Elizabeth, Mary, Joseph, Simeon, Anna—were the true heirs of the Law and the Prophets. So were the kind of people who followed him. These true heirs of the Old Testament recognized and welcomed Jesus as the promised Messiah (2:29-38; 9:20).

The Jews who rejected Jesus also rejected the noblest and best of their own heritage. The Book of Acts explains the hostility toward Paul as anger over the inclusion of Gentiles on equal footing with Jews (Acts 22:21-22). Luke 4:16-30 foreshadows this future rejection: initial rejection turned to skeptical questioning, and this in turn became angry rejection when Jesus mentioned Old Testament examples of inclusion of Gentiles. Jesus himself did not launch a personal ministry to the larger Gentile world, but he foreshadowed it in his ministry to the outcasts of his own society. He was criticized and rejected for this ministry to outcasts in the same way Paul later was rejected when he launched a mission to Gentiles (Luke 5:29-33; 15:1-2; 19:1-10). Jesus predicted a coming rejection of the gospel by many Jews and its acceptance by Gentiles (13:28-33; 14:23-24; 20:16).

Why should Gentiles follow a Jewish teacher, especially one who was executed as a rebel against Rome?—This was a crucial question for first-century Christians. They faced it whenever they tried to witness to an educated Gentile of the Greco-Roman world. Luke's basic purpose was to present Jesus Christ in such a way that people like Theophilus would know the truth and certainty of the good news (see comments on 1:3-4). He wanted to write a historically credible account that presents Jesus as the Savior of the world (2:10-11).

Luke, therefore, set the gospel story within the context of what was going on in the Roman Empire (2:1; 3:1). He presented Jesus as Savior, Lord, Son of God—all titles ascribed to the deified Roman emperors. Luke pointed to Jesus as the true divine Benefactor of humanity, who gave himself in life and in death. He is the risen Lord who can meet the deepest human needs. Luke used the words *save* and *salvation* more than any other Evangelist.

Luke dealt with the scandal of a crucified Savior. Jesus was executed on the charge of sedition, but the Roman procurator pronounced him innocent. In fact, Jesus' ignominious death actually was his greatest glory (see comments on 23:26-56). Long before he was crucified, the shadow of the cross fell across his path (2:35; 3:22). He freely committed himself to this way (4:1-13). His face was set toward Jerusalem long before he actually arrived there (9:51). His death was the inevitable outcome of a life of total self-giving and obedience to the will of God. The resurrection of Jesus from the dead showed that Jesus was indeed the Savior, Lord, and Son of God.

Special Themes

Luke had more than one purpose in writing, and he emphasized more than one theme. Here are some of the other distinctive themes found in Luke's Gospel.

Love for outcasts.—Christians believe that God revealed himself in Jesus Christ. Jesus' actions reveal what God is like. The Gospel of Luke shows God to be empathetic and compassionate toward people, whoever they are and whatever their needs (4:18; 7:13,22). This is especially seen in Jesus' compassion toward the outcasts of his day (7:36-50; 15:1-32; 19:1-10).

Women.—Luke presents women frequently and sympathetically (2:36-38; 8:1-3; 10:38-42; 13:10-17; 18:1-8). Jesus' treatment of women stands out in the male-oriented society of that day.

Holy Spirit.—Luke had much to say about the Spirit in Acts, but he also frequently mentioned the Spirit in the Gospel (1:15,35,41,67; 2:25; 4:14,18; 11:13; 12:12).

Prayer.—Luke's Gospel emphasizes the prayer life of Jesus (3:21; 5:16; 6:12; 9:18,28-29; 11:1; 22:32,42; 23:34,46) and Jesus' teachings about prayer (11:1-13; 18:1-14).

Praise.—Joyful praise is a distinctive theme of Luke's Gospel. The first two chapters record three hymn-like passages (1:46-55,67-79; 2:29-32). Luke also records many other instances of people praising God (2:20; 5:25-26; 13:13; 17:15; 18:43). In addition the words *joy* and *rejoice* recur throughout the Gospel (1:14,44; 10:21; 15:6-7,9-10; 19:6; 24:52).

Possessions.—Luke emphasizes Jesus' concern for the poor (4:18;

6:20,30; 14:13,21). Jesus also had much to say about the proper use of possessions (12:13-34; 16:1-31; 18:18-30).

Structure and Contents

Prologue (1:1-4)
I. Good News of Christ's Coming (1:5 to 2:52)
II. Preparation and Commitment (3:1 to 4:13)
III. Ministry in Galilee (4:14 to 9:50)
IV. Journeying to Jerusalem (9:51 to 19:27)
V. Final Ministry in Jerusalem (19:28 to 24:53)

This outline shows the overall structure of Luke's Gospel. Following the prologue are two introductions. One tells of the events related to Jesus' birth and childhood. The other tells how the work of John the Baptist provided the setting for Jesus' commitment to his ministry.

The first large segment of Luke's Gospel records Jesus' ministry in Galilee. Luke's account of the Galilean ministry is more like Matthew and Mark than is any other segment of the Third Gospel. The rejection at Nazareth (4:16-30) sets the tone for Jesus' ministry. Jesus ministered to the needs of people through word and deed. He called the twelve and began to train them. He faced increasing opposition from the Pharisees. The climax of the Galilean ministry was Peter's confession and Jesus' prediction of his own death and resurrection.

The theme of the longest segment of Luke is Jesus' journey to Jerusalem. The theme is introduced in 9:51 and recurs throughout. This segment, however, is not a travel journal; the theme has to do with Jesus' commitment to the way of the cross rather than with geography or chronology. Most of the material in Luke 9:51 to 19:27 is found only in Luke. Some of the most memorable of Jesus' teachings are found in these chapters: the good Samaritan, the prodigal son, the rich man and Lazarus.

The final segment tells what happened when Jesus arrived in Jerusalem. His confrontation with his enemies set the stage for his arrest, trials, crucifixion, and resurrection. Luke emphasized the reality of Jesus' resurrection and the difference it made in the lives of the disciples.

See the introductions to each section for more details about the structure of the Gospel. Also see the "Contents" for a more detailed outline of Luke's Gospel.

Prologue (1:1-4)

The opening verses of Luke's Gospel provide a brief description of how and why the Gospel was written. These verses are important not only for the study of Luke's Gospel but also for an understanding of the period in which the New Testament was written.

The Period in Which the Gospels Were Written (1:1-2)

Early period of writing about Jesus (v. 1).—Luke 1:1 reveals that Luke was not the first to write about what God in Christ had caused to be accomplished among the believers. Mark's Gospel was probably one of the writings that preceded Luke. The essence of over 50 percent of the verses in Mark is found in Luke. The percentage of Mark in Matthew is even higher—about 90 percent. Most careful students of the New Testament believe that Matthew and Luke had copies of Mark's Gospel. (See the commentaries on Mark and Matthew.)

Very likely, many of the writings were not what might be called complete accounts of the coming, teachings, ministry, death, and resurrection of Jesus. Luke 1:3 implies as much. Many of the early writings probably were about only one or a few aspects of the gospel.

For example, some of the writings probably recorded only Jesus' teachings. Luke and Matthew include in their Gospels many of Jesus' teachings—many more than are found in Mark. Some of these teachings are found both in Matthew and in Luke. This evidence causes many students of the New Testament to think that there was a written record of the sayings of Jesus and that Matthew and Luke had copies.

The testimony of eyewitnesses (v. 2).—The period of writing followed a period of teaching and preaching by those who had been with Jesus. The people of first-century Palestine were literate people, but they relied much less than we do on written communication. They were skilled at memorization. They and their forefathers had practiced this art for centuries. God used this skill in the early period of transmitting the gospel.

The apostles told and retold what Jesus had said and done. Others heard, learned, and told. Later some people began to write these things. During this period the apostles were on hand to be sure that others were speaking and writing the truth.

We do not know when the first written accounts were made. We do know some of the factors that encouraged more and more writing. One factor was the spread of the gospel to the Greco-Roman world. The Greeks and Romans were less skilled than the Jews at memorization. They relied more on written communication.

Another factor was the precedent of letters by Paul and the other apostles. Most of the New Testament Epistles were written before the Gospels. The apostles used this method of communicating the mind of Christ to persons in places the apostles could not personally visit at a given time. The extent of their influence thus was greatly enlarged.

The key factor in the writing of the Gospels, however, was that the era of the apostles was passing. As the apostles grew older and as some of them passed from the scene, the Christians realized that the witness and teachings of the eyewitnesses needed to be preserved in written form.

Luke and the other Gospel writers did not write something they had concocted on their own or some vision only they had experienced. They recorded the witness of the apostles, which had become the faith and practice of the Christian churches.

The Writing of Luke's Gospel (1:3-4)

Luke and his Gospel (v. 3).—"Therefore, since I myself have carefully investigated everything from the beginning, it seemed good also to me to write an orderly account for you, most excellent Theophilus" (v. 3, NIV). The word "also" shows that Luke considered himself in the same general category as the "many" (v. 1) who already had written. Why then did Luke write? What unique contribution did he hope to make?

For one thing, he wanted to write an account that was complete. His own research had included "everything from the beginning," not just one or a few aspects of Jesus' life or teachings. Luke's Gospel is longer and more complete than the Gospel of Mark. For example, Luke went back to the events related to Jesus' birth; whereas Mark began with the ministry of John the Baptist.

Luke, of course, did not literally include everything about Jesus in his Gospel. He, like other Gospel writers, was selective in what he recorded. He was a writer and witness, not just a compiler. Everything he had found in his careful research did not become part of his book, only what fitted his purpose.

Part of his goal was to write an orderly account. He wanted to take the things he had read and heard and to put them in an orderly account of the coming, teachings, miracles, ministry, death, and resurrection of Jesus. The word "orderly," however, does not mean that Luke intended an exact chronological sequence at every point. The word has more to do with a logical and meaningful flow of teachings and events than it does with exact chronology. (See comments on 4:16.)

Luke 1:1-4 shows that there is no contradiction between divine inspiration of the Scriptures and the full utilization of human skills and human processes. God used the careful research of a scholar like Luke, whose goal was to use a variety of sources as the basis for a well-written and faith-inspiring account of "all that Jesus began to do and to teach" (Acts 1:1).

The Gospel of Luke and the Book of Acts were both addressed to Theophilus (Acts 1:1). All we know about Theophilus is found in these two verses. The word translated "most excellent" in Luke 1:3 suggests that he was a person of authority, perhaps a government official. Theophilus may have been a convert who had been taught many things about Christ, or he may have been an open-minded seeker who had heard these things.

The certainty of the gospel (v. 4).—Luke wrote so that Theophilus would know the truth and certainty of the Christian gospel. Luke was a careful writer and historian of the life and work of Jesus Christ, but he was, first of all, a witness. In relatively modern times, some historians set as their goal to be purely objective in recording the events of history. Some of these "objective" historians were critical of Luke because he wrote from the perspective of faith. More recently, most historians have come to recognize that no historian is ever purely detached and objective. A historian's point of view always influences what he writes. Most modern historians strive to be as objective as possible, but they acknowledge the perspective from which they write. Luke was a careful historian, but he made no secret of his faith and of his purpose to seek to persuade others to have faith in Christ. (For other information about Luke's purpose, see "Introduction: The Gospel of Luke.")

Good News of Christ's Coming
1:5 to 2:52

The first major portion of Luke's Gospel is an introduction to the theme of good news. The word for *good news* in Greek is the word from which we get our word *evangelism*. The word is found in 1:29 and 2:10, and the idea is found throughout both chapters.

Most of the themes that are developed more fully in later chapters are introduced in 1:5 to 2:52: fulfillment of the Old Testament in Christ; prayer; the Holy Spirit; salvation as forgiveness; hope for outcasts; light for all people; the dawning of a new day; the prominent role of women in God's work.

The events described in 1:5 to 2:52 relate to Christ's coming. Jesus' birth and early years are intertwined with the birth of John. The relation between the roles of Jesus and John is one of the major concerns of these early chapters. John is the last and greatest of the prophets, but Jesus is the promised Messiah, Son of God, and Savior.

The drama of Christ's coming unfolds in seven scenes:
1. The announcement of John's birth to Zechariah (1:5-25).
2. The announcement of Jesus' birth to Mary (1:26-38).
3. Mary's visit to Elizabeth (1:39-56).
4. The birth of John (1:57-80).
5. The birth of Jesus (2:1-20).
6. Jesus as an infant in the Temple (2:21-39).
7. Jesus as a boy in the Temple (2:40-52).

The mystery of the miraculous pervades these events. Angels

delivered messages. A child was born to an elderly couple, and a virgin conceived and bore a son. These were people of a prescientific age; but they knew as well as we that what happened to Elizabeth was amazing, if not impossible, and that what happened to Mary was miraculous.

Some people think the Bible has miracles on every page. Actually the Bible is very judicious in its accounts of the miraculous. Most of the biblical miracles came in three crucial periods of redemptive history; the deliverance from Egypt under Moses, the encounters of the prophets Elijah and Elisha with the menace of Baal worship, and the events connected with the coming of Christ and the proclamation of the gospel in a pagan world.

The Bible declares the reality of a God who created heaven and earth and who is active in history on our behalf. Anyone who accepts this basic revelation has opened the door to the miraculous. Some people are offended and embarrassed at the miraculous element in the account of Christ's coming. Many of us would be more surprised if events of this cosmic significance were unaccompanied by signs and wonders.

An Answer to Prayer (1:5-25)

True righteousness (vv. 5-7).—Zechariah and Elizabeth represent the true piety that existed in Israel. They were righteous (v. 6) in the best sense of the word, not in the sense of the meticulous legalism that characterized some in Israel. They were of priestly families, but they were different in every way from the priestly families that controlled the Temple for their own advantage. Zechariah and Elizabeth believed in and practiced prayer; they hoped for the coming of the Messiah.

They are typical of the kind of people mentioned in Luke 1:5 to 2:52 as most closely connected with the coming of Christ. They, along with Mary, Joseph, Simeon, and Anna, were the true Israel of righteousness and faith. They were not wealthy or famous by worldly standards, but they were the salt-of-the-earth sort of truly godly people.

Rebirth of prophecy (vv. 8-17).—Zechariah was offering incense in the Temple when the angel appeared to him. Although Zechariah was an old man, this was his only time to perform this priestly service. Priests were chosen by lot to officiate at certain rituals; and because there were so many priests, no one offered incense more than once in a lifetime.

This would have been a high point in Zechariah's life under normal circumstances; but, as he officiated, suddenly an angel appeared to him. The angel told the terrified priest, "Do not be afraid, Zechariah, for your prayer is heard, and your wife Elizabeth will bear you a son, and you shall call his name John" (v. 13).

This does not mean that Zechariah was using his opportunity at the altar to pray for a child of his own. No doubt he and his wife had often prayed such a prayer; but as an officiating priest, Zechariah was praying for the coming of the Messiah to Israel. Zechariah's prayer and countless other prayers down through the centuries had been heard; God was sending the Messiah. His more personal prayer, however, also was being answered. The angel made this announcement to the elderly priest because he was to be the father of the prophet who would call people to repentance before the coming of the Lord.

The angel's description of John in 1:15 was a way of pointing to his prophetic mission. Being filled with the Spirit was often associated in the Old Testament with the work of prophets. And the Old Testament foretold a renewal of the Spirit and a rebirth of prophecy in connection with the coming of the Messiah (Joel 2:28).

The angel used the final promise of the Old Testament to describe John's mission. Verses 16-17 reflect Malachi's promise of the return of Elijah to call people to repentance in preparation for the coming of the Lord (Mal. 4:5-6). Later in Luke's Gospel, Jesus himself is closely identified with the work of Elijah (4:25-27); but John continues to be described as a prophet who fulfills Malachi's promise of a messenger to prepare the way for the Lord (4:25-27; Mal. 3:1).

Too good to be true (vv. 18-25).—Zechariah responded to the angel with a question reminiscent of Abraham's words under similar circumstances (v. 18; Gen. 15:8), but he lacked Abraham's faith. The angel's prophecy must have seemed too good to be true. He was not the first nor the last to doubt that God would really answer his prayers. Because of his unbelief, Zechariah was struck dumb until John's birth.

Elizabeth viewed her childlessness as a stigma; therefore, she rejoiced when she realized she was pregnant (v. 25). She already was experiencing in anticipation the joy and gladness of which Gabriel had spoken in verse 14.

The Miraculous Conception (1:26-38)

Like Zechariah and Elizabeth, Mary was not wealthy, powerful, or famous; but she was a person of true faith and integrity. It is significant that God chose such people to be the parents of Jesus and John.

There are a number of parallels between the announcements to Zechariah and to Mary. In each case Gabriel appeared and announced the birth of a son who was to play a crucial role in God's plan, a son who was named by the angel and who was to be born under unusual circumstances. However, in spite of the parallels, there are three significant differences.

Messenger and Messiah.—For one thing, there was a difference between John, who was to be a prophetic messenger, and Jesus, who was to be the Messiah and Son of God. Each was called "great" (vv. 15,32), but Jesus was by far the greatest. Notice the titles and descriptions of Jesus in verses 32-33,35. Verses 32-33 use the terminology of such messianic passages as 2 Samuel 7:13-16; Psalm 2:7; and Isaiah 9:6-7. Verse 35 refers to Jesus as the Son of God, a title later repeated by the voice from heaven at his baptism (3:22) and at the transfiguration (9:35).

Virgin birth.—The second difference is between a child born to an old couple and a child born to a virgin. The text is clear. Mary was engaged to Joseph, but she was not his wife. She was a virgin (v. 27). After the angel's announcement that she was to be the mother of the Messiah, she asked, "I am a virgin. How, then, can this be?" (v. 34, GNB).

The angel's answer in verse 35 is that the Holy Spirit would overshadow Mary in such a way that the child would be the Son of God. Some ancient stories told of procreation as a result of a union of a god and a woman. The language of Luke 1:35 does not describe God as the male partner in a sexual union; rather the language is that of Genesis 1, where the Spirit of God was active in creation. John's conception has its Old Testament parallel in Isaac, the child of promise born to Abraham and Sarah in their old age; but the conception of Jesus has its parallel in the miracle of divine creation.

Jesus was born to a virgin, but he was *born*. Some ancient stories told of divine beings that sprang full-grown into life. This was not the way God's Son came. He was divinely conceived; but once conceived, he was formed within Mary's womb and was born through the normal processes of birth. Thus there was a blending of the divine and the human in Jesus' conception and birth, just as there was throughout his life and ministry.

The virgin birth was not something the early Christians preached on street corners for all to hear, but something they told in hushed and reverent tones within the family of faith. They did not build their case for Christianity on this doctrine. When they preached to unbelievers, they built their case on the death and resurrection of Jesus (see sermons in Acts). However, when people became believers in the risen Lord, they could appreciate this account of Jesus' coming.

The handmaid of the Lord.—The third difference between 1:5-25 and 1:26-38 is the difference between the responses of Zechariah and Mary. Each was initially troubled and afraid, and each questioned how such a thing could be; but there the similarities end. Zechariah was struck dumb because of his unbelief. Mary, by contrast, believed. The angel told Mary of Elizabeth's conception in her old age (v. 36) and used words reminiscent of God's words to Abraham and Sarah, "With God, nothing will be impossible" (v. 37; Gen. 18:14). Mary responded with trust and submission to God's will (v. 38).

Exalting the Lowly (1:39-56)

Elizabeth's prophecy (vv. 39-45).—Mary hastened to visit her kinswoman Elizabeth. As soon as Mary greeted her, Elizabeth was filled with the Spirit and spoke as a prophet. She referred to Mary as "the mother of my Lord" (v. 43) and blessed her for believing God's word (v. 45). This scene thus reinforces the theme of the superiority of Mary's son to Elizabeth's.

Elizabeth's words in verse 42, like Gabriel's in verse 28, were used in later centuries to exalt Mary to a divine-like role of her own. This misses the point not only of these passages but also of the whole New Testament. Mary was a recipient of grace, not a source of grace.

Her blessedness was the blessedness of one who became a willing channel of divine blessings to others.

Mary's song (vv. 46-56).—Mary's response in verses 46-55 reflects humble trust. This passage is a kind of hymnlike poem. It often is called the Magnificat, its first word in the Latin Bible. The passage is made up largely of Old Testament materials, especially Hannah's prayer in 1 Samuel 2:1-10. Mary rejoiced that God had regarded her low estate. This was the basis on which she would be called blessed by future generations (vv. 47-49). What had happened to Mary was a sign of what God was doing among all people (vv. 50-53) and on behalf of his servant Israel (vv. 54-55).

Mary's song celebrated the reversal of positions that would come under God's new order. God's merciful help is given not to the proud, mighty, and rich of the world. Such people generally think they need nothing beyond themselves. People like Mary, however, are the poor and lowly who are open to God's grace and help. God's exaltation of Mary from her low estate thus was a sign of what God would do for his oppressed people and for all who are open to his grace.

The Dawning of a New Day (1:57-80)

His name is John (vv. 57-66).—The naming of a child had special meaning in Bible times. Verses 57-66 record the drama connected with the naming of John. Neighbors and relatives assumed the child would be named for his father, but Elizabeth and Zechariah remembered the angel's words and named him John. All of this was done in such a way that everyone who heard it was impressed. They wondered what special destiny awaited this child: "What then will this child be?" (v. 66).

Light in the darkness (vv. 67-79).—These verses provide a prophetic answer to the question of verse 66. Earlier Elizabeth had been filled with the Spirit and had spoken prophetically of Mary's child (vv. 41-45). Now Zechariah was filled with the Spirit and prophesied of the new day about to dawn. His poem or song is often called the Benedictus, the first word in the Latin Bible.

Zechariah spoke not so much of John as of the new day to dawn with the Messiah's coming. John was mentioned as the one who was to prepare the Lord's way, but Zechariah, like Elizabeth, clearly recognized that John's role was not the main one. He was "the prophet of the Most High" (v. 76), but he was not the Messiah, whom Gabriel had called "the Son of the Most High" (v. 32).

The first half of Zechariah's song, in verses 68-75, weaves together a number of Old Testament promises that stand fulfilled in the Messiah's coming. Using language reminiscent of the deliverance from Egypt, Zechariah spoke of a new visitation and deliverance by the Lord (v. 68). This would fulfill the promises to Abraham (v. 73), to David (v. 69), and those that came through the prophets to Israel (vv. 70-72).

The second half of the hymn has a more spiritual and universal tone. Words about victory over enemies give way to words about salvation in terms of forgiveness of sins (vv. 76-77). The analogy in verses 78b-79 is difficult to translate, but the idea seems to be that a sunrise is about to spread light over the world. Verse 78b says literally, "The sunrise from on high shall visit us."

Verse 79 expresses what the coming of Jesus Christ meant to the ancient world. The surviving records of that day show that the people dwelt "in darkness and in the shadow of death." Christ's coming was a light piercing that darkness.

The analogy likely was intended to include Gentiles as well as Jews. The universal note in Luke and Acts becomes clear later on. Luke probably saw this idea implicitly in the description of a new day spreading its light over a world where people cowered in the fear of pagan superstition, in the darkness of sin, and under the hopeless, relentless shadow of death.

In the wilderness (v. 80).—John's childhood is summed up in this verse. The last part of the verse is laden with anticipation. John went into the wilderness. There later the word of the Lord would come to him (3:2), and he would begin his call for repentance.

Good News of Great Joy (2:1-20)

Augustus Caesar ruled as emperor over most of the civilized world. He was honored as a great benefactor. Under his reign the world enjoyed a period of peace. Yet the first-century philosopher Epictetus wrote: "While the emperor may give peace from war on land and sea, he is unable to give peace from passion, grief, and envy. He cannot give peace of heart, for which man yearns more than even for outward peace." Luke 2:1-20 tells of the coming of One who could offer the kind of peace that lay beyond the power of the most powerful man on earth.

The fullness of time (vv. 1-7).—Luke's purpose in mentioning Caesar Augustus' decree (v. 1) probably was to show that God moves in the affairs of nations to accomplish his own purposes. The Old Testament tells how the Lord used Cyrus to achieve his purpose for his people (Isa. 45:1). In the same way God used the emperor's tax decree to bring Mary and Joseph to the place appointed for the Messiah's birth. The prophecy of Micah 5:2 is not mentioned in the passage, but it clearly stands in the background.

In Galatians 4:4 Paul referred to Christ's birth "when the time had fully come." His point was that God sent his Son into the world in his own way and at his own appointed time. People like Caesar Augustus may have thought they were in control of human destiny, but God was in control—using events to work out his own eternal purposes.

Heaven touches earth (vv. 8-14).—At many points in Luke 1:5 to 2:52 signs herald the divine intervention into history, but none is more dramatic than the angels' announcement to the shepherds on the night of Jesus' birth. Three verses focus on the significance of this unique event: verses 10,11, and 14.

Verse 10 is the angel's announcement of "good news of a great joy which will come to all the people." Earlier announcements had been to individuals personally involved in the dawning of God's new day—Zechariah and Mary. In Luke 2:8-14, however, the first public announcement was made.

Shepherds were among the lowest groups on the social scale. Thus the first public proclamation of the good news was to social outcasts. The choice was deliberate. Since the gospel is for all people, it was announced first of all to a group whom many would exclude from polite society. But God will not exclude them from the good news.

Verse 11 focuses on the One whose coming was heralded. Each of the three titles—Savior, Christ, Lord—is significant. The word *Savior* was familiar to Jews and Gentiles. It meant healer, deliverer, benefactor. It was a word often used of the great men of the day. Caesar Augustus, for example, was often heralded as a savior.

Christ means Messiah, the anointed one to rule as King in fulfillment of God's promises to David. *Lord* is the word used in the Greek translation of the Old Testament to represent Yahweh; thus it speaks of the divine nature of the One who was born.

The angel who spoke verses 10-12 was joined by a heavenly host who praised God with these words: "Glory to God in the highest, and on earth peace to men on whom his favor rests" (v. 14, NIV).

Some manuscripts have "peace, good will to men," but the best manuscripts have "peace to men of good will." The word translated "good will" is consistently used of God's goodwill, not humanity's. A paraphrase of this passage would be, "peace to people who are the objects of God's good will." The angels were not distinguishing a select group of people of goodwill on whom God bestowed his blessings. Rather the heavenly host praised God for his gracious offer of peace to all people. Thus verse 14 praised God for the good news of great joy to all people described in verse 10.

Witnesses of the good news (vv. 15-20).—The shepherds were not only the first to hear the proclamation of the good news, but they also were the first humans to tell others. They were quick to respond to the announcement by the heavenly messengers, and they were equally diligent to make this known to others. They also returned praising God for what they had seen and heard.

The reference to Mary's pondering all these things in her heart (v. 19) probably means that Luke considered her the source of much of what is told in Luke 1:5 to 2:52. (The same kind of statement is also made in 2:51).

Light to Gentiles and Glory to Israel (2:21-39)

The Temple was central in Israel's worship and hopes. The opening episode in Luke 1:5 to 2:52 took place in the Temple; so did the last two episodes. Luke 2:22-38 tells how Jesus was presented in the Temple as an infant.

According to the law (vv. 21-24).—Five times in this episode the writer mentions that Mary and Joseph acted according to the law (vv. 22,23,24,27,39). They performed three ceremonies prescribed by the law. They circumcised their eight-day-old son (see Gen. 17:9-14) and named him Jesus as the angel had instructed (v. 21). Mary went to the Temple for purification as prescribed in Leviticus

12 (vv. 22*a*,24). She and Joseph presented Jesus in the Temple, following the instructions in Exodus 13:2,12-15 about the redemption of a first-born son. Presentation in the Temple was not required in the last case, but Mary and Joseph felt it was appropriate.

The offering made for Mary's purification in verse 24 is the one prescribed in Leviticus 12:8 for those who could not afford a lamb. The passage, therefore, reveals that Jesus was born into a home of poor, modest means but a home of deep loyalty to the religion of the Old Testament.

The shadow of the cross (vv. 25-39).—Three times the text refers to the Spirit's influence on Simeon (vv. 25,26,27). As Elizabeth (1:41) and Zechariah (1:67) spoke Spirit-inspired prophecies before Jesus' birth, so Simeon (vv. 25-35) and Anna (vv. 36-38) spoke prophetically when the infant was brought to the Temple.

These two godly old people represented Old Testament faith at its best. Both of them recognized the infant Jesus as the promised Messiah. All the first believers were Jews. The Gospel of Luke presents Jesus as the Messiah of Israel, whom true Israelites recognized as such.

Simeon's prophecy in verses 29-32 blessed God for allowing him to see God's salvation, which God had "prepared in the presence of all peoples." This salvation would be not only glory to Israel but also light for revelation to the Gentiles.

This revelation to all people, including Gentiles, is one of the strong themes in Luke's Gospel, and even more so in the Book of Acts. This universal scope of God's salvation was implied in 1:79 and was made more explicit in 2:10, but 2:32 is the first clear statement of inclusion of Gentiles by name.

Simeon's prediction to Mary in verses 34-35 is the first connection in Luke's Gospel between Jesus' mission and suffering. For the first time the shadow of the cross fell across Jesus' path. Later in her life Mary often must have recalled Simeon's strange prophecy.

Anna's prophecy reinforced the basic thrust of Simeon's words. One of the characteristics of Luke's Gospel is the prominence of women. Elizabeth, Mary, and Anna are mentioned in connection with Christ's coming.

Verse 39 tells of the family's return to Nazareth.

In His Father's House (2:40-52)

Apart from the summary statements about Jesus' growth in 2:40 and 2:52 the only knowledge of Jesus' childhood comes from the episode recorded in 2:41-51. Some later writings told fanciful stories that supposedly happened in the years of Jesus' childhood and youth. From books telling of Jesus' childhood and youth, the early Christians selected as Scripture only Luke's Gospel.

As in earlier episodes, Luke's Gospel stresses the mystery of the human and the divine in Jesus Christ. This mystery constitutes the paradox of the incarnation. Jesus was fully divine; yet he was also fully human. He was born to a virgin, but he was born. He grew through the normal processes of human growth, but at the age of twelve he was aware of his unique sonship.

When Mary and Joseph returned to Jerusalem looking for the missing boy, they were astonished at what they found. Jesus was in the Temple sitting among the teachers. Teachers of that day combined methods of lecturing, answering questions asked by their pupils, and asking questions of their pupils. The teachers in the Temple were amazed at the careful attention, insightful questions, and wise answers of the boy from Galilee.

Mary's anxious question (v. 48) and Jesus' answer (v. 49) are the heart of the passage. Verse 49 may be translated either "in my Father's house" (that is, the Temple) or "about my Father's business" (KJV). The setting of the saying in the Temple makes the former more likely.

In either case Jesus' reply reveals an awareness of his unique relationship with his Heavenly Father. In her question Mary had said to Jesus: "Son, why have you treated us so? Behold, your father and I have been looking for you anxiously" (v. 48). The text is very careful to show that Jesus went with them and was obedient to them (v. 51), but first he gently yet firmly asserted his sense of sonship to his Father.

This brief glimpse of Jesus as a child forms a kind of bridge between the events connected with his birth and the account of his adult ministry. Throughout his life he was a respectful son; but as an adult he took up a mission that neither his family nor his followers

understood. The anxiety of his mother in the Temple thus foreshadowed much future misunderstanding as Jesus undertook to do
the will of his Father.

Some people wonder why Mary marveled at Simeon's prophecy
(2:33) and was astonished at Jesus' words in the Temple. She had
been intimately involved in the wonders connected with his coming
How could she ever be astonished at what he did?

This overlooks the fact that Mary did not have a clear understanding of how Jesus' mission would unfold. Like many others close to
Jesus, she was sometimes puzzled by the way Jesus set about to
fulfill his mission (Mark 3:21,31-35; John 2:3-5). She was a pilgrim of
faith who marveled as the drama unfolded, and sometimes, like all
pilgrims, she had more questions than answers.

Preparation and Commitment
3:1 to 4:13

Luke 3:1 to 4:13 is a prelude to Jesus' ministry. It has much in
common with Luke 1:5 to 2:52. Both sections serve as introductions
to the main body of the Gospel beginning at 4:14. The first
introduction tells of the birth and early years of John and Jesus. The
second introduction tells what happened just before Jesus began his
public ministry.

In each of these two introductory sections of the Gospel, events in
the lives of John and Jesus are intertwined. As the Gospel begins
with the announcement of John's birth (1:5-25), so Luke 3:1 to 4:13
begins with the ministry of John (3:1-20). This is followed by Jesus'
commitment to his ministry (3:21 to 4:13).

A Man Who Was a Sermon (3:1-20)

Alfred Plummer says of John the Baptist: "The whole man was a
sermon." Luke 3:1-20 shows how John was consumed with his

awesome mission. Luke tells of his prophetic call (vv. 1-6), his message (vv. 7-14), his words about the Messiah (vv. 15-17), and his arrest (vv. 18-20).

A Man Whose Time Had Come (3:1-6)

Called onto the stage of history (vv. 1-2).—Luke took special pains to set his Gospel within the framework of world history. Luke 1:5 begins with the words "in the days of Herod, king of Judea." Luke 2:1-2 mentions Caesar Augustus and Quirinius, the governor of Syria. Luke 3:1-2 is the longest historical reference. Luke mentioned Tiberius Caesar, Pontius Pilate, Herod Antipas, Philip, Lysanius, Annas, and Caiaphas.

Part of Luke's purpose was to help his readers date the events. There were several methods of reckoning the years of an emperor's reign. Estimates of the beginning of John's ministry range from AD 26 to 29. Luke's primary concern in 3:1-2, however, was to stress the worldwide significance of John's call. Luke was writing a Gospel about a Savior for all people. He wanted Theophilus (1:3) and other Gentile readers to see that world salvation was inherent in the gospel from the beginning.

Luke 3:2*b* picks up John's trail after he went into the wilderness in 1:80. The years of waiting and preparing were over. His time had come. He was called onto the stage of world history to prepare for history's most momentous events.

Preparing the way for the Lord (vv. 3-6).—John not only preached repentance before the Lord's coming, he also signified this message with baptism. The Old Testament prophets had used various kinds of prophetic symbolism. John's prophetic sign was baptism. This was a way of signifying repentance and forgiveness.

Several New Testament texts refer to repentance, baptism, and forgiveness (see, for example, Acts 2:38). John clearly did not think of baptism as a ritual that achieved forgiveness in itself. Baptism was a sign of the forgiveness that results from genuine repentance (see the comments on vv. 7-9).

All the Gospels refer to John's ministry by quoting portions of Isaiah 40:3-5 (Matt. 3:3; Mark 1:2-3; Luke 3:4-6; John 1:23). Luke, however, is the only one of the four to quote the words "all flesh shall see the salvation of God" (v. 6). This is consistent with Luke's emphasis on the worldwide mission of the Savior.

What Is Repentance? (3:7-14)

Baptism and repentance (vv. 7-9).—John's message was repentance. Baptism was its sign. This is clear from verses 7-9. These people came for baptism. They obviously needed forgiveness; John called them "a brood of vipers" (v. 7). Yet John refused to baptize them because he saw no evidence of repentance. Without a change of heart, baptism would have been a farce. It was meaningful only as a sign of genuine repentance. Repentance, not baptism, is what brings forgiveness.

When a Gentile became a Jew, one of the requirements was a kind of baptism. The Gentile immersed himself in water as a part of his entrance rites into Judaism as a proselyte.

John's baptism was different from proselyte baptism in at least two ways. First of all, John himself did the baptizing. He was called John the Baptist, which means the baptizer (Matt. 3:1; Mark 1:4; Luke 7:20,33). Second, and more important, John's baptism had a strong moral and universal basis. Proselyte baptism assumed Gentiles were outsiders who needed to be baptized in order to become insiders. John's baptism assumed that everyone needed repentance in order to be an insider.

He warned his fellow Jews about presuming on their ancestry. Claiming Abraham as an ancestor was no guarantee of being right with God. Apart from repentance, all people stand under the wrath of God as sinners. This applies as much to Jews as to Gentiles. The positive side of this is that God's power can create sons of Abraham. If he can do it out of stones, he can surely do it out of people, whatever their ancestry. Paul made much of this point (Rom. 2:25-29).

Changing how you live (vv. 10-14).—There is a striking contrast between the people of verses 7-9 and those of verses 10-14. The former group presumed on their ancestry and did not repent. The latter group were typical of those who earnestly heeded John's call for repentance.

The groups in verses 10-14 represented the moral and social outcasts of the day. The tax collectors and soldiers who enforced the tax were despised. Yet they were the ones who repented and were baptized by John, not the supposedly righteous and religious people of the day (see Luke 7:29-30).

John explained repentance in simple, practical terms. For the average person, repentance meant turning from a life of looking out for oneself to a life of sharing with others (v. 11). This meant sharing one's food and clothing with those who had none.

John was even more pointed in focusing on the sins of the tax collectors, who often were guilty of graft. They were told to collect no more than was due (vv. 12-13). The soldiers probably were Jewish soldier-police who helped enforce the will of the tax collectors. They had a tendency to use force to extort what was not rightfully theirs. Repentance for them included living within their own income and not taking what was not theirs (v. 14).

The Spirit and Fire (3:15-17)

John's activity aroused great interest and speculation. It was only natural that some wondered whether he was the Messiah (v. 15). John quickly denied this. In that day one of a slave's duties was to remove his master's shoes. Thus John said he was like a slave in comparison to the Messiah (v. 16).

John pictured his inferiority to the Messiah in two other ways: He baptized with water, but the Messiah would baptize with the Holy Spirit and fire (v. 16). He preached judgment, but the Messiah would bring the judgment (v. 17).

The picture of judgment in verse 9 was the Messiah with an ax poised to cut down the tree that does not bear good fruit. The picture in verse 17 is the thresher who separates the chaff from the good grain and then burns the chaff. John's understanding of the Messiah as a judge caused him later to wonder about the approach Jesus was taking. (See comments on Luke 7:21-23.)

The Truth Hurts (3:18-20)

Herod Antipas was one of the sons of Herod the Great, who was in his last evil days when John (Luke 1:5) and Jesus were born (Matt. 2:1). Herod Antipas was subject to Roman authority, but he ruled as tetrarch of Galilee during the ministries of John and Jesus (Luke 3:1). Both Herod and Herodias had been married to other people—he to the daughter of the king of Arabia and she to Herod's half-brother

Philip. Herod persuaded Herodias to leave Philip and marry him. Meanwhile he divorced his own wife.

A prophet like John could not be silent about such a flagrant evil by the royal couple. He followed in the noble train of earlier prophets like Nathan and Elijah. The truth hurt Herod and Herodias, so Herod added to earlier evils by imprisoning the bold prophet.

The truth also hurt John. He was jailed and eventually executed because of his commitment to truth. Jesus' later tribute to John recognized this quality of prophetic boldness (Luke 7:24-30).

Committed to Service (3:21 to 4:13)

This prelude to Jesus' public ministry shows Jesus committing himself to a mission of service and sacrifice. He made such a commitment in his baptism (3:21-22). His genealogy stresses his ties not only to Israel but also to all humanity (3:22-38). His resistance to temptations shows how he remained true to his own sense of mission (4:1-13).

A Voice from Heaven (3:21-22)

Luke's account of Jesus' baptism stresses that it happened when all the people were being baptized. This shows clearly his intent to identify with those he had come to serve and to save.

Luke also is our source for the fact that Jesus was praying when the Spirit descended and the voice spoke. This is consistent with Luke's emphasis on prayer, especially the prayer life of Jesus (see 6:12; 9:18,28; 10:21; 11:1; 22:32; 23:34,46).

On two significant occasions the voice from heaven spoke basically the same message. At his baptism the voice spoke to Jesus, and at his transfiguration the voice spoke to Peter, James, and John (9:35).

The words "from heaven" quoted portions of two important Old Testament passages. Psalm 2:7 and Isaiah 42:1 show God's approval of his Messiah (anointed, Ps. 2:2). Luke understood Jesus to be God's Messiah and Servant.

Later events in Jesus' life show that he saw his mission as a continuation of these roles. He intended his baptism as a public commitment to this mission. He was not baptized as others were—to signify repentance; he had no sins from which to turn. Rather he was baptized as the Suffering Servant who took his stand with the sinners he had come to save. The voice from heaven was a divine benediction and assurance on this mission of service and sacrifice.

A Mission to Humanity (3:23-38)

Matthew included a genealogy of Jesus at the beginning of his Gospel (1:1-17). Luke's placement of the genealogy may be designed to stress Jesus' unique mission, as he prepared to begin his public ministry.

Luke's emphasis is on Jesus' universal ministry to all people. Matthew's genealogy begins with Abraham; the emphasis is on Jesus as one who fulfilled God's promises to Abraham and David. Luke traced Jesus' genealogy all the way back to Adam. This shows that Jesus was linked by ties not only to Israel but also to all humanity. His mission was ultimately to all people.

Other differences between Matthew 1:1-17 and Luke 3:23-38 are more difficult to explain. Some of the names are different, especially from David to Jesus. Matthew traced the descent from David through Nathan, while Luke traced it through Solomon.

Several solutions have been proposed. One is that Matthew traced Jesus' lineage through Joseph and Luke through Mary. Another is that Matthew traced the royal line of David—those who would have been rulers had David's line continued on an actual throne—while Luke gives the line to which Joseph belonged. Still another proposed solution is that a levirate marriage had taken place by Joseph's mother. According to this view, Heli died childless, and his widow married Jacob. Thus Matthew lists Joseph's line through Jacob, his actual father, and Luke uses Heli, his legal father.

Matthew and Luke both clearly believed in the virgin birth. However, the normal custom was to trace a genealogy through the father. Thus Luke wrote that Jesus was "the son (as was supposed) of Joseph" (3:23).

Tempted As We Are (4:1-13)

Hebrews 4:15 says of Jesus that he was "tempted as we are, yet without sin." This statement underscores the reality of Jesus' temptations. Matthew and Luke record Jesus' virgin birth, but neither ties Jesus' sinlessness to being virgin-born. Jesus was sinless because he met and resisted temptation.

Jesus' temptations were like ours in that they were real, but his experience with temptation was unique in two ways: For one thing, only he resisted temptation and did not sin. He met temptation on the field of battle and emerged victorious. The rest of us at some points have yielded to the tempter. Who knows more about temptation—the one who yields or the one who endures? Surely it is the one who endures. Thus only Jesus really knows the full fury of temptation, for only he has successfully endured all its power and subtlety.

Jesus' temptations are also unique in another way: He was the Son of God committed to a role as Suffering Servant. Only he, therefore, could be tempted to compromise his mission. Each of us can be tempted to fail to fulfill God's will for us, but only Jesus as God's Son could be tempted to misuse his power for selfish ends rather than for God's glory and the salvation of humanity.

This is the clue to understanding Luke 4:1-13. Jesus had just committed himself to a mission of self-giving service that would ultimately lead to the cross. Throughout his ministry he would encounter many who would acclaim him as Messiah if he was willing to be their kind of messiah. Even his closest followers would misunderstand the lonely mission to which he had been called.

Therefore, before beginning his ministry he went through a period of testing. He was led by the Spirit into this time of testing (v. 1), which could strengthen his resolve for the task ahead. The devil, however, sought to make this a time when Jesus would yield to subtle temptations to abort his mission (v. 2).

Physical needs (vv. 3-4).—The first temptation was to use his power to meet physical needs. This was more than a temptation to feed himself miraculously; it was a temptation to embark on a mission to feed hungry people. After all, God had given manna through Moses during the Exodus. Should not he do the same as he launched a new exodus? Jesus' hunger reminded him of the desperate all-consuming plight of a world of hungry people. His compassion made this a powerful temptation.

He resisted by quoting Deuteronomy 8:3. As desperate as human hunger is, people have a more desperate need—a life lived in communion with and obedience to God.

Power (vv. 5-8).—The second temptation was to seek the power of a world ruler. The subtle appeal of this temptation—like the other two—was that it matched popular expectations about the Messiah. Many looked for a glorious king to restore and enlarge the glory of David's kingdom. The Messiah would be a king who would defeat Israel's enemies and make Israel a world empire.

The strength of this temptation was the element of truth in it: Jesus was the Messiah, son of David, heir to a universal kingdom. Jesus, however, knew there was a vast difference between his kingdom and the one many of his countrymen wanted. (John 6:15 tells how Jesus later refused to be such a king. John 18:36 tells how Jesus tried to explain this to Pilate.)

All devil worshipers are not people who literally pray to the devil or participate in some dark rite. For Jesus to have worshiped the devil would have meant laying claim to all that he could have had without regard for the will of God or the needs of others.

Again Jesus resisted by quoting a verse from Deuteronomy (6:13). Service to God demands wholehearted devotion. Just as worshiping the devil meant selfish grasping for power, so worshiping God means a commitment to God's mission of self-giving service for others.

Popularity (vv. 9-12).—The third temptation was to perform a dazzling miracle at the Temple. Many people were anxiously awaiting a Messiah who would perform spectacular signs. What better place to gain popular support than at the Temple, the heartland of national faith and worship?

Satan bolstered the third temptation with a quotation of Psalm 91:11-12: If Jesus was the Son of God, then God surely would not allow him to suffer harm in jumping from the pinnacle of the Temple.

Once again Jesus quoted Deuteronomy (6:16). He refused to put God to this kind of test. Faith is trust and obedience to God, not presumptuous grandstanding.

Verse 13 shows that Jesus had won a crucial victory, but that the devil found other opportunities to tempt Jesus with many of these same temptations. The temptations returned with a final fury during his last days (22:3,31); however, he faced temptation on more than one occasion during his ministry. At the Last Supper Jesus said to the disciples, "You are those who have continued with me in my trials" (Luke 22:28). The rod for "trials" also means "temptations."

Ministry in Galilee
4:14 to 9:50

Luke 4:14 to 9:50 records Jesus' ministry in Galilee. Many of the events of this part of Jesus' ministry are also recorded in Mark. Many of the teachings are recorded in some form in Matthew.

A wide variety of subjects are dealt with in these chapters, but three main themes run through this part of Jesus' ministry. Each ties in with later parts of Luke-Acts.

The nature of Jesus' ministry.—Jesus conducted a Spirit-led life of service to people. The way of the cross is implicit in this kind of ministry, and it became explicit near the end of this part of Jesus' life (Luke 9:22-23).

The response to Jesus' ministry.—People responded in different ways to Jesus' ministry. In general, however, initial popularity gave way to growing misunderstanding and opposition. This set the stage for ultimate rejection and crucifixion.

Witnesses to Jesus' ministry.—Jesus called and began to train his disciples. Most of them were from Galilee. These men of Galilee continued with him in the latter part of his ministry, and they became the core of his first witnesses after his death and resurrection (see Acts 1:11,13,21-22).

Ministry in Miniature (4:14-30)

At the beginning of Jesus' ministry, Luke recorded an incident that has all the basic characteristics of his later ministry—both his personal ministry in Luke and his continuing work through his followers in Acts. Jesus presented himself in his hometown synagogue as the Spirit-led Servant prophesied in Isaiah. Initial amazement turned to skepticism and demands for signs. Jesus then compared himself to Elijah and Elisha, whom God had sent to help Gentiles. The people of Nazareth reacted violently to this statement of a mission to Gentiles, but Jesus went on to do his work.

A Good Start (4:14-15)

These verses summarize three facts about Jesus' earliest days of ministry: (1) He ministered in the power of the Spirit. (2) He taught in the synagogues. (3) He was well known and highly praised.

The reference to the Spirit in verse 14 ties this to what precedes and to what follows (see 3:22; 4:1,18).

Jesus' early ministry centered in the synagogues of Galilee. These were the local meeting places for worship and religious instruction. Even in the early days Jesus did not confine his ministry to synagogues; however, as opposition grew, we read less and less of Jesus teaching in the synagogues.

What a contrast exists between his early popularity and the hostility that soon developed (4:28-29; 6:11)!

A Mission to People (4:16-21)

In his hometown synagogue (v. 16).—This verse gives us another bit of information about Jesus' childhood and youth. As he grew up, his custom had been to go to the synagogue on the sabbath day.

Matthew 13:54-58 and Mark 6:1-6 record a visit by Jesus to the synagogue in Nazareth. They place this visit later in Jesus' ministry. Because of this, some Bible students believe Luke recorded a different visit to Nazareth. More likely, however, Luke recorded the same incident. Luke's account is longest, but all three tell the same basic story with the same general outcome. Each Synoptic Gospel, for example, quotes the proverb about a prophet not being acceptable in his own country (Mark 6:4; Matt. 13:57; Luke 4:24).

The most likely explanation is that Luke's inspired plan for presenting the gospel story included using this incident as an introduction to Jesus' ministry. Luke's definition of "an orderly account" (1:3) did not include an exact chronological sequence at every point. For example, he told about John's imprisonment (3:19-20) before he told about Jesus' baptism (3:21-22).

The servant of the Lord (vv. 17-21).—This is one of the earliest records of what took place in a Jewish synagogue service. Later sources speak of two Scripture readings: one from the Law and the other from the Prophets. Jesus read Isaiah 61:1-2 and 58:6. This may have been a prescribed passage for the day, or Jesus himself may have selected the verses. The word "found" in verse 17 could mean either.

Verses 18-19 are among the most important verses in the Gospel. Only Luke records this summary of Jesus' understanding of his mission. The verses are from some of the Servant passages of Isaiah. The voice from heaven at his baptism had used language from Isaiah 42:1. Here Jesus referred to himself by quoting another Servant passage. Whatever the "servant" may have meant to the prophet and his first readers, the early Christians followed Jesus in seeing him as the ultimate Servant.

The Servant was anointed by the Spirit to help people. His was a mission of proclamation and liberation. The help was given to such groups as the poor, the captives, the blind, and the oppressed. Later, Jesus replied to John's question by describing his ministry in similar terms (7:22).

As was the custom, Jesus stood to read the Scriptures and sat to teach (v. 20). Verse 21 records the beginning of his sermon. No one but Jesus could have begun a sermon in such a way. He claimed to be the fulfillment of the prophet's words, and he claimed the fulfillment was a present reality.

His Own Received Him Not (4:22-30)

Skeptical hearers (vv. 22-24).—The initial reaction of Jesus' hearers was favorable. They were impressed by his speaking ability. Since verse 21 records only Jesus' beginning words, verse 22 may reflect their changing emotions as they listened. At first they were impressed; but as he continued, they began to wonder and raise questions in their minds. They wondered at the discrepancy between the man and his message: *They knew him. He had grown up among them. He was Joseph's son. How then could he be the Servant promised by Isaiah?*

Jesus sensed their skepticism and used two proverbs to illustrate their feelings. "Physician, heal yourself" (v. 23) ordinarily would mean that a physician who healed others couldn't heal himself. In this case, however, it meant that Jesus had healed elsewhere; why not heal in Nazareth? Jesus expected they would want him to prove himself by doing miracles at Nazareth as he had done in Capernaum.

The second proverb was, "No prophet is acceptable in his own country" (v. 24).

Sent to help outsiders (vv. 25-27).—Jesus followed up on the proverb about prophets by reminding them of two Old Testament prophets. There were many widows in Israel during the famine of Elijah's day, but the prophet was sent to a woman who lived in Sidon. There were many lepers in Israel during Elisha's day, but the prophet healed Naaman the Syrian. The widow and Naaman were Gentiles.

This was Jesus' way of responding to their demand for signs of wonder among his own neighbors. His ministry, which was as broad as human need, could not be confined to his hometown, nor even to his own nation. Jesus did not mention Israel's rejection in verses 25-27. However, when these verses are taken along with verse 24 the message is twofold: (1) As Israel often had refused its own prophets, so would they refuse Jesus. (2) As Elijah and Elisha had ministered to Gentiles, so would Jesus.

From worshipers to mob (vv. 28-29).—They became so angry that they ran Jesus out of town and even tried to kill him.

What turned this group of worshipers into a bloodthirsty mob? Jesus told how two revered prophets went to Gentiles rather than to their own people. The scene is similar to several episodes in the Book of Acts, especially Acts 22:21-22. Paul had been addressing the mob in Jerusalem. They listened until he told of his commission to go to Gentiles. Then they went berserk.

Going on his way (v. 30).—The significance of verse 30 is its foreshadowing of future events, its epitomizing of the outcome of a gospel for all people. Jesus passed through the mob and went on his way to complete his heaven-sent mission. This does not mean he always would escape his enemies, but it means that God's purposes will not be thwarted. Beyond his death was resurrection. Beyond the rejection by many of his own people was a mission to all people. Thus in a way verse 30 foreshadows the rest of Luke and Acts.

Mighty Works and the Word (4:31 to 5:16)

Jesus embarked on a ministry like that described in Luke 4:18-19. Luke 4:31 to 5:16 tells of some of his early miracles. These were acts of compassion toward persons with various kinds of desperate needs. The miracles also were signs of the good news of the kingdom of God. Most of the miracles involved Jesus' authoritative word; others involved his healing touch.

The responses to his early miracles were mostly on a superficial level. He was popular. Many thought he was a miracle worker, and they thronged about him seeking cures. The conflicts with religious leaders, which are found in Luke 5:17 to 6:11, are absent from 4:31 to 5:16. The people were not opposed to him, but neither were they committed to him. The outstanding exception to this was Simon Peter, whose response in 5:1-11 marks a crucial step not only in his life but also in the history of Christianity.

Power of the Authoritative Word (4:31-44)

"What is this word?" (vv. 31-37).—Capernaum, located on the Sea of Galilee, provided a kind of home base for Jesus' Galilean ministry. Luke 4:31-44 is centered in and around Capernaum. The events of 31-37 took place in the synagogue. He taught there in much the same way as 4:16-21 describes his teaching in the synagogue at Nazareth. The people were astonished at his authority (v. 32). They had heard many teachers, but Jesus was different. He did not cite others as authorities for what he taught. He spoke on his own authority.

While in the synagogue, he encountered "a man who had the spirit of an unclean demon" (v. 33). The demon speaking through the man called Jesus by name and implored him not to destroy them. The demon also claimed to know that Jesus was the Holy One of God (v. 34). Jesus' command in verse 35 resulted in the demon's exorcism.

Throughout his ministry Jesus often encountered demon-possessed people. He viewed them as possessed by hostile powers over which they had little or no control. The demons represented satanic power, which is always destructive to human welfare. Jesus had come to break the power of the devil in human lives. His miracles of exorcism are signs of the larger struggle with Satan.

Called to a larger ministry (vv. 38-44).—On the same sabbath Jesus healed Simon's mother-in-law of a high fever (vv. 38-39). By the time the sabbath ended at sunset, Simon's house and the street outside were as crowded as any doctor's waiting room. People with all kinds of diseases had heard of Jesus' miracles and thronged to him for help and healing. Although this happened after a long, tiring day, Jesus laid his hands on them and healed them (v. 40).

When day came, Jesus went away to a lonely place. Mark 1:35 says he went there to pray. The people followed him and tried to keep him from leaving the area (v. 42). Jesus' answer is important: "I must preach the good news of the kingdom of God to the other cities also; for I was sent for this purpose" (v. 43).

This shows that Jesus refused to have his ministry dictated to him by others. It also shows that he refused to have his work limited to one area. He intended to go to all the Jewish territory (see "Judea" in v. 44). Later his followers would be told to go into all the world with the good news.

The incident also shows Jesus did not want to be known primarily as a miracle-worker. He performed some miracles as acts of compassion and as signs of the kingdom, but he had come to preach and make real the good news of God's grace and presence.

Basic Steps in Following Jesus (5:1-11)

Obedience (vv. 1-5).—Simon already had some kind of relationship with Jesus, but until this incident he was basically a fisherman. He fished as a business, not as a hobby; and he was good at it. He and his partners James and John were successful owners of a fishing business.

Jesus' command in verse 4 probably took Peter by surprise. His answer is typical of Peter's later responses to Jesus. He said what he thought, but he ended up doing as Jesus commanded.

Confession (vv. 6-8).—The miracle of the great shoal of fish overwhelmed not only Peter's nets and boats but also Peter himself. It brought together much of what Peter already had been feeling. He had observed Jesus' earlier miracles as a result of Jesus' authoritative word. This plus the power of Jesus' presence brought Simon to his knees.

His confession in verse 8 is reminiscent of Isaiah's words in Isaiah 6:5. At this moment of special closeness to Jesus, Peter felt keenly the difference between himself and Jesus. The grace and power of Jesus produced in him a deep sense of his own sinfulness. Overwhelmed with his own unworthiness, Peter asked Jesus to depart from him.

Commitment (vv. 9-11).—Fortunately for Peter, Jesus did not go away. Instead he spoke words of comfort and challenge. He dealt kindly with Peter's fear and agitation of spirit. Then he called Peter to become a different kind of fisherman. No longer was he to catch fish. Now he was to catch human beings.

One of the themes in Luke's Gospel is Jesus' acceptance of the unacceptable. This was Peter's experience. The acceptance was seen not only in Jesus' words of assurance but also in his words calling Peter to service. This is typical of God's amazing grace. Not only does he accept us into his presence, but he also calls us to serve him.

Peter's response was total commitment (v. 11). He probably already had been wrestling with this decision. Peter was established in business. He was married. He had a house. Giving up his business to follow Jesus was not easy, but his experience with Jesus brought him to the point of commitment. The die was cast. He cut his ties with the past. From now on he would follow Jesus.

We know from what happened later that this was only the first step in Peter's pilgrimage as a disciple, but it was a crucial step. There can be no pilgrimage without a beginning.

Touching the Untouchable (5:12-16)

No group in ancient society was more pitiful than lepers. Their disease was a slow, lingering death. They died inch by inch. And to make matters worse they were cut off from any contact with the rest of society, including their own families. Nothing but a corpse was more unclean than a leper. Yet Jesus dared to touch the leper and to speak the authoritative word that caused him to be cured. This is another example of Jesus' acceptance of the unacceptable.

Although Jesus asked the leper not to tell anyone except the priest, word got out, and multitudes flocked to him to hear and be healed. Jesus withdrew and prayed (v. 16). This again shows his reluctance to be known primarily as a miracle worker.

The "Sins" of Jesus (5:17 to 6:11)

The testimony of the New Testament is that Jesus was without sin. His opponents, however, accused him of a number of sins. Luke 5:17 to 6:11 records confrontations over four issues: forgiveness of sins, associating with sinners, fasting, and the sabbath.

Blasphemy (5:17-26)

A delegation of dignitaries (v. 17).—A new element is introduced in verse 17. Pharisees and teachers of the law showed up to hear and observe Jesus. They came from all over Galilee and Judea, including Jerusalem itself. No sinister intent is mentioned, but these religious leaders became Jesus' severest critics.

The Pharisees were a leading Jewish party of that day. They believed in a strict keeping of the law, as interpreted in their own traditions. They were separatists who sought to avoid contact with unclean things and unclean people. The teachers of the law, also called scribes (v. 21), were professional students of the law. Most of them were Pharisees.

Sins forgiven (vv. 18-20).—Why did Jesus deal with the man's sins before healing him? One possibility is that there was some connection—either real or imagined—between the man's physical plight and his sins. Many people in that day assumed such a connection (John 9:2). A more likely explanation, however, is that Jesus dealt with his sins first because that was the man's basic need. Jesus was concerned about the total person, but at the heart of human need is the problem of sin and guilt. His healings were signs of salvation from the moral and spiritual sickness of sin.

Blasphemer or Savior? (vv. 21-26).—The scribes and Pharisees accused Jesus of blasphemy. He claimed to be able to do something only God can do—forgive sins. They would have been right if Jesus were just another person. Any person who claimed to be God would be guilty of blasphemy—unless that person was the Messiah, Son of God. Jesus was not guilty of blasphemy precisely because he acted with divine authority to declare sins forgiven. He said, "The Son of man has authority on earth to forgive sins" (v. 24).

Jesus was obviously claiming for himself divine prerogatives, but he did not use any of the popular messianic titles. Instead he referred to himself as Son of man. Luke 5:24 is the first use of this title in Luke. Jesus used this title more than any other when he was speaking of who he was. He probably avoided the popular titles because the people had preconceived notions about what these titles meant. Jesus was able to take the less familiar title "Son of man" and fill it with his own meaning.

Some people assume this title stresses the humanity of Jesus while the title "Son of God" stresses his deity. As used in the New Testament, both titles include humanity and deity. Here, for example, Jesus used the title to declare his divine authority to forgive sins. Overall, Jesus used the title to stress two aspects of his redemptive work—death and resurrection (Luke 9:22). On one hand, the Son of man is a humble sufferer who seems weak and powerless; on the other hand, he is vindicated and glorified in divine power (Luke 9:26; see also Dan. 7:13).

Associating with Sinners (5:27-32)

Luke presents Jesus as the friend of sinners. He freely associated with all kinds of people. This placed him on a collision course with the Pharisees.

The first collision came after Jesus accepted Levi's dinner invitation (v. 29). Table fellowship is one of the closest forms of human association. The Pharisees, however, believed in close associations only with people who rigidly observed the laws about ritual cleanliness.

Two groups were guests of Levi, and neither group met the Pharisees' qualifications. The tax collectors were outcasts from respectable society. They were collaborators with a foreign-dominated government. Many of them were guilty of using their power to extort money for themselves. They had daily contact with all kinds of other "unclean" people. The word "sinners" here means the common people who paid little heed to the religious scruples of the Pharisees.

Someone has said that the Pharisees believed in salvation by separation while Jesus practiced salvation by association. The Pharisees made every effort to separate themselves from others. They would receive sinners, but only after the sinners repented and became Pharisees. Jesus befriended sinners. He did not become a sinner, but he associated with sinners in order to help them find the way to God and new life.

Jesus used the analogy of the physician who goes where the sick people are (v. 31). There is some irony in his use of the word "righteous" in verse 32. On occasion, Jesus tried to help the Pharisees see that they too needed to repent (Luke 11:39-52). However, in verse 32 he left it to the Pharisees to see this for themselves.

Jesus' attempt to help the Pharisees recognize that their attitude toward "sinners" was one of their own worst sins is recorded later in the Gospel of Luke. After being criticized by them for eating with sinners (Luke 15:2), Jesus told them not only about the sinful prodigal son but also about the peevish elder brother (15:11-32). They called him a sinner for associating with sinners; he called them sinners for not doing so.

Neglecting Religious Disciplines (5:33-39)

Fast or feast? (vv. 33-35).—The Old Testament required only one time of fasting, in connection with the Day of Atonement (Lev. 16:29). Voluntary fasting during a crisis also was practiced. Pious Pharisees, however, fasted twice each week (Luke 18:12). They apparently viewed fasting as a mark of special commitment and dedication. They were critical of Jesus because his followers did not fast (v. 33).

Jesus explained that fasting during a wedding is inappropriate (v. 34). The Bible refers to the messianic age as a wedding feast. This was Jesus' way of claiming to be the Bridegroom for whom the feast is held.

They accused Jesus of frivolity and neglecting basic spiritual disciplines. Jesus on occasion fasted, and he often spent time in prayer. However, he did not make fasting into a prescribed ritual. The kind of fasting he practiced was a natural fasting that resulted from preoccupation with more important matters (see John 4:31-34).

The old and the new (vv. 36-39).—Jesus broadened the application with another analogy, which Luke called a parable. The issue was the relationship between the new way of Jesus and the old way of Judaism. Jesus' way cannot simply be patched onto Judaism like a piece of cloth (v. 36).

Jesus also used the analogy of old and new wine. Pouring the new way of the gospel into the wineskins of Judaism would result in spilling the new wine and ruining the old wineskins (vv. 37-38).

Only Luke records verse 39. Jesus seems to have been speaking to those who cling to the old. They argue that religion is like wine; the old is best.

Sabbath-Breaking (6:1-11)

Lord of the sabbath (vv. 1-5).—During the Interbiblical Period, keeping the sabbath became one of the most obvious marks of a believer in the God of the Old Testament. It was near the top of the list of pharisaic virtues. As in other areas, the Pharisees had their own rigid definitions and requirements.

They were determined to avoid even the appearance of working on the sabbath. They had developed a meticulous list of things that constituted work. The disciples ran afoul of this list by plucking grain and rubbing it in their hands (vv. 1-2). To the Pharisees, this was harvesting and threshing.

Jesus kept the sabbath as the Old Testament had intended (Luke 4:16), but he made no effort to conform to the rigid scruples of the Pharisees. He referred the critics to the example of David. When David was desperately hungry, he broke the law by eating the bread of the Presence (vv. 3-4). If David could do this, how much more could the Son of David? Jesus did not use that title, but that seems to have been his point.

Verse 5 is clear enough: "The Son of man is lord of the sabbath." Just as the Son of man had authority to forgive sins (5:24), so did he have authority over the sabbath.

Doing good on the sabbath (vv. 6-11).—Mark's account of the preceding incident includes the saying of Jesus "The sabbath was made for man, not man for the sabbath" (Mark 2:27). Luke does not record this saying, but Luke 6:6-11 makes the same point. (See the comments on Luke 13:10-17).

On this occasion Jesus did not wait for his critics to launch their attack; he took the offensive and put them on the spot. He called to his side a man with a withered hand (v. 8). According to the Pharisees, healing on the sabbath was wrong unless there was an actual danger to life itself. This man's case was not such an emergency, so they would want healing to be put off till the next day.

Jesus asked them, "Is it lawful on the sabbath to do good or to do harm, to save life or to destroy it?" (v. 9). Even their tradition allowed treatment of emergency cases. In other words, even they could not deny that it was lawful on the sabbath to save life and prevent death. Jesus took this principle and applied it more broadly to helping rather than harming. He stated the question in such a way that they couldn't afford to answer his question. Therefore, Jesus proceeded to heal the man (v. 10). They had focused all their attention on the negatives—what *not* to do on the sabbath. Jesus focused on the positives.

The original intent of the sabbath was to provide a day of rest that would free people from the tyranny of a life of ceaseless toil. In other words, God instituted the sabbath for the good of humanity. Any set of rules that thwarts God's purpose deserves to be treated as Jesus treated the tradition about not healing on the sabbath. Doing good is always in season.

Verse 11 describes the deep fury of Jesus' critics. They felt humiliated. They now were more than critics; they were enemies.

Discipleship As a Way of Life (6:12-49)

In this section of the Gospel, Jesus selected his closest followers and instructed them and his other disciples. Verses 20-49 make up what sometimes is called the Sermon on the Plain. There are many similarities between this and the Sermon on the Mount in Matthew 5—7. Each of these passages includes some of Jesus' most important teachings on how his followers should live.

Occasionally a person says, "My religion is the Sermon on the Mount," or "I don't need religion; I just practice the Golden Rule." Such a person overlooks an important fact about Jesus' ethical teachings: Jesus' teachings were given to disciples. He assumed a commitment to him and his way. The Sermon on the Mount and the Golden Rule are not simple ethical guidelines for the man-on-the-street; rather they are highly demanding principles for committed followers of Christ.

Call to Special Service (6:12-19)

Luke's account of the choosing of the twelve stresses the all-night praying preceding the choice (v. 12). The selection of *twelve* signified the new Israel that Jesus was creating. The twelve apostles corresponded to the twelve tribes of Israel.

The word "disciples" means learners or followers. Jesus chose the twelve from a larger group of disciples (vv. 13,17). Mark 3:14 says that Jesus chose the twelve "to be with him and to be sent out to preach." The word *apostles* means messengers sent out under the authority of another. The word was most often used later of those whom the risen Christ sent out as witnesses of his resurrection. The twelve formed the core of these special witnesses. After Judas' death a replacement was chosen from the larger group of those who followed Jesus during his ministry and were witnesses of his resurrection (Acts 1:21-22).

Things Are Not What They Seem (6:20-26)

Blessed means happy or fortunate. Jesus pronounced as blessed the poor (v. 20), the hungry (v. 21*a*), the sad (v. 21*b*), and the persecuted (vv. 22-23). He also pronounced woes on their counterparts: the rich (v. 24), the well-fed (v. 25*a*), the merry (v. 25*b*), and the popular (v. 26).

His list is the exact opposite of our list of the fortunate and the unfortunate. Jesus turned everything upside down to make an important point: the kingdom of God is the ultimate good. Blessed are those whose poverty, hunger, or distress makes them open to God's reign in their lives. Blessed are those whose commitment to God's will is so active that they arouse the anger of evildoers.

By the same token, woe to those whose wealth, full stomach, or carefree life blinds them to their need for the good news of the kingdom. And woe to those who value popularity so much that they never take the risk of commitment to God and his way.

A Different Kind of Love (6:27-36)

Love your enemies (vv. 27-30).—Love is the heart of Jesus' teachings, and these verses are crucial in understanding what he meant. He obviously meant something more than a warm sentiment. By definition, enemies are persons we do not feel good about.

And if we wait until we like our enemies, most of us will never love our enemies. Jesus defined love as action, not emotion. Whatever we may feel about our enemies, we are to act for good on their behalf. Jesus himself defined how to love our enemies when he said: "Do good to those who hate you, bless those who curse you, pray for those who abuse you" (vv. 27-28).

Often our feelings toward our enemies change as we do good for them, bless them, and pray for them. But the feelings usually follow the actions, not precede them. We must not wait for the feelings before doing good to our enemies.

By definition, our enemies have hurt us in some way. The natural impulse toward those who hurt us is to get back at them. Jesus, however, taught that we should not only absorb the hurt without seeking to retaliate but also give back good for the evil we have received (v. 29).

This principle applies to more than our enemies. Three of the four examples in verses 29-30 apply to possessions. In each case, Jesus taught giving, not grasping.

The four applications of love in verses 29-30 cannot always be practiced literally, but they always must be taken seriously. No list of specific applications can fit all the complex situations in which Christian love needs to be practiced. For example, acting for the good of others at times may call for *not* turning the other cheek or for *not* giving a person everything he asks for. In this passage, Jesus was not saying everything about Christian love, but he was stressing the heart of love—doing good to others even at risk or cost to self.

The Golden Rule (v. 31).—This sums up Jesus' main point. Notice that the rule is stated positively, not negatively. It is not "don't do to others what you wouldn't want them to do to you." Rather the Golden Rule calls on followers of Jesus to take the initiative. How do you want others to treat you? What do you want them to do for you? Treat them as you want to be treated. Do the good for them you want done for you.

God's kind of love (vv. 32-36).—Evil people do evil to others, no matter how others treat them. They give back evil for evil, and evil for good. The normal pattern for most people is evil for evil, and good for good. Jesus' pattern is good for evil as well as for good. This is God's way of love. There is nothing unusual or difficult about liking people who like us or doing good to those who do good to us. This is how most people act. Jesus calls us to God's kind of love. Those who practice God's kind of love are recognized as sons of God (v. 35).

Good in the Best Sense of the Word (6:37-42)

Someone described a certain religious person as "good in the *worst* sense of the word." People who are concerned about doing right sometimes are tempted to become rigid and judgmental. In verses 37-42 Jesus described persons who are good in the *best* sense of the word.

On one hand, they avoid the temptation to pass judgment on the sins of others. On the other hand, they practice a forgiving spirit (v. 37). They are openhanded and generous toward others (v. 38*a*).

In life we reap what we sow. What we give to life is what we receive back. Constant critics lay themselves open to criticism. The merciful receive mercy. The generous receive as freely as they give.

The blind are not qualified to lead. They will only lead others astray (v. 39). Pupils tend to become like their teachers (v. 40). In this context, verses 39-40 may refer to the blindness of leaders or teachers who can see the faults of others but not their own sins.

Verses 41-42 is an example of Jesus' use of irony and humor. The person who is overly concerned about his brother's faults is often blind to personal sins that are much more serious. The rule of thumb is always to be aware of our own sins. This keeps us aware of our own continual need for God's grace. Nothing is a better antidote for false pride and a judgmental spirit. At the same time we can forgive others because we have experienced God's forgiving love in Christ (Eph. 4:32).

Tests of Goodness (6:43-49)

The fruit test (vv. 43-45).—A person's character is revealed by what that person says and does. Trees are known by their fruits (vv. 43-44). Likewise, good people or evil people reveal their inner attitudes and values by their actions and words (v. 45).

The obedience test (vv. 46-49).—Those who call Jesus "Lord" are not really his unless they practice what he tells them to do (v. 46). What they profess should match what they practice. This is probably the greatest indictment against professing Christians. Our daily practice too often undercuts what we profess.

The parable in verses 47-49 reinforces the point in verse 46. The difference between the two kinds of people is not a failure to hear. Both groups hear the word and know what Christ would have them do. The difference is that one hears and obeys while the other hears but does not obey.

Love in Action (7:1 to 8:3)

Jesus taught the way of love not only by words (6:27-36) but also by deeds. He responded to the faith of a Gentile centurion by healing his servant (7:1-10). He restored to life the only son of a widow (7:11-17). He responded to the perplexity of the imprisoned John the Baptist by telling of his ministry of help and healing (7:18-35). He assured a sinful woman of the reality of the forgiveness of her sins (7:36-50). He included among his followers a number of women (8:1-3).

Helping an Outsider (7:1-10)

A centurion was an officer who commanded about one hundred men. The centurion in this passage was a Gentile who had a deep respect for the Jews and their religion. He may have been a God-fearer like Cornelius (Acts 10:1-2,28); that is, he had not become an official convert to Judaism, but he believed in many of its teachings. This particular centurion had even built the local synagogue for the Jews.

He was a man of humility and faith. Others said of him, "He is *worthy* to have you do this for him" (v. 4); but he sent word to Jesus saying, "I am *not worthy* to have you come under my roof" (v. 6, author's italics). He had heard of Jesus and believed that Jesus could exercise his authority over disease just as he himself could exercise his authority over his troops (vv. 3,7-8).

Jesus marveled at the faith of this Gentile, a faith greater than he had found in Israel (v. 9). This incident has special significance in Luke-Acts. Luke's second volume tells of many Gentiles who later responded in faith in Jesus.

Stopping a Funeral (7:11-17)

Part of Jesus' ministry involved restoring the dead to life (Luke 7:22). The Gospels record three specific instances: Jairus' daughter (Matt. 9:18-26; Mark 5:21-43; Luke 8:40-56), the son of the widow of Nain (Luke 7:11-17), and Lazarus (John 11:1-44). These people were restored to life, but later they died. Jesus' power over death in their lives, however, pointed to his own unique resurrection. He was raised as conqueror of death, never again to die (Rom. 6:9).

Jesus restored the widow's son because of his compassion on her (v. 13). A widow's plight in any generation is difficult, but in that day a widow without a son was in a desperate situation. This young man was the widow's only son. She was dependent on him for support, protection, and companionship. He was her hope for the future. Without him there would be no grandchildren, no one to carry on the family line.

Helping a Perplexed Friend (7:18-35)

A question (vv. 18-20).—John the Baptist had been imprisoned because he boldly spoke the truth (Luke 3:19-20). While in prison, his disciples brought him word of what Jesus was doing (v. 18). John then sent two of his disciples to Jesus with this question: "Are you he who is to come, or shall we look for another?" (v. 19).

How could John, who spoke earlier with such boldness and certainty, ask such a question? Sometimes faith is expressed in bold certainty; at other times it is expressed in honest questions that express perplexity and doubt. Such questions are not like the questions of confirmed skeptics whose normal approach to life is cynical unbelief. Keep in mind that John sent his question *to Jesus.* His was the perplexity of a genuine believer who was struggling to match part of his experience with the affirmations of his faith.

An answer (vv. 21-23).—Keep in mind also that our faith at best is immature. We see through a glass darkly precisely because we walk by faith, not sight. John's earlier statements show that he thought of the Messiah's work primarily in terms of judgment on evil (Luke 3:9,16-17). John apparently was perplexed because Jesus was not acting as he had expected.

Jesus' answer supports this interpretation of John's perplexity. Jesus continued his ministry of help and healing in the presence of John's disciples (v. 21). Then he sent them back with this answer to John's question: "Go and tell John what you have seen and heard: the blind receive their sight, the lame walk, lepers are cleansed, and the deaf hear, the dead are raised up, the poor have the good news preached to them" (v. 22).

The similarities to Luke 4:18-19 are obvious. Jesus knew that John was familiar with the Old Testament. John had emphasized some Old Testament passages that spoke of the coming work of judgment. Jesus was reminding him of other Old Testament passages that spoke of the Messiah as one who was moved with compassion to help people with their deepest needs. In other words, John's perplexity grew out of his incomplete understanding of what the Messiah was to do.

A commendation (vv. 24-28).—After the messengers of John had gone, Jesus delivered a powerful and lyrical tribute to John. He was a bold, courageous prophet. It never occurred to John to let outside forces determine his direction as the wind does a reed (v. 24). His power was not the power of wealth or royalty, but of truth (v. 25). Yes, he was a prophet, but he was "more than a prophet" (v. 26). He was the messenger prophesied by Malachi as preparing the way of the Lord (v. 27; Mal. 3:1).

Verse 28 is the most enigmatic part of this passage. How could Jesus say, on one hand, "among those born of women none is greater than John"; yet add, "he who is least in the kingdom of God is greater than he"? John was the last and greatest of the Old Testament prophets; but he was of the old order, not the new. He was a bold prophet who prepared the way for the Messiah, but he was not privileged to stand in the full light of God's new day. The least in the kingdom is "greater" than John only in one respect. No one is greater than John when judged in light of opportunity and understanding. He stood in the last lingering moments of darkness and prophesied the coming dawn, but he did not understand all that the light of day would reveal. We are privileged to stand in the full light of the day John foretold.

A parable (vv. 29-35).—The common people and the tax collectors had responded to John's mission as the work of God (v. 29), but the Pharisees and the scribes had rejected John and his message (v. 30). The latter response prompted Jesus to compare those who rejected John to children at play. The parable in verse 32 seems to picture two groups of children at play. One group refused to play any of the games suggested by the other group. They would not play wedding, and they also refused to play funeral.

God had sent John the Baptist, who lived in isolation from human society, and some people said he was demon-possessed (v. 33). God sent Jesus, who associated with all kinds of people, and the same ones who rejected the austere John rejected the sociable Jesus. They accused Jesus of the sins of the people he associated with (v. 34). Fortunately, there were some, like the people of verse 29, who saw the hand of God in the work of John and in the work of Jesus (v. 35).

Befriending a Sinful Outcast (7:36-50)

This incident, which is recorded only in this Gospel, presents one of Luke's favorite themes: the compassion of Jesus toward sinners contrasted with the self-righteous attitude of the Pharisees (see 5:27-32; 15; 19:1-10).

Eating with a Pharisee (vv. 36-39).—Just as Jesus sometimes ate with tax collectors and sinners, so he sometimes ate with Pharisees (see 11:37; 14:1). He did not discriminate against persons from any group; he offered his friendship to all. Simon the Pharisee had invited Jesus to dinner, and Jesus accepted.

Although it was not uncommon for people from the street to come in and observe such festivities, Simon was shocked to see a sinful woman come in and proceed to anoint Jesus' feet as described in verse 38. She was able to anoint his feet because people of that day reclined as they ate.

Simon quickly formed his own conclusion based on what he saw. He assumed two things about a prophet: (1) A prophet would have special insight into a person's character. (2) A prophet would not knowingly let an immoral woman anoint his feet. He, therefore, concluded Jesus was no prophet (v. 39).

The parable of two debtors (vv. 40-43).—Jesus showed his true prophetic insight by reading the thoughts of Simon. He told the parable of two debtors (vv. 41-42). The main point of the parable is obvious in light of Jesus' words in verses 44-47. There is, however, a subtle point that Simon may have missed.

Both debtors owed a debt they could not pay. The creditor forgave them both. Each should have been grateful. Differences between what each was forgiven are relative. Each should have been grateful based on what he had been forgiven, not based on comparing his debt with the debts of others.

With regard to forgiveness of sins, each of us has been forgiven a debt none of us could pay. The degree of our love and gratitude depends on our own estimate of the amount of that debt and of the grace of God in forgiving us. A person, therefore, does not have to have been a sinful reprobate in order to appreciate the love of God.

Forgiveness and love (vv. 44-47).—Jesus called Simon's attention to the sharp contrast between the woman's expressions of love and Simon's neglect of the usual courtesies of a good host (vv. 44-46).

Verse 47 is the most difficult verse in the passage. As usually translated, the first part of the verse seems to imply that the woman's many sins were forgiven because of her great love. This interpretation, however, is contrary not only to the New Testament as a whole but also to the rest of this passage. Everything else in the passage assumes that the woman was expressing great love out of gratitude for Jesus' forgiveness of her sins. That fact that she came with an alabaster flask of ointment (v. 37) implies that she already had met Jesus and had her sins forgiven. The parable of the two debtors (vv. 41-42) puts the forgiveness before the gratitude. Later Jesus declared that her faith, not her love, had saved her (v. 50). And even in the last part of verse 47 forgiveness precedes love.

The usual translation of verse 47 is, "Therefore, I tell you, her sins, which are many, are forgiven, for she loved much; but he who is forgiven little, loves little." The *Good News Bible* brings out the meaning more clearly: "I tell you, then, the great love she has shown proves that her many sins have been forgiven. But whoever has been forgiven little shows only a little love."

Reassurance to a forgiven sinner (vv. 48-50).—If the interpretation offered above is correct, Jesus' words in verse 48 were not the

first time he had said this to the woman. She had felt the scorn of
Simon. Jesus, therefore, reassured her that her sins had been
forgiven, whatever people like Simon chose to think.

Liberating Some Women (8:1-3)

As Jesus continued his ministry of preaching and bringing the
good news of the kingdom of God, he was accompanied by the
twelve and by some women. These women had been healed of evil
spirits and other infirmities. Among these women were Mary
Magdalene, Joanna, and Susanna. The woman "used their own
resources to help Jesus and his disciples" (v. 3, GNB).

Both Mark (15:41) and Matthew (27:55) in describing the crucifixion mentioned the women who had followed Jesus from Galilee and
ministered to him. Luke, who characteristically emphasized the role
of women, gives his brief but significant reference in the midst of his
description of Jesus' ministry in Galilee.

Luke 8:1-3 signifies the higher plane to which Jesus lifted women.
It was a man's world. Only males fully participated in synagogue
services. Jesus treated women as persons in their own right. As in
this case, he not only liberated them from what afflicted them but
also included them among his followers. The latter relationship was
reciprocal; it included not only his help for them but also the help
they could give to him and the others.

Gospel for the Ear (8:4-21)

Hearing Is Not Enough (8:4-18)

Parable of the soils (vv. 4-8).—Three major groups are mentioned
at this stage in Jesus' ministry. One was the religious leaders, whose
opposition to Jesus was hardening. Then there were the disciples,
which included not only the twelve but a larger number of followers
(8:2-3). Finally there were the crowds (vv. 4,19,40).

In this setting Jesus told the parable of the soils, also sometimes
called the parable of the sower. The former title is more accurate
because the difference was not in the sower or his seed but in the

soils. Jesus concluded the story with these words: "He who has ears to hear, let him hear" (v. 8). His parables were signs of the kingdom. So were his miracles. The parables were signs for the ear, and the miracles were signs for the eye.

Purpose of parables (vv. 9-15).—Luke 8:10 and its parallels in Mark 4:12 and Matthew 13:13 are among the most difficult verses in the New Testament. On the surface, Jesus seems to have been saying that he used parables to hide the truth from some hearers; however, this interpretation is contrary not only to the New Testament as a whole but also to the meaning of the parable. The point of the passage is the importance of hearing and responding in the right way to the word (vv. 8,18,21).

Jesus taught in parables so that people would have the best opportunity to respond to his word. He went forth like the sower intending that all the seed bear fruit; but as in the case of the sower's seed, some of Jesus' words fell on hard ground (vv. 5, 12). These people included his enemies who had closed their eyes to the light and their ears to the truth. Likewise, some seed fell in shallow soil, and some of Jesus' words were heard by superficial followers, whose early enthusiasm faded and disappeared in times of trouble (vv. 6,13). Still other seed fell in the weed-filled corners of the field, and some of Jesus' words gained a sympathetic hearing but never bore fruit because the hearers allowed cares and pleasures to predominate (vv. 7,14). Fortunately, some seed fell on good soil and yielded much fruit, and some of Jesus' words were heard by genuine followers whose lives testified to the reality of their faith (vv. 8,15).

In a sense, therefore, Jesus' parables separated the true followers from the curious crowds. All heard his teachings, but only some heard with faith and commitment. Others missed the point even of the story form of parables. Even the disciples did not immediately understand in every case, but they persisted in seeking the truth (v. 9). Others heard only a story. Yet the story form of the parables had this additional advantage: many people remembered the story even if they did not understand its point. There was hope that some day the moral and spiritual truth of the parable might pierce their darkened minds and hearts like a ray of divine light.

The word "secrets" in verse 10 does not mean something God

wants to hide from some people. The word in the New Testament means a truth made known by divine revelation, and God's ultimate intent is to reveal, not hide (v. 17).

Watch how you hear (vv. 16-18).—These three verses are found elsewhere in Luke in three separate places (11:33; 12:2; 19:26). As used here, they reinforce the message of the parable of the soils. Those who have heard the word with faith and commitment have the light, and light is for sharing that others may see (v. 16). God's intention is that the light be seen, not hid (v. 17). Each person, therefore, should be careful to hear as God intends (v. 18a). Hearing involves a twofold responsibility—to receive and share the light (v. 18b).

We Are Family (8:19-21)

This incident further reinforces the lesson about hearing. Jesus taught that the members of his larger family are those who hear the word of God and do it (v. 21).

The occasion was the coming of his mother and brothers. Mark's account of this incident reveals that his family had come to try to take him home because they thought he was losing his mind (Mark 3:21,31-35). This is understandable, for John 7:5 states that his brothers did not believe in him. Jesus was everything a brother and a son should be; but when family interests threatened his mission, he put first the will of his Father (see Luke 2:48-51). Thus he practiced what he taught others (Luke 9:57-62; 11:27-28; 14:26).

The positive message is that all of us by faith can be part of the family of God. We are family.

Faith and Fear (8:22-56)

Luke 8:22-56 records four of Jesus' miracles: the stilling of the storm (vv. 22-25), the deliverance of the demoniac (vv. 26-39), the healing of the woman with the flow of blood (vv. 43-48), and the restoration to life of Jairus' daughter (vv. 40-42,49-56). As the parables were the gospel for the ear, so were the miracles the gospel for the eye. They were signs of the kingdom of divine grace and power. These four miracles show God's grace and power in four areas that threaten human life and welfare: nature's sometimes destructive force, the enslavement resulting from the power of evil, the pain and helplessness of lingering illness, and the fearful reality of bereavement and death.

Christ's miracles show the divine authority over each of these areas. They are signs that God ultimately will destroy and remove each of these threats. This final deliverance is part of the ultimate coming of the kingdom. Jesus' acts of grace and power are signs of this ultimate victory and show that God's grace and power are already at work in and through his Son.

Fear Mixed with Faith (8:22-25)

The heart of this incident is Jesus' question to the disciples, "Where is your faith?" (v. 25). He was rebuking them for not trusting God to watch over them as they went about doing his will. God does not always shield us from the destructiveness of all life's storms, but he always can be trusted. This was the trust they lacked when they panicked and awakened Jesus with their cries (v. 24).

The disciples' fear of the storm was replaced with a different fear. After Jesus' demonstration of power, they felt fear and amazement in the presence of one who could command obedience from the winds and water (v. 25).

Fear That Rejects Jesus (8:26-39)

A desperate man (vv. 26-30).—The plight of the demoniac is described in these verses. Imagine how the disciples felt when they saw this man. They were approaching the shoreline of Gentile territory (v. 26). To make matters worse, they were landing near a cemetery (v. 27). Then just as they stepped on land this wild man ran toward them.

The man was under the power of forces over which he had no control. Society had tried to restrain him with chains, but he had broken these and fled into the desert (v. 29). He had no home but the tombs (v. 27). The demonic powers that possessed him were so strong that the man called himself "Legion" (v. 30), from a Roman army unit of six thousand men. Something in the man drew him to Jesus, but the demons saw Jesus as an enemy (v. 28).

A dramatic exorcism (vv. 31-33).—These are difficult verses.

There have been many attempts to try to explain why Jesus allowed the demons to enter the swine. One explanation is that Jesus did this so that the man would have some dramatic proof that the evil powers had departed from him.

A request to leave (vv. 34-37).—The sad part of the story is the reaction of the people. They asked Jesus to leave (v. 37). Many of them either knew the man or knew of him. They came out to see what had happened and found the man "sitting at the feet of Jesus, clothed and in his right mind" (v. 35). They could have had any one of many reactions. They could have been grateful and happy, but they were afraid (v. 35). Luke mentions their great fear as the reason for asking Jesus to leave (v. 37). This kind of superstitious fear rejects Jesus and the help he offers.

A new witness (vv. 38-39).—The man himself asked to go with Jesus (v. 38). He may have felt fearful about trying to reenter society in his own land. Jesus told him to go home and tell others what God had done for him (v. 39). This man, who was probably a Gentile, became the first witness for Jesus in Gentile territory. He was a sign of what was coming after the death and resurrection of Jesus. Luke tells this exciting story of proclamation to Gentiles in the second volume of his writings—the Book of Acts.

Acting by Faith in Spite of Fear (8:40-48)

Two miracles are woven together in Luke 8:40-56. Jesus returned to Galilee to find the crowds waiting (v. 40). Jairus fell at his feet and asked him to come to his house to help his daughter (vv. 41-42). On his way he healed the woman with the flow of blood.

Hers was a pitiful plight. She had been ill for twelve years and had been pronounced incurable (v. 43). In addition, her malady caused her to be considered permanently unclean by her people. She was treated in much the same way as a leper. To make matters worse, many people assumed her plight was evidence of an immoral life.

As the crowd pressed about Jesus, she had touched his garment and felt herself healed (v. 44). When Jesus asked who had touched him, Peter objected that nearly everyone in that crowd was touching him (v. 45). Jesus explained that he had felt power go out from him at someone's touch (v. 46).

The woman was terrified. *What would happen if people knew*

what she had done? She was unclean and untouchable; yet she had dared to touch Jesus. In spite of her fear, she fell at Jesus' feet and told everyone "why she had touched him, and how she had been immediately healed" (v. 47).

Then Jesus said to her the same thing he had said to the sinful woman in Luke 7:50. Many of the English translations differ, but the words are the same in Greek. The word translated "saved" also means "made . . . well."

Faith That Casts Out Fear (8:49-56)

Jairus had heard what the woman said. Jesus built on this experience when the numbing news came that the girl was dead. Those who brought the news (v. 49) said in effect, "Death, which always has the last word, has spoken. Jesus might as well go on his way." Jesus then spoke to Jairus: "Do not fear; only believe, and she shall be made well" (v. 50). The word translated "made well" is the same word as in Luke 7:50 and 8:48. Jairus had seen the woman saved from her illness through faith. Jesus challenged him to have the same faith that Jesus could save his daughter from death's clutches.

Many people died whom Jesus did not bring back to life. Some people loved their dead loved ones as much as Jairus did, and some had as much faith. The raising of the widow's son, Jairus' daughter, and Lazarus were exceptional miracles, but they showed the authority of Jesus over death. What happened to them points to the Christian hope of final victory over death itself, which is based on the resurrection of Jesus himself from death. The mourners laughed at Jesus' claim that the girl was not dead but sleeping (vv. 52-53). They laughed because death always has the last word. They were wrong that day, for Jesus showed that he had the last word.

The Way of the Cross (9:1-50)

Luke 9:1-50 is the climactic part of Luke's account of Jesus' Galilean ministry. The heart of the passage is Jesus' prediction of his coming death (v. 22) and his call for others to follow him in the way of the cross (vv. 23-27). The mission of the twelve (vv. 1-9) and the feeding of the five thousand (vv. 10-17) provide the background for the theme. (Mark's Gospel in 6:45 to 8:27 provides additional background events not recorded in Luke.) The occasion for Jesus' prediction was Peter's confession of Jesus as the Christ (vv. 18-22). The events on the mount of transfiguration (vv. 28-36) and at the foot of the mountain (vv. 37-45) give further emphasis to the theme. The section concludes with two episodes that show how far the disciples had to go before they practiced the way of the cross (vv. 46-50).

On the Master's Mission (9:1-9)

The mission of the twelve (vv. 1-6).—The disciples had been with Jesus during much of his Galilean ministry. Now Jesus sent them out to do what they had seen him do. They were to declare the reality of God's reign and to demonstrate this by acts of compassion (vv. 1-2). This was good preparation for the time when the apostles would be called on to continue the work of the risen Lord in the power of his Spirit.

The mission of the twelve in Galilee was to be a short-term missionary tour. They were not to spend time preparing provisions for the journey; they simply were to go (v. 3). They were to accept the hospitality of those who received them (v. 4), and they were to move quickly on when they were rejected (v. 5). The twelve did as they were told (v. 6).

Herod's perplexity (vv. 7-9).—Herod Antipas was tetrarch of Galilee and Perea (see 3:18-20). He heard reports of what Jesus and the twelve were doing. He was aware of three explanations about who Jesus was. Some thought Jesus was John the Baptist raised from the dead; others thought he was Elijah; still others believed one of the other ancient prophets had been brought back from the dead.

The report that perplexed Herod was the one about John the Baptist, whom Herod had ordered to be beheaded. Perhaps there was a certain amount of guilt in Herod's heart. He wanted to see Jesus (v. 9), perhaps to reassure himself that Jesus was not John. Luke 23:6-12 records the sad scene when Jesus and Herod finally met.

Breaking Bread (9:10-17)

After the return of the twelve from their mission, they reported to Jesus. Jesus and the twelve then withdrew (v. 10) to what is called a "lonely place" (v. 12). Jesus apparently felt the need for such a time; however, when the crowds heard of it, they followed. Notice how Jesus responded to what many would have viewed as an intrusion: he welcomed them and helped them (v. 11).

The feeding of the five thousand (vv. 12-17) is one of the few miracles recorded in all four Gospels. It was a typical act of compassion on Jesus' part. He also intended it as a sign of God's reign. John 6 records the aftermath of the miracle. Jesus had wanted the people to see him as the Bread of life offering himself for them. Instead they insisted on seeing him only as a king who could fill their empty stomachs.

A Different Kind of King (9:18-22)

The Christ of God (vv. 18-20).—Each of the Synoptic Gospels records the confession of Peter (Matt. 16:13-23; Mark 8:27-33), but only Luke places it in the context of Jesus' prayer life (v. 18; compare 3:21; 6:12; 9:28).

The people in general had not come to think of Jesus as the promised Messiah. They thought of him as John the Baptist, Elijah, or one of the prophets (v. 19; compare 9:7-8). Therefore, Peter's confession was all the more significant. He declared Jesus to be God's promised Messiah. ("Christ" is Greek for the Hebrew "Messiah.") Messiah means anointed one. Ancient kings were anointed. God had promised David that his throne would be established forever (2 Sam. 7). After the fall of Judah and the end of David's dynasty on an actual throne, the Jews looked for a future son of David to reestablish the reign of David's family over Israel.

Tell no one (v. 21).—Peter was right; Jesus was the Christ of God (Matt. 16:17-19). Why then did Jesus instruct the twelve not to tell anyone? The problem was that most people were looking for one kind of Messiah, but Jesus had come to be a different kind of King. The popular idea of messiah was a military leader and an economic benefactor. *He would deliver the Jews from Roman domination and restore Israel to a powerful nation. The Messiah would bring a time of prosperity.* Many people had come to expect everything that was wrong to be set right when the Messiah came.

What would have happened if the disciples had spread the word that Jesus was the Messiah? Most people would have read into this their own ideas of the Messiah. They would have falsely assumed that Jesus was the king they were expecting, not the King he had come to be.

The suffering Son of man (v. 22).—Jesus did not refer to himself as Messiah. Instead he spoke of himself, as he had before, as the Son of man (see comments on 5:24). Without using the title "Messiah," he proceeded to declare the kind of Messiah he had come to be. He would be different from what the people were expecting. He "must suffer . . . be rejected . . . be killed . . . be raised." Jesus seems to have combined two Old Testament ideas. On one hand, he saw himself as the Suffering Servant of Isaiah 53; on the other hand he was the vindicated, triumphant Son of man of Daniel 7 (see 9:26). Beyond his suffering, rejection, and death was resurrection.

The disciples obviously were not expecting him to be raised from the dead (24:11). Why were they surprised by his resurrection if he had predicted it ahead of time? He had told them, but they had not really heard him. They were so confused by his words about suffering and death that they missed his words about resurrection. The Gospels of Matthew and Mark tell how Peter tried to rebuke Jesus for this prediction of death and resurrection, and Jesus in turn rebuked Peter (Matt. 22-23; Mark 8:32-33). Luke did not record this exchange, but he did show how the disciples misunderstood Jesus (9:45) and missed the whole point about crossbearing (9:46). They had confessed Jesus as the Christ, but at this stage in their understanding they thought he was the Messiah of popular Jewish expectations.

The Cross as a Way of Life (9:23-27)

Jesus followed up on the prediction of his cross by explaining that following him involves taking up a cross (v. 23). In that day taking up a cross meant carrying a cross to the place of one's execution. A follower of Christ's must be willing to die with him and for him. This primary meaning lies in the background of Jesus' words about saving one's life (v. 24) and being ashamed of Jesus (v. 26); however, the word "daily" in verse 23 shows that Jesus meant more than a willingness to endure martyrdom for his sake. A follower of Christ must be willing to live a cross-way-of-life day by day.

Jesus meant more than what is often referred to as crossbearing.

He meant more than enduring some burden or trial over which we have little or no control. This is part of the Christian life, but it is not crossbearing. Jesus was referring to a voluntary commitment to live by the principle of self-giving love.

Verses 24-25 express the paradox of this way of life. A cautious, self-centered approach to life is not life at all. On the other hand, the person who risks all for God and others finds life (v. 24). Those who go through life grasping everything for themselves end up losing everything (v. 25).

Verse 23 is a difficult verse to practice; verse 27 is a difficult verse to understand. To what does seeing the kingdom of God refer in this verse? Some interpreters say that Jesus was speaking ironically; the kingdom was already there if only they had eyes to see (17:20-21). Others believe Jesus was referring to one or more of the significant events of the near future: the transfiguration, resurrection, ascension, Pentecost, the spread of the gospel as recorded in Acts, the fall of Jerusalem in AD 70.

A Voice from Heaven—Again! (9:28-36)

When Jesus was baptized, a voice from heaven had said, "Thou art my beloved Son; with thee I am well pleased" (Luke 3:22). The voice spoke to Jesus to confirm him in his chosen mission. At the transfiguration, a voice from heaven spoke to Peter, James, and John: "This is my Son, my Chosen; listen to him" (v. 35).

The transfiguration was to strengthen and reassure Jesus in his commitment to the way of the cross. It also was to challenge the three disciples to accept what Jesus was trying to tell them about the way of the cross.

Each of the Synoptics records the transfiguration (Matt. 17:1-8; Mark 9:2-8), but only Luke tells us that it took place while Jesus was praying (vv. 28-29). Luke also is the only one who recorded what Moses, Elijah, and Jesus talked about, "his departure, which he was to accomplish at Jerusalem" (v. 31). The Greek word translated "departure" is *exodus*. Moses led the people of Israel in a trumphant Exodus from Egypt to the Promised Land. Elijah had a triumphant exit from earth to heaven. These two also represented the Old Testament Law and Prophets, which Jesus came to fulfill. Fulfill how? Through a triumphant exodus that involved death and resurrection. God sent Moses and Elijah to reassure Jesus in this mission.

Peter and the others had been awakened from a sound sleep when this took place (v. 32). Peter's suggestion about the three booths was inappropriate because Jesus had his own mission to perform. It would not be accomplished by camping on the mount to remember past triumphs and to savor present revelations. Jesus had to come down from the mountain and set his face toward Jerusalem. The voice from heaven challenged Peter, James, and John to listen to Jesus when he told them what lay ahead.

Great Need and Weak Faith (9:37-45)

At the foot of the mountain (vv. 37-43a).—A painting by Raphael shows the contrast between the glory of the mount and the desperate need below. There were the crowds (v. 37). There was the desperation and pitiful plight of the father and his only son (vv. 38-40). There was the helplessness of the disciples (v. 40).

Jesus' words in verse 41 probably were directed to the disciples and to the crowds. Apparently some of the crowd were using the plight of the boy to try to embarrass Jesus and the disciples. Jesus healed the boy and left the people astonished (vv. 42-43a).

Failure to understand the cross (vv. 43b-45).—The voice had told the disciples to listen to Jesus (v. 35). Now Jesus said, "Let these words sink into your ears; for the Son of man is to be delivered into the hands of men" (v. 44). However, they still did not understand (v. 45). Verse 45 might mean that they did not understand because something or someone hid the meaning from them. More likely, the point is that their own preconceived notions were so strong that they could not understand what Jesus said about his death.

What Makes a Person Great? (9:46-50)

Humble service (vv. 46-48).—Verse 46 shows clearly how far the twelve were from an understanding of or commitment to the way of the cross. They were arguing about which of them was the greatest.

Often during his ministry Jesus used a child to teach the disciples a lesson. In Luke 18:17 he spoke of children as having the kind of humble trust needed to receive the kingdom. This may be part of his purpose in verses 47-48. The child was least and willing to be least.

However, Jesus probably intended to emphasize the humble service of receiving a child in his name. He put the child by his side (and probably hugged the child). He said in essence that whoever takes the time to love and help a child is great in the kingdom.

A tolerant spirit (vv. 49-50).—At first sight verse 50 appears to contradict Luke 11:23. Both, however, are true. Luke 11:23 stresses that a person is either with Christ or against him. It also implies, when compared with verse 50, that this is a judgment people make about themselves, not about others. Verse 50 is talking about our judgments about others.

This verse also refers to a different issue than Luke 11:23. The disciples were critical of the exorcist because he was not following with them. He wasn't of their group, and he probably wasn't going about it in their way. Jesus' point is that not everyone who serves him belongs to the same group or goes about it in the same way. The issue here is not commitment. That is between Christ and the person. The issue is a tolerant and glad spirit toward all persons who are striving to serve Jesus. How different Christian history would have been had Christ's followers learned this lesson!

Journeying to Jerusalem
9:51 to 19:27

Luke 9:51 to 19:27 is the longest section of the Gospel. The theme of these chapters is introduced in 9:51: "When the days drew near for him to be received up, he set his face to go to Jerusalem." The same theme recurs in 9:53; 13:22,33; 17:11; 18:31; 19:11; and in 19:28 when he prepared to enter the city.

This theme does not mean that Jesus headed directly to Jerusalem by the shortest route. The theme has to do with Jesus' commitment to go to Jerusalem, not with geography or chronology. The point is that every step Jesus took in any direction was actually a step closer to the climax of his mission. Toward the end of the Galilean ministry,

Jesus had clearly told the twelve what awaited him in Jerusalem (9:22). At the transfiguration Moses and Elijah came to speak to Jesus about the same thing (9:31).

Rejection and crucifixion lay ahead, but so did resurrection. From this point the shadow of the cross lay across Jesus' path. However, the victory of resurrection and ascension lay beyond the suffering of the cross. "Received up" in verse 51 referred to being received up in victory and vindication to God the Father.

A Strong Sense of Mission (9:51 to 10:24)

Handling Rejection (9:51-56)

This is the first mention of the Samaritans in Luke's Gospel. The people of a village refused to welcome Jesus because he was a Jew on his way to Jerusalem (v. 53). The response of James and John in verse 54 shows how far they were from sharing Jesus' commitment to the way of the cross. Wanting to call down fire on those who had rejected them is an understandable reaction, but Jesus rebuked them (v. 55). Earlier Jesus had told them: "Love your enemies, do good to those who hate you, bless those who curse you, pray for those who abuse you" (Luke 6:27-28). Jesus' actions as he journeyed to and arrived at Jerusalem showed he practiced what he preached.

Would-Be Followers (9:57-62)

Those who would follow Jesus must follow him in the way of the cross (Luke 9:23-24). Luke 9:57-62 tells of three men who expressed interest in following Jesus but who lacked the commitment. The ways Jesus dealt with these would-be followers sound almost as if he were trying to discourage them. Actually he was trying to challenge them truly to follow him.

Jesus tried to help the first man face the cost of true commitment. The man's profession in verse 57 sounded glib to Jesus. The man needed to realize that following Jesus means following him in his way of sacrifice and self-giving (v. 58).

The other two men expressed their intentions to follow Jesus, but each had something else he had to do *first* (vv. 59-61). Verse 59 may mean that the man's father actually had died, or it may mean that the son felt an obligation to stay at home during his father's lifetime. If the latter was the case, Jesus challenged what may have been only an excuse for an indefinite delay. If the former was true, Jesus was stressing the absolute priority that must be given to following him.

Even the closest of family ties must not take precedence over following Jesus. This is the point of Jesus' strong responses in verses 60 and 62. As in Luke 14:26 where Jesus spoke of "hate" toward family, verse 60 can be understood as a shocking way to stress the priority that must be given to following him.

Training for Missionary Service (10:1-16)

The appointing of seventy missionaries in verse 1 foreshadowed the time when Jesus' followers would be sent forth on a mission to all nations (Acts 1:8). Seventy Gentile nations were mentioned in Genesis 10. Some of the instructions in this passage applied only to the seventy missionaries, but the principles apply to all mission work.

One of the principles is the necessity of trust in God. The first instruction was to pray, for the laborers and the harvest are in the hands of the Lord (v. 2). Reliance on the Lord is essential because of the hostility sometimes faced by missionaries (v. 3). Even the unusual instructions about not taking extra provisions were to help them learn the lesson of trust (v. 4). The ambassadors of peace were to stay where they were welcomed and to accept whatever hospitality and provisions they received (vv. 5-8). They were to declare the presence of the kingdom of God by word and deed (v. 9).

Verse 8 probably is another foreshadowing of the future mission to Gentiles. The Jewish Christian missionaries had to learn to set aside their traditions about clean and unclean foods (see Acts 10). Verses 10-15 also imply the future Gentile mission. Shaking the dust from one's feet was a Jewish practice after leaving Gentile territory. Jesus used it as a symbol of judgment on those who rejected the kingdom. He mentioned especially the Galilean cities that had rejected him. If the sinful Gentile cities of the past had had such opportunity, they would have repented. The implication is that Gentile cities will have an opportunity to respond to the good news.

Cause for Rejoicing (10:17-24)

The words *joy* (v. 17) and *rejoice* (vv. 20-21) are the keys to this passage. The seventy returned with joy after their successful mission. Jesus shared their joy, but reminded them to rejoice primarily not in being empowered for service but in having been saved by God's grace (v. 20). Then Jesus rejoiced that God's message was accepted. Although most of the important people of the day missed God's grace, many of the ordinary people accepted God's revelation of himself in Jesus (vv. 21-22). Jesus told the disciples that they had been privileged to see and hear what the kings and prophets of the old order had yearned to see and hear (vv. 23-24).

Part of Jesus' joy was in his vision of Satan's defeat (v. 18). The subjection of the demons in Jesus' name was part of the incarnate victory over Satan (see Heb. 2:14). Jesus also promised his servants that the power of the enemy (Satan) would not be able to harm them. The "authority to tread upon serpents and scorpions" (v. 19) is a symbolic way of expressing this assurance. Satan of course could cause them much harm, even to the point of death itself; but Satan could not really hurt them (compare Luke 21:16-18).

Service and Prayer (10:25 to 11:13)

Service and prayer go together. Service without prayer lacks proper motivation, direction, and power. Prayer without service is sterile and self-centered. Jesus' example and teachings linked the two in indissoluble union. Thus Luke's Gospel puts the parable of the good Samaritan (10:25-37) in immediate context with the incident in the home of Mary and Martha (10:38-42) and with the teachings about prayer in Luke 11:1-13.

How Big Is Your Neighborhood? (10:25-37)

A man with a small neighborhood (vv. 25-29).—The lawyer's questions reveal more about him than his answers. He was properly concerned about eternal life (v. 25). He gave the right answer (v. 27) to Jesus' question about the law (v. 26). On another occasion, Jesus commended a scribe for recognizing that wholehearted love for

God and love for neighbors summarize the heart of the law (Mark 12:28-34). The question of the lawyer in Luke 10:29, however, showed a limited view of love.

His question gave him away. He had trouble with the command to love his neighbor unless he could limit the definition of *neighbor.* Apparently he didn't think of some people as neighbors; however, he wanted some way to show that his definition of *neighbor* was realistic and adequate.

A man with a big neighborhood (vv. 30-35).—Modern readers miss the shock Jesus' hearers must have felt when he first told this story. Jesus made a despised Samaritan the hero of the story. The priest and Levite in the parable had the same limited view of neighbor as the lawyer. Nothing is said in the story about the victim's race or nationality. Presumably he was a Jew, but the Samaritan saw him as a human being.

The priest and the Levite viewed the victim only from a distance and then moved quickly by on the other side of the road. They could have rationalized their behavior in many ways: *The man was unclean. They would risk their own lives because the thieves might still be near. They had important duties elsewhere. Someone else would help the man.*

The Samaritan showed by his actions what love is. The reality of his compassion is seen in what he did to help the man. Christian love is acting for the good of other persons—whoever they are, whatever the cost, and however we may feel.

Whose neighbor am I? (vv. 36-37).—Jesus' question in verse 36 shows that the lawyer had asked the wrong question. He should have asked, "Whose neighbor can I be?" He was concerned to excuse his narrow view of the love commandment. He wondered: *Whom must I treat as my neighbor?* and *Whom can I ignore?* Jesus tried to help him see that he should have been taking the initiative in recognizing every person as his neighbor and in responding to human need as he encountered it. The lawyer seems not to have learned this lesson, for he could not bring himself even to admit that a Samaritan acted more nobly than two of his own kind. He referred to the Samaritan only as "the one who showed mercy" (v. 37), making no mention of his nationality.

Choosing the Best (10:38-42)

The parable in 10:25-27 stresses the importance of service to others in daily life. The incident in 10:38-42 shows that we must receive from Christ in order adequately to give of ourselves for others.

John 11—12 tells us that Martha and Mary lived in Bethany and had a brother named Lazarus. The tone of Luke 10:38-42 suggests that Jesus was no stranger to this home.

Martha's service was proper and commendable in many ways; however, Jesus rebuked her for the anxiety and distraction shown by her rebuke of Mary. The word translated "anxious" (v. 41) is the same word Jesus used in warning against worry that results from not trusting God and not putting first things first (Luke 12:22-31; Matt. 6:25-34).

Martha was anxious about "many things" (v. 41), but Jesus said that "one thing is needful" (v. 42). Some scholars see this as a contrast between the many dishes Martha had prepared and a simpler, adequate meal. This may have been in the background, but the last part of verse 42 shows Jesus applied it much more broadly. The one essential is the good portion chosen by Mary—to receive the word from Jesus.

Luke 10:38-42, therefore, teaches that service for Christ grows out of receiving the word of life from Christ. If we would be good Samaritans, we first of all must follow Mary's example and sit at Jesus' feet. A life of effective service is a life rooted in prayer, worship, and study of the Scriptures.

Teach Us to Pray (11:1-13)

A model prayer (vv. 1-4).—Luke's Gospel stresses Jesus' prayer life. The disciples' awareness of this caused them to make the request in verse 1. He answered, first of all, by giving them a model prayer.

Matthew's account of the Model Prayer is longer and more familiar. The setting also is different; Matthew 6:9-15 is part of the Sermon on the Mount. The shorter version of the prayer in Luke was given by Jesus in response to the disciples' request that he teach them to pray. This shows that the Model Prayer was given primarily as a model for praying rather than as a formal prayer to recite.

Verse 2 stressed the paradox of closeness and distance to the God to whom we pray. On one hand, he is our Heavenly Father with whom we have intimate communion; on the other hand, he is the holy God whose name is hallowed above all things.

Our first petition is for the coming of his kingdom. We pray for the completion of what God has done, is doing, and will do in Jesus Christ. Our petitions range all the way from the coming of God's kingdom to the provision for our daily need for bread (v. 3).

Prayer includes confession of sins and commitment to show the same kind of forgiveness to others (v. 4). Forgiveness is a two-way street. The heart that is open to receive God's forgiveness also is open to give forgiveness to others. By the same token, a heart that is closed toward others is closed toward God.

Prayer acknowledges our dependence on God for strength and guidance. At first sight the last part of verse 4 looks like a contradiction to James 1:13. God allows us to be tested, but his intent is never that we fall into evil because of some temptation. The prayer of Luke 11:4 is the opposite of a spirit of self-confidence that assumes we are capable of handling every situation in our own strength.

The need to pray (vv. 5-10).—After teaching the disciples how to pray, Jesus turned to a more difficult task: to teach them the need to pray. This is the point of the parable of the friend at midnight (vv. 5-8). The disciples had asked Jesus to teach them how to pray, which may imply that the main need is knowing what to say when praying. The key, however, is recognizing the need to pray. We learn to pray by praying. The one who prays out of a sense of need is the one who truly learns to pray.

The man's sense of need was great. Hospitality was a sacred duty in that society; and the host had nothing to set before the hungry traveler, who arrived unexpectedly and late. The host's sense of need was so great that he disturbed his friend and neighbor's sleep to ask for help. "Importunity" in verse 8 refers to his shameless knocking at his neighbor's door so late at night.

Verses 9-10 apply the story in verses 5-8. Just as the man's deep need drove him to seek help from his friend, so should our need drive us to God. When it does, we can be sure God will hear us.

The parable of the friend at midnight (Luke 11:5-8) has much in common with the parable of the unjust judge in Luke 18:1-8. Each teaches the need for continuing in prayer. Each is told in a form which on the surface seems to imply that God must be persuaded to answer our prayers by our continual and persistent requests. This, however, misses the point in both parables. The need for persistence in praying is our need, not God's.

The point, therefore, is definitely *not* that God must be persuaded to hear our prayers by our persistence. The man in the parable was persistent because (1) his need was desperate and (2) his relationship with his neighbor was good. Prayer is persistent for the same two reasons. When the need is real, no one needs to tell us to keep praying about it. Likewise, because we know that God loves us, we continue to pray to him even when the specific requests do not seem to be answered.

Encouragement to pray (vv. 11-13).—The analogy in verses 11-13 is like a parable. Verses 5-8 and verses 11-13 are "how-much-more" parables. If a friend inconvenienced himself because of persistent cries for help, *how much more* will our loving Heavenly Father give us what we need? If an earthly father does his best to respond to his child's request for something to eat, "*how much more* will the heavenly Father give the Holy Spirit to those who ask him"? (v. 13, author's italics).

God is the giver of every good gift. He gives many of his gifts apart from prayer, but our deepest needs can only be met through prayer. The best gift God ever gives is the gift of his own presence to be with us. The gift of his Spirit's presence and power in our lives is the best answer to prayer, and this gift is continually given even when many of our requests seem to have gone unanswered.

This points up another reason why genuine prayer is persistent. Some needs change from day to day, but communion with God is an unchanging characteristic of a life of faith. Whatever the urgency of specific petitions, the need for daily communion with God remains constant.

The Danger of Closed Minds (11:14-54)

A closed mind is a deadly thing. By this time in Jesus' ministry, opposition had begun to harden. Luke 11:14-54 shows that some of his enemies had made up their minds to reject him, and nothing he said or did would change them. In Luke 11:14-28 Jesus responded to the irrational charge that he cast out demons by the power of the devil. Luke 11:29-36 records his response to their demand for signs. Luke 11:37-54 lists a series of charges Jesus made against the Pharisees and lawyers (scribes).

Who Is on the Lord's Side? (11:14-28)

Three kinds of responses (vv. 14-16).—Here are three responses to Jesus' act of casting out a demon: (1) The people marveled, but apparently did little else (v. 14). (2) Some of those present (Matt. 12:24 calls them Pharisees) accused Jesus of casting out demons by Beelzebul (v. 15; v. 18 shows this is another name for Satan). (3) Still others demanded that Jesus show them a sign from heaven (v. 16).

These responses, especially the last two, show the danger of closed minds. They already had made up their minds; therefore, they resorted to ridiculous charges and demands, and they refused to consider the possibility that Jesus' exorcisms were the work of God.

In the verses that follow, Jesus responded to each of these groups: Verses 17-22 are a response to verse 15; verses 23-28, to verse 14; and verses 29-36, to verse 16.

The finger of God (vv. 17-22).—Jesus pointed out how ridiculous was the charge in verse 15. Satan would not be waging war on his own troops (vv. 17-18). Jesus also pointed out that there were other Jewish exorcists, but no one had accused them of being allies of Satan (v. 19).

Then Jesus turned the argument around and focused it on his accusers. They had conceded that he cast out demons. If Satan did not help him, who did? Jesus used language reminiscent of Exodus 8:19 to point to the irresistible conclusion that God's power was at work. The *finger of God* seems to refer to the Holy Spirit (Matt. 12:28). God was using the casting out of demons to press his sovereign claims on those who saw these signs.

In the analogy of the strong man (Satan), Jesus was the stronger one who overcame Satan (vv. 21-22).

With Jesus or against him? (v. 23).—Everyone is on one side or the other in the struggle between good and evil, God and Satan. No one can remain neutral. People who try to remain uncommitted actually contribute aid and comfort to the side of evil. In this context, Jesus may have been addressing those in verse 14 who were impressed by Jesus, but not impressed enough to commit themselves.

See the comments on Luke 9:50 for the relationship between 11:23 and Jesus' saying, "He that is not against you is for you."

Don't underestimate evil (vv. 24-26).—Casting out evil is not enough unless the emptiness is filled with the presence and power of God. The power of evil is deceptive and untiring. When a life is left empty, evil seeps back into the vacancy.

The real issue (vv. 27-28).—A woman in the crowd, apparently impressed by Jesus, declared a blessing on his mother (v. 27). Jesus' response in verse 28 did not question the truth of the woman's statement, but it did indicate she had missed the main point of what she had observed. The woman intended to pay a tribute to Jesus and his mother, but Jesus refocused the real issue: Those who are truly with Jesus are those who are committed to him because they have heard and heeded the word of God. The point in 11:28 is the same as in 8:21.

Missing the Obvious (11:29-36)

The sign of Jonah (vv. 29-30).—Beginning in verse 29 Jesus responded to the people mentioned in verse 16. They tested him by demanding a sign from heaven. Jesus branded them an evil generation for demanding signs. They were evil because they did not have an honest desire to know the truth; rather they were blind to the obvious fact that God was at work in the ministry of Jesus.

Jesus promised to give them only the sign of Jonah. He would be to his generation what Jonah had been to Nineveh (v. 30). That is, he himself was the sign as he called people to repent.

Some people claim they would believe if God would only show them special miraculous signs. Faith is not the result of special proofs. If people will not respond to the clear call of God through his word, they would not believe even if they were given special signs. (See the comments on Luke 16:27-31.)

Greater than Solomon (vv. 31-32).—Judgment is according to light and opportunity. Some people stand in the full light of God's revelation in Christ and turn away. They will be more accountable in the day of judgment than people with less opportunity. The queen of Sheba came many miles to hear the wisdom of Solomon, but the people of Jesus' day rejected the revelation of God in Christ— something far greater than Solomon. Nineveh repented at the preaching of Jonah, but the people of Jesus' generation did not respond to God's call in Christ.

Bad light or poor eyesight? *(vv. 33-36).*—A lamp is made to shine (v. 33). The eye is like a lamp for the body: Good eyes illumine, but diseased eyes distort and darken (v. 34). In the area of spiritual perception, the ultimate tragedy is spiritual blindness, which darkens everything (v. 35). By contrast, when the eyes of the soul are healthy, everything is illumined (v. 36).

The sign-seekers claimed they needed more light in order to see, but their problem was not bad light but poor eyesight. They closed their eyes to the light. Extra light cannot help that condition.

When Religion Is Sinful (11:37-54)

Relying on superficial morality (vv. 37-41).—One of the Pharisees' traditions was ritual washing of hands before meals. The purpose was ceremonial cleanliness, not hygiene. They were astonished that a religious teacher like Jesus would ignore this. Jesus tried to show them that preoccupation with externals has nothing to do with real moral issues (compare Mark 7:1-23). Sin is too deeply rooted to be cleansed by washing the hands. Real cleansing from sin must be internal (vv. 40-41).

Neglecting the things that count (v. 42).—This verse introduces a series of three woes against the Pharisees (vv. 42-44), followed by three woes against the lawyers or scribes (vv. 45-52). *Woe* as used by Jesus was not a curse but an expression of deep regret. He exposed the sins of the Pharisees and scribes to try to help them and the people influenced by them.

The Pharisees tithed beyond what the law required, but they missed the point. Tithing is an expression of total commitment, not a substitute for it. They were meticulous in paying their tithes, but they neglected justice toward people and love toward God (compare Mic. 6:6-8).

Feeding on human praise (v. 43).—Pharisaic religion fed the basic human sin, pride. In spite of being filled with inner sin (v. 39) and neglecting the things that count (v. 42), they were confident of their righteousness because of such things as their hand washings and their tithing. They loved the special attention that came to people of such righteousness and religious devotion.

Corrupting others (v. 44).—Touching the dead was considered especially defiling; even walking over a grave was defiling. Jesus said that the Pharisees were like unmarked graves. Unsuspecting people became corrupted and defiled by their contact with these men who were supposed to be righteous but actually were guilty of the worst of sins.

Burdening others (vv. 45-46).—The lawyers were professional experts in the law. Many of them were Pharisees, but not all Pharisees were lawyers. Verse 46 is the first of three woes directed against the lawyers. (Compare Matt. 23 where a series of woes is directed against the scribes *and* Pharisees.)

Religion is supposed to lift burdens or make them easier to bear (Ps. 55:22; Gal. 6:2). The lawyers, however, loaded people with burdens and did nothing to lighten any burden. They controlled the interpretation of the laws and the intricate system of traditions. This maze of religious legalism was a heavy burden for people who took religion seriously.

Resisting the truth (vv. 47-51).—The lawyers built tombs for the ancient prophets, but their actions were no different from those of their forefathers who had killed the prophets (vv. 47-48). Honoring dead prophets is easier than responding to the truth presented by living prophets. Jesus declared that his generation would kill its own share of prophets (v. 49). Abel and Zechariah (2 Chron. 24:21) represent the first and the last martyrs in the Old Testament, since 2 Chronicles is the last book in the Hebrew Scriptures. The people of that generation would be held accountable for the blood of all the martyred prophets because they ignored the truth for which the dead prophets died, and they rejected and killed the prophets of their own day (vv. 50-51).

Keeping others from God (vv. 52-54).—The lawyers robbed the people of their opportunity of knowing God and his will (v. 52). They turned religion into a maze of obscure and impossible laws. The

Scriptures, which should have pointed to God, were distorted and misapplied.

The scribes and Pharisees showed the truth of what Jesus had said about resisting the truth. They continued to do their best to lay a trap for Jesus (vv. 53-54).

Requirements for Disciples (12:1-53)

Luke 12:1-53 consists primarily of teachings of Jesus addressed to his followers. The three main themes are courageous confession (vv. 1-12), proper perspective on possessions (vv. 13-34), and faithful stewardship (vv. 35-53).

Courageous Confession (12:1-12)

Beware hypocrisy (vv. 1-3).—Hypocrites try to hide the truth by pretending to be something they are not. Jesus charged the Pharisees with hypocrisy because they tried to hide what they really were behind masks of outward religious practices (11:39-44). Why did he warn his disciples against "the leaven of the Pharisees, which is hypocrisy" (v. 1)? Was he warning against danger of opposition from the Pharisees, or was he warning against the danger of becoming hypocrites like the Pharisees? If it was the former, his point was that the Pharisees would be among those who would try to silence the truth by persecuting believers. If it was the latter, Jesus was focusing on the ever-present danger of religious pretense.

Verses 2-3 emphasize that the truth eventually will be revealed. These verses sometimes are taken to refer to the inevitable judgment coming on every kind of pretense. Others take them to refer to the need for courageous proclamation of the truth in the face of persecution (compare Matt. 10:26-27).

Jesus' point in verses 1-3 may be that the disciples will be tempted to hide the truth about themselves and what they believe. In a sense, this is a form of hypocrisy, because it tries to hide the truth. The truth will come out. Believers live and speak the truth.

Fear and trust (vv. 4-7).—Verses 4-12 clearly refer to a persecution situation. In such a time disciples will be tempted to fear their persecutors. Why fear them when all they can do is kill you (v. 4)? Rather fear only God (v. 5). Some people have all kinds of fears. The Bible consistently declares that only one fear is justified. If people fear God, they need fear nothing else.

Jesus, however, clearly did not mean a slavish, cringing fear. Rather he emphasized trust in God who cares for us. If God is aware of the tiny sparrows, how much more aware is he of each of us (vv. 6-7)?

Speaking up for Christ (vv. 8-12).—In situations when believers are tempted to fail to confess Christ, they must be on their guard against denying him in word or deed (vv. 8-9). This does not mean that denial is an unforgivable sin. Jesus can and does forgive those who repent of this sin. Consider Peter, for example. This is the meaning of the first part of verse 10.

The rest of the verse, however, warns of a sin for which there is no forgiveness. The person who persists in rejecting light and truth stands in danger of becoming so hardened that he attributes the work of the Spirit to Satan (compare Matt. 12:24-32). This is more than a personal affront against Jesus; it is a hardening of the heart against every attempt by God's Spirit to bring in mercy, grace, and truth. Only those who thus refuse forgiveness are unforgivable.

Believers need not worry about how to respond when they are unexpectedly brought to trial for their faith. At such times the Spirit will make us equal to the challenge (vv. 11-12). Some people quote verse 12 in trying to justify their failure to prepare for preaching or teaching opportunities. This completely perverts the Scriptures in an attempt to excuse laziness and ignorance.

Proper Perspective on Possessions (12:13-34)

Beware covetousness (vv. 13-15).—Jesus refused to act as judge in a family dispute about inheritance. This does not mean that the issue was unimportant, nor does it mean that the brother in verse 13 did not have a legitimate case. Jesus chose to deal with a more basic issue than the legality of an inheritance claim. He dealt with the moral issue in the dispute. Covetousness is a combination of greed and envy. It is the desire for more and more, which often is activated by wanting what someone else has.

Nothing Jesus said is more relevant than verse 15. He attacked the basic premise of many people's philosophy of life. They assume that abundant possessions guarantee the good life. Jesus warned that wealth does not equal life. Jesus knew that covetousness is an insatiable thirst that destroys what makes life worth living. Right relationships and inner contentment are more valuable than an abundance of possessions.

Parable of the rich fool (vv. 16-21).—Jesus told a story to illustrate his point. The farmer in his story had abundant possessions, but he missed life. He apparently was a hardworking, honest man—commendable qualities. What then was his problem? He assumed that abundant possessions ensure abundant living. As a result, he spent his life seeking to get more and more.

One night he laid his plans for a pleasant and secure retirement. That night he died. His preoccupation with possessions had robbed him of life while he was alive and left him unprepared for death and judgment.

He had lived as though he were some kind of immortal god who had no need for the true and living God. Notice the repetition of *my* in verses 17-18. He had spent all his energies to possess what slipped from his grasp when his heart ceased to beat. One night he spoke of "my crops . . . my barns . . . my grain . . . my goods" (vv. 17-18). After that night they were no longer his; and after the estate was settled, some other fool very likely would be saying of the same possessions "my crops, my barns, my grain, my goods."

Don't be anxious (vv. 22-31).—Preoccupation with possessions can rob a person of life whether he be rich or poor. Verses 13-21 warn against one form of preoccupation—covetousness; verses 22-31 warn against another form of preoccupation—anxiety. Covetousness is the desire for more and more, but never getting enough. Anxiety is the crippling fear that there may not be enough. For the poor, anxiety focuses on having enough for survival; for others, anxiety is concerned about having enough to maintain a certain standard of living.

Jesus warned against anxiety about food and clothing (v. 22). Just as life does not consist in abundant possessions (v. 15), neither does it consist of food and clothing, the most basic of physical possessions (v. 23).

The passage shows why anxiety is wrong. Anxiety, like covetousness, robs of life (v. 23). It is futile. Anxiety cannot add any time to our span of life (v. 25). To the contrary, studies show that it actually shortens life. Anxiety shows a lack of faith in God (v. 28). It is responding to life as unbelieving pagans do, not as people of faith should (vv. 29-30).

Jesus presented the antidote to worldly anxiety. It is real life, which involves knowing and serving God. God feeds the birds (v. 24), and he adorns the flowers of the field (vv. 27-28). Surely he can be trusted to care for the needs of those committed to seek his kingdom (v. 31).

The passage does not deny that believers should work and make plans for the future. There is often a thin line between planning for the future, on the one hand, and being fretful about the outcome, on the other hand. Seeking God's kingdom puts things in proper perspective. People of faith learn to do what they can do and leave the outcome in God's hands.

True wealth (vv. 32-34).—Verse 32 is a beautiful word of assurance. God is the Shepherd of the flock and our Heavenly Father. He desires to give us the kingdom. Those who seek the kingdom, therefore, can be sure of finding it. And to find the kingdom is to find life and true riches.

Those who receive God's gift of the kingdom are able to see possessions in proper perspective. They discover that they are trustees who have the privilege of sharing with others (v. 33a). What a contrast is shown between the generous person and the rich fool. The fool tightly grasped at more and more possessions and called them his own, with no mention of God and others (vv. 17-18).

Those who share with others make an investment that time and circumstances cannot destroy. Theirs are the purses that do not grow old. Theirs is the treasure that lies beyond the hands of any thief (v. 33b). How people use their possessions is a crucial issue—a moral and spiritual issue. How we use our possessions shows clearly what are our real priorities and commitments (v. 34).

Faithful Stewardship (12:35-53)

Ready for the Master's coming (vv. 35-40).—Stewardship of possessions is implicit in the preceding verses; most of the rest of chapter 12 deals with stewardship of life and service, and it does so in connection with the Lord's coming. Although the fact of his coming is certain, the time is uncertain (v. 40).

Jesus used two analogies to stress the need for his followers to be ready for his coming. The first analogy is that disciples are like servants of a master who is away at a marriage feast (v. 36). Since the servants do not know when he is returning, they must remain vigilant.

Girding one's loins meant to tuck the long robes into their belts to be ready for quick movement (v. 35). The Jews divided the night into three watches. Even if the master returned as late as the second or third watch, the servants were to be ready (v. 38).

Ordinarily when a master returned, the servants would feed him. Jesus, however, used the analogy to refer to his coming. Therefore, he told how the Master will gird himself and serve those who have faithfully waited for him (v. 37). His kingdom has different standards than earthly kingdoms. Humble service is the ultimate measure of success (Luke 22:24-27; John 13:12-15).

The second analogy concerns the homeowner who does not know when the thief is coming (v. 39). Jesus used this only to show how uncertain is the time of his coming.

Judgment according to opportunity (vv. 41-48).—Jesus did not answer Peter's question (v. 41) directly; instead he asked another question (v. 42). Jesus did not deny that his teachings about faithful stewardship had special application to the apostles and other leaders; however, he refused to restrict the application to them.

Throughout verses 35-48, Jesus used the word for *servant* or *slave*. The one exception is in verse 42, where he used the word *steward*. Verses 42-48 provide insight into the duties of a steward. The steward was a servant or slave in charge of his master's household. When the master was away, the steward was expected to handle the household consistently with the master's instructions. When the owner returned, the steward would be held accountable.

Verses 42-44 describe the faithful steward and his reward. His reward is a larger responsibility in the master's service.

Verses 45-48 describe the unfaithful steward and his punishment. He forgot that he was the master's servant and steward, and proceeded to lord it over the other servants and to act in other ways unbecoming his master (v. 45). It is easy to see why Christians in later times have seen these verses as applying especially to persons in places of leadership.

Some commentators distinguish between the punishment in verse 46 and that in verses 47-48. They see the servant in verse 46 as so unfaithful that he was treated as no servant at all. By contrast, the servants in verses 47-48 were punished, but they were still treated as servants.

There is one clear contrast in the passage. It is between verse 47 and verse 48. One servant had a clearer understanding of his master's will than the other; therefore, he was punished more severely than the other. Luke 12:47-48 teaches the principle of judgment according to opportunity.

Christ the divider (vv. 49-53).—In verses 49-50, Jesus used words to describe his mission similar to the words used earlier by John the Baptist (3:15-17). When John spoke of fire, he meant judgment. What did Jesus mean?

Jesus had not instituted the kind of judgment John had expected. Instead Jesus had undertaken a mission of service and redemption. (See the comments on 7:18-28.) Jesus, however, saw that the outcome of his mission would be a crisis out of which would come judgment and division. He also realized that he himself would pass through a baptism of suffering, rejection, and death. The Old Testament often refers to passing through the fire of testing and the sea of troubles (compare Pss. 66:12; 69:2-3; 124:3-5; Isa. 43:2). Jesus had mixed feelings about this. On one hand, he wanted the mission and its outcome to be accomplished; on the other hand, he was burdened with the thought of how it would be accomplished (compare 22:42).

In one sense Jesus had come to bring peace (2:14), but he had not come to bring the easy peace and prosperity anticipated in many messianic hopes. Jesus faced the crisis of the cross; his followers faced the crisis of commitment to the way of the cross. As it involved rejection for him, so would it involve misunderstanding and rejection for his followers. His ultimate intent was not to bring the kind of division described in verses 51-53, but such division is inevitable when some choose to follow Christ and others to reject him. This sets up strong conflicts even in families.

The Urgency of Ultimate Issues (12:54 to 13:35)

Luke 12:54 to 13:35 records a series of incidents in which Jesus spoke primarily to persons other than his followers. He responded to what some person or group said: a report of a tragedy (13:1), a criticism of Jesus' action (13:14), a question (13:23), and a warning (13:31).

Jesus' teachings and responses focus on the urgency of ultimate issues: human tragedy and the need for repentance (12:54 to 13:9), human need (13:10-17), and entering the kingdom (13:18-30). All of this happened during Jesus' final journey to Jerusalem (13:22) and the fulfillment of his mission (13:31-35). This added to the sense of urgency.

Repent or Perish (12:54 to 13:9)

A time for decision (12:54-59).—Jesus was speaking primarily to the multitudes (v. 54). The people had an amazing lack of awareness of what was going on about them. They could read nature's signs, but they did not read the signs of the times in which they lived (vv. 54-56).

Theirs was a unique opportunity. People in that age were privileged to see and hear what the ancient prophets and kings had longed for (see 10:23-24). Why then could they not recognize their unique opportunity? The word *hypocrites* suggests they only pretended to be blind to the signs. If they were blind it was the result of refusing to see (compare 11:35-36).

In rejecting Christ they chose a path that would lead to inevitable judgment. Many of the people were choosing a way of self-assertion and violence that eventually led to war with Rome and the destruction of Jerusalem. The signs of that violent end were already clear.

Yet even as he spoke, Jesus used an analogy to show it was not yet too late. The people still had enough moral sensitivity to know what was the right thing to do (v. 57). They were like a guilty man about to be dragged into court by his accuser. He still had time to settle out of court; but if he delayed much longer, he would be taken to court, convicted, and imprisoned (vv. 58-59). They faced certain judgment, but they still had time to repent.

One clear lesson from tragedy (13:1-5).—While a group of Galileans were in the Temple, they were slain at Pilate's orders (v. 1). The most likely explanation is that they were considered revolutionaries against Roman rule. Why was this report brought to Jesus? Jesus' response (v. 2) indicates the reporters assumed the Galileans got no more than they deserved. Their smug self-righteousness caused them to draw the wrong conclusion. Jesus spelled out for them the only proper conclusion. The tragedy should have reminded each of his own sin and need for repentance (v. 3).

Jesus then mentioned a tragedy of a different kind—an accident in Jerusalem that killed eighteen people (v. 4). The first-century Jewish historian Josephus recorded that Pilate financed an aqueduct to Jerusalem with funds from the Temple. This was an unpopular project for pious Jews. Perhaps Luke 13:4 refers to an accident that occurred during this unpopular construction project. If so, many pious Jews would have assumed the accident was a divine judgment on workers willing to be paid with sacred money.

Jesus was enlarging and reinforcing his point with a tragedy that was obviously more of an accident than Pilate's execution order. Popular theology assumed that such accidents were divine judgments on sinners. Many would have reached this conclusion whether or not the accident was part of Pilate's aqueduct project.

Jesus denied the basic premise of this kind of thinking. He did not deny that the victims were sinners, nor did he deny that tragic death is ever the result of a person's sins. What he did, however, was to refocus the whole issue on the smug bystanders who passed quick judgment on hapless victims while ignoring their own sins.

When tragedy befalls others, the only clear lesson to be learned is our own need for a right relationship with God. Rather than passing judgment on others, let us look to our own moral and spiritual needs.

Coming judgment on fruitlessness (13:6-9).—The parable in verses 6-9 complements the teaching in verses 1-5. The only alternatives are repentance or judgment (vv. 1-5). The opportunity for repenting is almost over; then will come sure judgment (vv. 6-9).

The owner of the fig tree had every right to expect fruit after three years. He ordered it cut down not only because it was useless but also because it exhausted the soil. The owner agreed to an extra year of grace, during which every possible action would be taken to encourage fruitbearing.

Verses 6-9 is a parable, not an allegory. The point is that although God is patient and forbearing, continued refusal to repent spells sure doom (compare 2 Pet. 3:8-10). The immediate application was to Israel (compare Isa. 5:1-7). The ministries of John the Baptist and Jesus were the time of great opportunity. The opportunity was not yet past, but soon it would be—then it would be too late.

Although the immediate application of the entire section—Luke 12:54 to 13:9—was to Israel, the principles apply to persons and groups in every generation. No issue is more urgent than the need to repent; the alternative is inevitable judgment.

Is This an Emergency? (13:10-17)

This is the last instance in Luke when Jesus taught in a synagogue (see comments on 4:14-15). Luke 6:6-11 records an earlier sabbath healing in a synagogue (see 14:1-6 for a later sabbath healing). The basic issue was the same in both cases. Jewish tradition allowed treatment of life-threatening diseases on the sabbath, but Jesus healed persons whose problems the authorities did not consider emergencies.

This explains the peevish anger of the ruler of the synagogue (v. 14). He believed the Fourth Commandment had been broken. He obviously was angry with Jesus, but he addressed himself to the people. He accused them of coming for healing on the sabbath, although the text gives no hint of this. Jesus took the initiative in seeking out and healing the woman (vv. 11-13).

Such a view as the ruler's was pure hypocrisy. Traditional interpretation of the Fourth Commandment allowed animals to be cared for on the sabbath. They could be untied and watered (v. 15). The sabbath regulations even allowed a person to draw water, provided it was not carried to the animal.

Jesus forced them to face this question: *Are animals better than people?* The woman had been bound by a crippling disease for eighteen years; if an animal could be loosed from its bonds on the sabbath, why not a human being (v. 16)?

"Ought" used by Jesus in verse 16 is the same word used by the ruler in verse 14. It refers to a moral necessity. Each man used the word *ought* to refer to what he believed to be the moral obligation of the sabbath. Jesus broke current rules about the sabbath, but he restored its original intent. God gave the sabbath as a sign of liberation (compare Deut. 5:15; Mark 2:27). Therefore, it is not only lawful to do good on the sabbath (Luke 6:9), it is a moral obligation to do so (Luke 13:16).

The woman's case was an emergency, but not because she would die if she waited another day. It was an emergency to Jesus because she had suffered for eighteen years, and he had the opportunity to loose her burden on the sabbath—a day set aside as a sign of God's liberating grace and power. No wonder Jesus' answer shamed his adversaries and thrilled the people (v. 17).

Enter While You Can (13:18-30)

God's kingdom will come (vv. 18-21).—Jesus told the parables of the mustard seed (vv. 18-19) and the leaven (vv. 20-21) to affirm the certainty of God's purpose.

The mustard seed grows into a tree large enough for many nesting birds. Even so will the kingdom's influence extend like a large tree to encompass many. The birds may refer to the inclusion of Gentiles (compare 13:29).

Only a tiny amount of leaven permeates a large amount of dough. Even so will the influence of God's work permeate human lives and society.

Will the number of the saved be few? (vv. 22-27).—The question in verse 23 was a favorite topic for speculation. Persons who enjoy discussing this question nearly always consider themselves among the saved. Jesus' answer (vv. 24-30) indicates this probably was the situation here.

As he often did, Jesus refocused the issue: from the future to the present, and from others to self. He did not answer the question. In essence, he asked another question: *Are you among the saved?*

The door to salvation stood open to any who would enter. "Strive" and "narrow" in verse 24 do not refer to a works-salvation. Rather Jesus referred to the difficulties faced in being willing to make a total commitment to the way of the cross (compare Luke 9:57-62; 18:18-30). The difficulty of entering is from the human side, not from God's side (compare Luke 14:15-24; 15).

There is no reference to anyone striving to enter but failing to do so. The "many" who "will seek to enter and will not be able" (v. 24) are those who wait until the door is closed before trying to enter. No amount of effort or excuses will avail once the door is closed (vv. 25-27).

Guess who's coming to dinner? (vv. 28-30).—Jesus' reference to "many" in verse 24 might seem to imply that few will be saved. On the other hand, verses 28-30 refer to many who will be among the saved. The point is that many who expected to be inside will be outside, and their places will be taken by many whom the former group never expected. In this sense verses 28-30 are parallel in teaching to the parables in verses 18-21.

God's kingdom, like God himself, is bigger than most people's conception. Thus Jesus warned that a twofold shock awaited many with regard to future salvation. Many who expected to be saved would not be, and many unlikely people would be.

Verse 28 shows that Israelites could not presume on their ancestry to be saved. The patriarchs and prophets will be inside, but many other Israelites will be outside. Verse 29 uses the language of Isaiah 45:6 and 49:12 to describe the inclusion of Gentiles in the future feast in God's kingdom (compare 14:15-24). Those who had assumed they would be first ended up last, while the last became first (v. 30).

The Tragedy of Rejected Love (13:31-35)

Reply to a death threat (vv. 31-33).—For other references to Herod Antipas, see 3:1,18-20; 9:7-9; 23:6-12. Most of Jesus' public ministry was in Galilee and Perea, areas under Herod's administration. Jerusalem was in Judea, where Pontius Pilate was procurator.

We are not told why the Pharisees reported Herod's death threat to Jesus (v. 31). Jesus' reply was directed to Herod (v. 32); therefore, he accepted the report as accurate. The Pharisees may have wanted Jesus to go to Judea, where their own power and influence was greater than in Herod's territory.

Why did Jesus call Herod "that fox" (v. 32)? He may have been referring to a fox's renowned cunning. If so, he was discounting Herod's death threat as a strategy to try to frighten Jesus away.

In that day, "fox" also meant an insignificant person, as contrasted to a "lion," a person of true greatness. Jesus had great disdain for

Herod. When the two finally met, Jesus did not even answer his questions (Luke 23:8-9).

Jesus' reply to Herod's threat shows that he would not be manipulated. He would continue his ministry and complete it on his own schedule, not Herod's (v. 32). This would eventually mean leaving Herod's territory, but this would be at Jesus' initiative, not Herod's. His death lay ahead, but it would be in Jerusalem, the traditional place for prophets to be killed (v. 33).

In the last part of verse 33 Jesus used irony. He did not mean that no prophet ever had been killed elsewhere. John the Baptist, for example, had been killed by Herod at a place miles from Jerusalem.

Love can be rejected (vv. 34-35).—Verse 34 is a poignant lament. No tragedy equals the tragedy of people rejecting God's love. Jesus said: "How often *would* I . . . and you *would* not" (v. 34, author's italics). The Lord's will and intent was to gather them unto himself. What thwarted that divine plan? He willed it, but they did not! Some aspects of divine will are absolute and unconditional. However, his will to draw people to himself always is conditioned on people's response. Love and relationship cannot be forced. Love can only be freely chosen. Therefore, love and freedom go together. Love can be accepted, but it also can be rejected.

Verse 35 begins by referring to the plight of those who reject God's love. God reluctantly gives them what they want—to be left alone. "House" may refer to the Temple or to the nation. The outward trappings of religion would be present, but God would not be.

The last part of the verse has been interpreted in a number of ways: the royal entry (19:38), the resurrection, the fall of Jerusalem, the second coming.

Although many reject God's love and God lets them do so, his work will continue to its completion. People can refuse God's kingdom, but they cannot stop it. His kingdom will come, and his will shall be done.

Invitation to Discipleship (14:1-35)

The general theme of Luke 14 is Jesus' invitation to discipleship. His words in verses 1-24 were spoken at a meal in the house of a leading Pharisee. Here he was dealing with persons whose pride caused them to presume they already were destined for the kingdom (v. 15). Jesus' invitation in verses 25-35 was addressed to the crowds who followed him about, but who had little idea of what was involved in becoming real followers.

Replace Self-Seeking Pride with Humble Love (14:1-14)

Ox in the ditch (vv. 1-6).—This is one of three sabbath healings recorded by Luke that provided Jesus an opportunity to explain his actions (see comments on 6:6-11 and 13:10-17).

Jesus was a guest, but "they were watching him" (v. 1), apparently in the hope he would do or say something wrong. The Pharisees may have been using the sick man to try to trap Jesus; but more likely, he came on his own (v. 2). This episode combines the points made after the two previous sabbath healings: It is lawful to help people on the sabbath (v. 3; see 6:9). If animals can be helped on the sabbath, surely people can (v. 5; see 13:15-16).

Jesus' use of *son* in verse 5 (some ancient anthorities have *ass*) adds another emphasis. Discussing who could be helped on the sabbath was an academic exercise for a Pharisee unless the person was someone close to him; however, if a Pharisee's son was the one in trouble, the Pharisee quickly decided this was an emergency. Jesus' implication was, *Isn't it the same thing when the person is someone else's son?*

Seeking the chief places (vv. 7-11).—Verses 7-11 are a parable, not instructions about social etiquette. Greater than any social embarrassment (v. 9) will be the shame of being excluded from the feast in the coming kingdom of God. The Pharisees' pride caused them to expect the chief seats at that feast (13:23; 14:15); but their pride will exclude them, and their places will be taken by those who make no claims for themselves (13:28-30; 14:21-24). Thus those who exalt themselves will be humbled, and those who humble themselves will be exalted (v. 11).

The point of the parable, therefore, is that self-seeking pride is contrary to God's order of things. The irony is that the Pharisees were supposed to be God's most faithful servants; yet they acted no differently than any pagan scrambling for places of honor. On other occasions, Jesus accused them of using religion to seek to satisfy their hunger for special praise and honor (Matt. 6:1-6,16-18; 23:5-12; Luke 11:43). More often than not, arrogant self-assertion gains the chief seats; but faith believes that the meek ultimately will inherit the earth (Matt. 5:5).

We miss the point, however, if we see verses 7-11 as just another strategy for ultimately gaining the chief seats. Genuine humility is not a strategy to get what we want. Humility is an approach to life that sees self in proper relationship to God and others. It is the opposite of self-seeking pride.

Making a guest list (vv. 12-14).—Unlike verses 7-11, verses 12-14 are not specifically labeled as a parable; however, they seem to be a kind of parable. In the background are Jesus' teachings about God accepting the unacceptable into his kingdom, while excluding those who presume on their status (13:28-30; 14:11,15-24). In Pharisaic religion, the poor, maimed, lame, and blind (v. 13) were excluded from full participation in religious privileges. Jesus taught that God accepts just such people into his kingdom. Those who truly have been accepted by God have been accepted by God's grace, whether they are rich and healthy or poor and sick. Those who have been accepted on this basis, therefore, should be as open as God is toward all kinds of people.

The Pharisees' social snobbishness was no different from that of ordinary pagans. The principle of reciprocity is the norm for human society, but the standards of the kingdom challenge this norm with a radically different way of treating others—the way of self-giving love (see 6:32-36). This is the standard by which God ultimately will judge our actions (v. 14).

Come to the Feast (14:15-24)

Presumptuous pride (v. 15).—The pious platitude in verse 15 shows that many of the Pharisees had missed the point of verses 7-14. The man understood enough to realize Jesus was speaking of the feast in the coming kingdom, but his beatitude glibly assumed he would be among those who break bread at that feast. The parable of the great supper in verses 16-24 was designed to challenge his presumptuous pride.

Come, all is ready (vv. 16-17).—Jesus viewed God's kingdom as a joyful, sumptuous feast to which God issues a gracious invitation. Verse 16 refers to an initial invitation; verse 17 refers to a later announcement when the feast was actually ready.

Making excuses (vv. 18-20).—Presumably they all accepted the initial invitation; but when the slave announced the feast, they joined in what appeared to be a conspiracy of excuses. The three excuses mentioned in the parable are examples of the lame excuses given by the entire group.

There is a kind of grim humor in the excuses. Who buys a field without first seeing it or oxen without examining them? The law allowed a married man one year's exemption from military service and business (Deut. 24:5), but this exemption did not extend to social occasions to which one already had accepted an invitation.

The invitation was God's invitation to his chosen people, an invitation they accepted when they accepted God's covenant. The announcement was the declaration by Jesus and John the Baptist that the kingdom of God was at hand. The excuse-makers were those like the Pharisees who found various pretexts for rejecting Jesus and John (Luke 7:31-35).

Still there is room (vv. 21-24).—Notice that Jesus referred in verse 21 to the same groups mentioned in verse 13. These represent Jews whom the Pharisees considered unworthy of the kingdom. Some were literally physically maimed; others were tax collectors and sinners who did not keep the religious traditions of the Pharisees. Jesus' point is that although the Pharisees excluded them, God invites them (see 5:29-32; 7:29-30; 15:1-32). The other side of it is that the Pharisees themselves will be excluded (v. 24).

Those in the highways and hedges (v. 23) represent those outside the city, thus the Gentiles to whom the message eventually would go (13:29). "Compel" has been used at times in Christian history to try to justify persecution as a means of forcing people into the kingdom, but this distorts what the New Testament teaches about God's invitation. In this context "compel" refers to the urgency of persuading others.

The form of the parable may seem to imply that the invitations in verses 21-23 were afterthoughts, for no parable can capture all aspects of the truth. The clear teaching of the Scriptures is that

God's intent from the beginning has been to include all people in his invitation. No one is excluded except those who refuse to accept the invitation.

Count the Cost (14:25-35)

Superficial followers (v. 25).—Jesus was still popular enough for great crowds to follow him about. His words in verses 26-35 were addressed to these crowds. Although they followed him about, they were not real followers. This explains the seeming harshness of verses 26-35. Jesus was not trying to frighten them away. He was challenging them to genuine commitment. Most of them, however, had not faced up to what is involved in commitment (see comments on 9:57-62).

Love and hate (v. 26).—This verse is an excellent example of the difference between taking the Bible literally and taking it seriously. Jesus never intended that this statement be taken literally, but he did intend that it be taken seriously. This was a kind of figure of speech often used to emphasize a strong point of view (compare Mal. 1:2-3). The same point is made in milder language in Matthew 10:37: "He who loves father or mother more than me is not worthy of me."

The statement refers to those times when family loyalty comes in conflict with commitment to Christ (Matt. 10:34-36; Luke 12:51-53). For example, it speaks to the man in verse 20 who said he could not come because of his wife and to the man in 9:59 who first had to bury his father. The New Testament leaves no doubt about the need for love and loyalty in families, but even family loyalties must not stand between a person and commitment to Christ. When this tragedy occurs, the person's love and loyalty to Christ must be so clear and strong that by comparison he seems to hate his family. This is actually how some families interpret the choice made by a family member who decides to follow Christ against the family's wishes.

Crossbearing (v. 27).—To bear a cross in that day meant to be willing to die a martyr's death. Jesus had used this challenge earlier in calling his disciples to deny self in total commitment to him and his way (see comments on 9:23-27). Verse 27 thus refers to the same idea as in the last part of verse 26. In this context, hating one's life means a willingness to give one's life for Christ's sake.

Total commitment (vv. 28-33).—The point of the two parables (the builder in vv. 28-30 and the king in vv. 31-32) is summed up in verse 33. The parables reinforce verses 26-27 in calling for total commitment. Jesus wanted these superficial followers (v. 25) to become real followers. He did not want them to delude themselves that they were real followers simply because they tagged along after him, listened to what he taught, and said good things about him.

The parable makes only one point: count the cost before enlisting as a follower of Christ. Discipleship is costly, and those who follow Christ must be willing to pay the cost. Salvation is free, but it is not cheap. It involves repentance, commitment, and renunciation of anything that stands in the way of the abundant life to which Christ calls. The great renunciation is to let Christ replace self as the center of life.

The parables were *not* intended to teach that no one should commit to follow Christ if there is the slightest possibility of failing somewhere along the way. This interpretation would undercut the whole meaning of faith. Faith without risk is not faith. Part of total commitment is trust that Christ will be sufficient for whatever the future holds.

Useless followers (vv. 34-35).—The salt of that day was not pure; therefore, it could lose its saltiness. The saying appears in different settings in Matthew 5:13 and Mark 9:50. The point here is that a professed discipleship without total commitment is useless.

God's Joy (15:1-32)

Luke 15 is among the most famous chapters in the Bible. The most familiar part is the story of the prodigal son (vv. 11-24). This story, however, needs to be seen in the context of the entire chapter, especially the story of the elder brother (vv. 25-32), which is part of the same parable of the loving father.

The scribes and Pharisees criticized Jesus for receiving sinners and eating with them (vv. 1-2). Jesus then told three parables: the good shepherd and the lost sheep (vv. 3-7); the diligent woman and the lost coin (vv. 8-10); and the loving father and his two sons (vv. 11-32). The theme of the parables is God's joy over the repentance of one sinner (vv. 7,10,22-24,32).

Friend of Sinners (15:1-2)

These verses provide the key to the chapter. Jesus and the Pharisees already had clashed over this issue (Luke 5:29-32; 7:36-50), but Luke 15 provides Jesus' longest response to the charge that he was a friend of sinners. The chapter focuses their sharp differences over the issue. Jesus' approach was to include others; the Pharisees' was to exclude. The Pharisees taught repentance, but they avoided all associations with sinners. The idea of eating with sinners was particularly abhorrent to them. They would accept sinners but only after the sinners had become penitents and proved themselves by good works. Jesus sought out and befriended sinners as the best way to lead them to repent. He showed by his actions the desire of God to welcome repentant sinners.

Seeking the Lost (15:3-10)

The shepherd and the sheep (vv. 3-7).—The parable focuses on the shepherd's concern for one lost sheep, his diligence in seeking it, and his joy in finding it. Jesus taught that these are God's attitudes and actions toward sinners. The revelation of a God who seeks sinners is implicit in the Old Testament (Gen. 3:9), but the emphasis is on the need for sinners to seek the Lord (Isa. 55:6-7). The Gospels clearly portray God as taking the initiative in seeking sinners. This is the whole point of Jesus' life and death. He said, "The Son of man came to seek and to save the lost" (Luke 19:10).

The "ninety-nine righteous persons who need no repentance" (v. 7) may refer to those who already had been found and were safely in the fold. On the other hand, Jesus may have been using irony in referring to the Pharisees, who were so sure they needed no repentance. The evangelical understanding of the Scriptures is that all of us are lost sheep until we are found by the good Shepherd (compare Isa. 53:6).

The woman and the coin (vv. 8-11).—Jesus sometimes used twin parables that teach essentially the same thing (see 14:28-33). This is true here. The woman was concerned over the loss of one coin, diligently sought it, and rejoiced when she found it. The lesson is spelled out: "Just so, I tell you, there is joy before the angels of God over one sinner who repents" (v. 10).

The Loving Father (15:11-32)

The prodigal's plight (vv. 11-16).—Verse 11 shows that both sons are part of the parable. The story of the prodigal represents God's reception of sinners (v. 1). The story of the elder brother represents the attitude of the self-righteous Pharisees, who were critical of Jesus' attitude toward sinners (v. 2).

Ordinarily a father did not give an inheritance before his death, but occasionally it was done. The extraordinary father in the story represents the Heavenly Father. Thus the action in verse 12 may have been intended to represent the freedom God gives to humanity. By the same token, the prodigal's actions in verses 13-16 may typify what sin is and what it does.

From a human point of view, the prodigal son can be faulted primarily for disregarding his responsibilities as a son toward his father. Insofar as his actions typify sinners, he shows the folly of misusing God-given freedom to seek freedom from a responsible relationship to God. Sinners squander God's gifts in a futile search for life and fulfillment on their own terms.

Jesus' Jewish hearers could imagine no plight worse than the prodigal's. He was feeding swine and envying the animals for what they ate. The fact that no one fed him shows the Gentile owners put more value on their animals than on the man who fed them.

The prodigal's decision (vv. 17-19).—This is the point in the parable most unlike the two parables of verses 3-10. No parable illustrates every aspect of the truth. The earlier parables focus on the seeking love of God, but they do not show the sinner's response to that love. When a shepherd finds a lost sheep, he needs only to pick it up. The same is true of a lost coin, but a lost person is different. When a person is lost, the person must choose to receive God's forgiving love. The father of the prodigal, therefore, is not depicted as going to the far country in search of his son. There was more involved in reclaiming a person than locating him. The son himself had to decide to return.

Jesus said the prodigal "came to himself" (v. 17). Like someone awakening from a dream, he came to grips with reality. He saw himself as he was and he remembered his father's house. As yet, he felt no hope of restoration to sonship. He dared to hope only that his father would hire him as a servant. He knew his father treated his servants much better than his current employer treated him.

The father's welcome (vv. 20-24).—Not every father would respond as this father did to this set of circumstances, but Jesus' point is that the Heavenly Father always responds this way. Just as the shepherd and the woman rejoiced over finding the sheep and the coin, the father rejoiced over finding his son.

The father seeks sinners, but he also awaits their response. The story uses a family scene to show how God responds to the repentance of one sinner. The waiting father rushed to welcome his son. Before the prodigal could finish his carefully rehearsed confession, the father gave orders for a welcome-home party.

The elder brother's complaints (vv. 25-30).—The elder brother's complaints about the father's treatment of the prodigal match the Pharisees' complaint about Jesus' treatment of sinners (v. 2). The character sketch of the elder brother is a portrait of Pharisaic religion.

The elder brother had stayed at home, but he was as lost to his father as the younger son had been. He had not shared his father's anguish when the prodigal was away; he certainly did not share his father's joy when his brother returned. In fact, he even refused to acknowledge his brother. In speaking about him to the father, the elder brother called him "this son of yours" (v. 30).

He pouted, "These many years I have served you, and I never disobeyed your command" (v. 29). Paul's reflection on his experience as a Pharisee shows that he had felt himself blameless before God (Phil. 3:6).

The word translated "served" in Luke 15:29 is actually the word *slaved.* The elder brother had stayed at home and worked the farm, but he viewed his work as that of a slave, not a son.

There may even have been a note of envy as well as judgment in the elder brother's charge to his father that the younger son had "devoured your living with harlots" (v. 30). Perhaps he had, but there is nothing about it in Jesus' description of what happened in the far country.

The father's entreaty (vv. 31-32).—The father's response was patient and gracious. The proud son had complained that he had been reduced to the status of a slave. If so, the father implied, this was by his own choice, not the father's. As far as the father was concerned, all the privileges of sonship were his if he would but recognize it. The father entreated his elder son to share in the joy of the restoration of the younger son and brother.

Jesus left the story open-ended. The curtain falls without hearing the elder son's response to his father's entreaty. This probably was deliberate. Jesus hoped some of the Pharisees would yet respond to the Father's entreaty, but the choice was theirs.

In many ways the Pharisees were not far from the kingdom. They knew the Scriptures, they wanted to be pleasing to God, and they took their moral responsibilities seriously. In other ways, however, they were much farther from the kingdom than the out-and-out sinner or irreligious person. Ironically, the Pharisees were separated from God by their "goodness"; whereas others often responded more quickly to God's loving call. Another parable—the Pharisee and the publican (Luke 18:9-14)—makes this point in a memorable way.

Money—Bridge or Barrier? (16:1-31)

The proper use of money is one of the themes in Luke's Gospel. All of chapter 16 is devoted to this theme. The chapter begins with the parable of the dishonest steward and several lessons about stewardship (vv. 1-13). When the Pharisees scoffed at Jesus' teachings about money, Jesus accused them of justifying themselves (vv. 14-18). Following up on this, Jesus told the story of the rich man and Lazarus (vv. 19-31).

The general theme is that money and possessions can build bridges or create barriers. Our use of money is temporary, but how we use it has eternal consequences. Rightly used, it can create a fellowship that is eternal; wrongly used, it separates and alienates—here and hereafter.

Investing for the Future (16:1-13)

A shrewd scoundrel (vv. 1-8a).—This is among the most difficult of Jesus' parables. Part of the problem is the uncertainty of some of the circumstances described in the parable. The main question, however, is this: In what sense did Jesus intend for the dishonest steward to be an example for his followers?

This steward was the manager of the rich man's estate. He was accused of wasting his employer's possessions (v. 1). This wastefulness may have resulted from incompetence or dishonesty or both. His employer told him to turn over the records of the estate as part of giving up his position as manager (v. 2).

Knowing he was soon to be unemployed, the manager began to plan for his future needs. He quickly ruled out manual labor and begging (v. 3). Instead he hit on a scheme to use his present position to make friends who would care for him when times got bad (v. 4).

He called in his employer's debtors one by one and reduced their debts (vv. 5-7). Whether he acted legally is not clear. He probably still possessed something like the power of attorney. If so, it was legal, at least on the surface, although it was done behind his employer's back. This would help explain why the rich man did not later repudiate the steward's actions. If the steward acted legally, there was little the master could do.

Another factor may have been involved. The law forbade one Israelite charging interest to another (Deut. 23:19-20). Most people got around this law by applying it only to the poor (Ex. 22:25; Lev. 25:35-36). The rich man probably had charged interest to his debtors. The amounts they owed shows they themselves were well-to-do.

The steward may have reduced the payments by the amounts of interest due. (Records of that day show interest on oil was much higher than on wheat.) This would provide another reason for the creditor not to undertake to recoup his losses. Outsiders who heard about the cancellation of the interest would have assumed the rich man authorized this action because of religious scruples. The rich man, therefore, did not want to lose his new reputation as a man who put principle above property.

It was in this spirit that the rich man commended the shrewdness of the dishonest steward. He had managed to ensure his future by his own clever manipulation. Very likely, it was a reluctant commendation, as if to say, "What a shrewd rascal he is!"

A lesson for sons of light (vv. 8b-9).—Verse 8 presents problems for interpreters. Who commended the steward—his master or Jesus? All of this is part of a parable Jesus told; therefore, he probably would not have referred to himself as "The master." The latter half of verse 8 begins Jesus' observations about the parable. In other words, the rich man in the story commended the shrewd scoundrel, and Jesus observed that the sons of light can learn a lesson from this son of darkness. Jesus did not commend the steward's dishonesty, but he did point to his initiative in planning for the future.

Verse 9 points to the lesson that should be learned from this parable. Someday money and possessions will fail us. This sometimes happens in life, but Jesus was speaking here about death—when possessions are utterly useless. On the other hand, money can be used now in ways that create an eternal fellowship.

The shrewd steward is an example for us only in an indirect way. Jesus was not talking about using money to "buy friends" in the usual sense of these words, but he was talking about using money to advance God's kingdom by meeting human needs. Money fails, but God's kingdom is eternal. When life comes to an end, the wisdom of lasting investments will become clear. God and his people will welcome us to the eternal abode of the family of God. Money will not be there, but money will have helped make possible what is there.

Money—the acid test (vv. 10-12).—A wealthy father may entrust his son with a small amount of responsibility before he comes of age. The son's faithfulness in a little shows he also will be faithful over all that ultimately will be entrusted to him (v. 10).

Even so does God entrust us with being trustees over what is his, not ours (v. 12). If we are faithful in using the possessions entrusted to us by God, we are shown fit for even larger responsibilities and ultimately for the full inheritance as children of God (v. 11).

Money—possession or possessor? (v. 13).—If people are not careful, they will be possessed by their possessions. A person can serve only one God. If a person's attitudes and actions are preoccupied with money, mammon is that person's master.

Like all false gods, trust in mammon is deceptive and destructive. No one is more tragic than a person who makes that discovery too late.

A Word to Lovers of Money (16:14-18)

Contrasting views about money (vv. 14-15).—Luke 16:1-13 was spoken to Jesus' followers (v. 1), but some Pharisees had been listening. When the Pharisees heard what Jesus said about money, they scoffed at him (v. 14). They viewed money differently. They saw money as evidence of God's favor, not as a false god threatening to take God's place.

Jesus accused the Pharisees of justifying themselves before men (v. 15a). They were so self-righteous that they never considered the possibility they were wrong. The parable of the Pharisee and the publican was directed to this fault of the Pharisees (Luke 18:9-14).

Jesus said, "What is exalted among men is an abomination in the sight of God" (v. 15b). The story of the rich man and Lazarus (Luke 16:19-31) illustrated the teaching of Jesus in verse 15. The rich man was exalted in human society, but he faced divine judgment beyond the grave.

The danger of self-justification (vv. 16-18).—John the Baptist was the dividing line between the old era of the law and the prophets and the new age of the good news of the kingdom (see comments on 7:28).

The last clause in verse 16 may have been intended as an accusation against those who tried to force the kingdom to fit their own selfish plans. More likely, it is a graphic description of the earnestness with which many people were responding to the good news and entering the kingdom. However, not many of the self-righteous Pharisees were among those pressing into the kingdom.

The Pharisees prided themselves on their careful observation of the law and often accused Jesus of disregarding their laws and traditions. In verse 17 Jesus affirmed the lasting importance of the moral truth in the law. In verse 18 he touched on an issue about which many Pharisees played games with moral truth—divorce.

The law recognized the realities of human frailty and allowed divorce (Deut. 24:1-4). On another occasion, Jesus showed that the divorce law was clearly set in the context of a revelation that affirmed the ideal of lasting marriage (Mark 10:2-12; Matt. 19:4-9). However, many Jewish men—including many of the Pharisees— had not maintained this tension between the actual and the ideal. They allowed a man to divorce his wife on trivial grounds, including finding a woman he liked better.

Jesus' point is that such a divorce is a legal fiction, a game people play to seek to justify their actions. Such a divorce may be legal, but it does not hide from God what is still an adulterous relationship. Interpreted in this way, verse 18 is an example of what happens when people try to justify themselves.

When Possessions Separate (16:19-31)

Rich man . . . poor man (vv. 19-21).—With a few words Jesus painted the sharp contrast between the rich man and the beggar at his gate. The rich man had everything money can buy; Lazarus had none of the things money can buy. He was helpless, hungry, sick—reduced to begging, hungrily devouring scraps from the rich man's garbage. His only companions were the unclean dogs of the street.

Beyond the grave (vv. 22-26).—The name Lazarus, which means "God helps," represented the beggar's trust in God. When he died, he was borne away by angels. On earth he had been excluded from the sumptuous feasts of the rich man. Beyond death he shared in the feast-like fellowship with Abraham and other people of faith. "Abraham's bosom" (v. 22) implies a place of honor at the heavenly feast.

The rich man died and was buried, no doubt with a lavish funeral and many eloquent eulogies. However, there were no ministering angels to bear him to heaven. Instead he found himself in the torment of Hades (v. 23).

The rich man's conversation with Abraham shows he was basically unchanged by his experience. Verse 24 implies that he still viewed Lazarus as an inferior person whose role was to serve his superiors.

Abraham's reply (v. 25) does not teach that eternity is always an exact reversal of a person's lot on earth. Rather the point is that nothing was allowed to intrude on Lazarus' bliss. C. S. Lewis wrestled with this question in his book *The Great Divorce:* Will those in heaven be grieved by their awareness of the fate of the wicked? He concluded that evil, not good, would be the victor if evil could intrude into heaven's joys.

Verse 26 refers to the vast impassable chasm between where

Lazarus was and where the rich man was. During his life the rich man had separated himself from Lazarus and others like him. He probably looked at his wealth and said to himself, "All of this is mine—mine to use and enjoy, to dispose of as I please." His attitude and his fate were similar to the rich farmer of Luke 12:13-21. Neither was accused of dishonesty, but each had made an idol of mammon. As a result, each separated himself from God and others.

According to the popular view of his day, the rich man was considered to be righteous and religious. He probably saw his wealth as a reward from God. Likewise he may have assumed that people like Lazarus also were getting what they deserved.

Jesus taught that money and possessions are gifts and trusts from God. God loans us these things with the expectation that we will use them to help others. When we do, we are drawn closer to God and to those who are helped. This closeness extends beyond death into eternity.

By contrast, hell is pictured as a place of separation and alienation—from God and others. The barriers built by pride, selfishness, greed, and indifference harden into an eternal destiny. The rich man could have been welcomed into "the eternal habitations" (v. 9) by Lazarus and others he had helped, but he doomed himself by selfishly grasping his possessions. In so doing, he separated himself from others; and, although he didn't know it at the time, he also separated himself from God.

Without excuse (vv. 27-31).—Verses 27-28 sometimes are seen as evidence of the rich man's change of heart. More likely, his words are evidence of his tendency to justify his own behavior. In essence, he was complaining that he would not be in hell if he had been adequately warned.

Abraham's response shows that the rich man could have seen the truth in the Scriptures (v. 29). The rich man's reply in verse 30 implies that the words of Moses and the prophets were not sufficient warning for him, nor would they be for his brothers. He insisted that a spectacular sign, like someone returning from the dead, would lead his brothers to repent.

Abraham refused to budge. The word of God was sufficient to call people to repent. Those who refused to heed God's Word would not be persuaded by a miraculous sign (v. 31). Those who demand signs are usually the first to explain them away.

Later events proved the truth of verse 31. When another person, Lazarus, was restored to life, some believed, but many hardened their hearts even further (John 11:45-53). When Jesus was raised from the dead, many found ways to continue unchanged and unrepentant (Matt. 28:11-15).

Faith and Faithfulness (17:1 to 18:8)

This part of Luke contains four blocks of material: several teachings about what Christ expects of his followers (17:1-10), the healing of ten lepers and the return of one to express gratitude (17:11-19), Jesus' teachings about the coming of the kingdom (17:20-37), and the parable of the unjust judge (18:1-8). Although no strong relationship exists between these blocks of material, faith is mentioned several times (17:5-6,19; 18:8). The coming of the kingdom is a link between 17:20-37 and 18:1-8.

What Christ Expects (17:1-10)

Beware leading others astray (vv. 1-2).—Jesus warned his disciples against doing anything that would cause others to fall into sin. "Little ones" (v. 2) are not only children but also persons of immature faith. The bad example of a Christian, especially a Christian leader, has a disastrous impact on those who are looking for an example of what a Christian should be.

When your brother sins against you (vv. 3-4).—The word "brother" shows the close ties that bind the members of the family of faith. Verses 1-2 warn against being an offending brother; verses 3-4 tell what an offended brother should do. What should you do when a brother has sinned against you? Jesus said, "Rebuke him, and if he repents, forgive him" (v. 3). Verse 4 shows that no limits are to be placed on this forgiveness.

This is consistent with other New Testament teachings on the subject (Matt. 18:15-35; Gal. 6:1; Eph. 4:32; Jas. 5:16). The motivation of the rebuke is love, and its goal is restoration. The spirit is not haughty and judgmental. Brothers in Christ have experienced the forgiving grace of God. We, therefore, should deal with one another as God has dealt with us.

God absorbed the hurt of our sins in the cross, and offers us forgiveness and reconciliation. Human forgiveness also involves absorbing the hurt and offering forgiveness and reconciliation. Repentance precedes forgiveness, but a forgiving spirit makes repentance possible. The forgiving spirit must be there even when repentance is not.

Increase our faith (vv. 5-6).—The demands of discipleship are great. For example, who has what it takes never to lead anyone astray (vv. 1-2) and always to practice forgiveness (vv. 3-4)? The disciples recognized they needed divine help to fulfill such demands; therefore, they said to Jesus, "Increase our faith!" (v. 5).

Jesus' answer clarifies the nature of true faith. The issue is not a need for greater faith—if by that we mean something we are capable of doing. Even faith as small as a tiny mustard seed opens the way for God to act out of his limitless resources.

On another occasion (Matt. 17:20) Jesus used a similar analogy, except that he spoke of moving a mountain rather than a tree. The point, however, is the same: faith, even a little faith, can channel God's unlimited grace and power.

Beware pride (vv. 7-10).—Pride is among the greatest dangers we face. Pride is such a subtle danger that it destroys the usefulness of God's most effective servants. The parable of the unprofitable servant is directed to the human tendency to say "What a great person I am" rather than "How great God is."

"Unworthy" in verse 10 is not a moral judgment. It does not depreciate either Christian servants or service. Rather it affirms that service is expected of us. God has called and equipped us for service. When we serve God, we are only doing what we are supposed to do. Neither God nor others are obligated to take special note of us for what we have done.

Like every parable, this parable should not be pressed beyond its intended purpose. It leaves much unsaid about Christian service. For example, it does not show the role of grace in service. God expects much of us; the demands are real and great; but God never asks us to give what he has not first given to us, and far more. Service, like life itself, is a gift of God.

Gratitude and Faith (17:11-19)

Verse 11 is a reminder to the reader that this took place as Jesus headed toward Jerusalem and the cross. The incident serves as a capsule of his ministry and a prophecy of what lay ahead.

The healing of the ten lepers was typical of his ministry of compassion. The failure of the nine to return to give thanks was typical of the response he was increasingly receiving. Many people came to him only for the help and healing they wanted, not for the deeper needs he came to meet. Even then, he was on his way to Jerusalem and rejection and crucifixion.

The positive response of one person, however, showed that not everyone would miss what he had come to do. The fact that the grateful leper was a Samaritan signaled the fact that many of those who would respond in the future would be Gentiles. This is the theme of Luke's second volume—the Book of Acts.

All the lepers had a certain kind of faith. They all obeyed Christ and were healed. However, verse 19 seems to indicate that only the Samaritan had the kind of faith that saves or makes a person truly whole. This has a sobering lesson: people can accept many of God's gracious gifts and yet completely miss the purpose for which the gifts are given. God's gifts are given that he might give himself to us and we might give ourselves to him in response. Expressing gratitude to God is one indication that a person has grasped the point of God's gracious goodness to us.

Thy Kingdom Come (17:20-37)

The kingdom has come (vv. 20-21).—The time of the kingdom's coming was a subject of great interest to the Pharisees; however, their understanding of the nature of the kingdom caused them to miss its present reality. They were expecting it to be an earthly realm, in a definite place and clearly observable. Jesus denied that the kingdom consists of outward signs to be seen or that it is to be found in some definite place. Rather, he taught that the kingdom was already among them.

Jesus used a word that can be translated either *within* you or *among* you. Jesus probably would not have told the Pharisees that the kingdom was within them. His point was that they had been blind to the presence of the kingdom among them. The kingdom was there in what Christ himself said and did. In Luke 11:20, Jesus told the Pharisees, "The kingdom of God has come upon you." That was also his point in Luke 17:21.

The kingdom is coming (vv. 22-24).—*Kingdom,* as used by Jesus, means reign, not realm. It is the reign of God as King. God has always been Sovereign, but many people have not acknowledged God as their Lord. The sovereignty of God was declared in a new and powerful way in the life and ministry of Jesus. Many people, however, still do not acknowledge God as their King. Thus the New Testament speaks of the coming of the kingdom as a future event as well as a present reality. Luke 17:20-21 refers to the present, and Luke 17:22-37 refers to the future coming of the kingdom. This is one of several passages in Luke that record Jesus' teachings about the future coming (12:35-48; 19:11-27; 21:5-36).

Luke's accounts of Jesus' teachings about the future have certain things in common. For one thing, Jesus taught that his future coming will be as clear as a flash of lightning across the night sky (v. 24). He said this to encourage his followers, who in dark times would be anxiously awaiting his coming (v. 22). He wanted them not to be led astray by persons who claimed that some secret coming already had taken place (v. 23).

First comes the cross (v. 25).—The climax of Jesus' incarnate mission is indispensable to God's redemptive plan. The cross is the heart of God's purpose and the key to his kingdom.

The time of his coming (vv. 26-30).—Jesus consistently taught the certainty of the fact but the uncertainty of the time. The future coming will be as unexpected for many people as the Flood was in Noah's day (vv. 26-27) or as the destruction of Sodom was in Lot's day (vv. 28-29). Persons were going about their usual pursuits when these judgments fell; even "so will it be on the day when the Son of man is revealed" (v. 30).

Effect on present actions (vv. 31-33).—The hope of the future coming should affect present actions and values. In verses 31-33 Jesus warned against the tendency to be preoccupied with earthly values and priorities. Lot's wife is a warning from the past. Her attachment to her possessions was so strong that judgment overtook her (Gen. 19:26). God's people should live by the values of God's eternal order, not the values of a transient world order.

Coming judgment (vv. 34-37).—The future coming will involve judgment. Verses 34-35 refer to the separation of persons with close earthly ties but with different ultimate allegiances.

Verse 37 usually is interpreted as a sign of coming judgment. The word for "eagles" may also be translated "vultures." The disciples wanted to know where this would take place. Once again Jesus rejected speculation about time or place. Instead he used a proverb to show that just as a dead body draws vultures even so will sin inevitably bring judgment.

Keep on Praying (18:1-8)

The parable of the unjust judge has some things in common with earlier parables. Like the parable of the friend at midnight (11:5-8), this parable teaches the need to persist in prayer (v. 1). Like the dishonest steward (16:1-9), the unjust judge was a rascal. In fact, the judge was everything the Old Testament says a judge shouldn't be (Ex. 23:6-8; Deut. 16:18-20). He had no fear of God and no concern for other people (v. 2).

Widows in that society were helpless and dependent. The judge was supposed to be there to help just such a person, but the only language he ordinarily heard was power and money. And the widow had neither. However, this widow was not the kind to give up easily. The judge's refusal to hear her case did not stop her from continuing to make her request (vv. 3-4a).

Finally the judge agreed to vindicate her against her adversary. He did so because she literally wore him down with her persistence. She annoyed him into granting her request. He reached the stage when he would do anything to get her out of his hair (vv. 4b-5).

Do not misunderstand Jesus' point. He was not saying that God is like the unjust judge and we must wear him down by our persistent praying. To the contrary, God is a loving Father who is sensitive to our needs (Matt. 6:7-8; Luke 11:9-13).

Part of the point, like the point of the parable of the friend at midnight, is that all real requests are persistent. The woman's need was desperate, and she refused to give up.

The Bible refers to God as the righteous Judge (2 Tim. 4:8). This is another "how much more" parable. If an unjust judge hears the persistent requests of a widow, how much more will the righteous

Judge hear and answer the cries of his people (vv. 6-7)? The last part of verse 7 is difficult to translate, but the main idea seems to reinforce the difference between God and the unjust judge. *The New English Bible* translates it this way: "And will not God vindicate his chosen, who cry out to him day and night, while he listens patiently to them?"

The specific application made of the parable was to difficult times as disciples await the Lord's coming. In times of persecution, evil people run roughshod over the righteous. In such times believers wonder why God allows evil to go unpunished. They pray for the Lord to come and deliver them, but their prayers seem to go unanswered. At such times believers need to be reminded of the need "always to pray and not lose heart" (v. 1). Vindication may seem to come slowly, but when judgment falls, it will fall quickly (v. 8a).

The last question in the parable is puzzling. There is absolutely no question about the faithfulness of God, but there is a question about the faith of human beings. Jesus already had said that the time of his coming will be like the Flood or the destruction of Sodom (17:26-30). Those were times of general but not total unbelief. His question in Luke 18:8, therefore, does not mean that there will be no faith when he returns. The intent of his question was not to raise doubts but to challenge his followers to persevere in faith in the difficult times ahead. The question reinforced the point of the parable expressed in verse 1.

Receiving the Kingdom (18:9 to 19:27)

This part of Luke continues the emphasis on the kingdom from the preceding passage. The kingdom of God is mentioned several times in Luke 18:9 to 19:27. Jesus spoke of receiving the kingdom (18:16-17), entering the kingdom (18:25), and forsaking all for the sake of the kingdom (18:29). Luke records a parable Jesus told to those who "supposed that the kingdom of God was to appear immediately" (19:11).

Luke 18:9 to 19:27 highlights a series of contrasts between right and wrong responses to the kingdom. The proud Pharisee is contrasted not only with the repentant tax collector (18:9-14) but also with the trusting children (18:15-17). The rich ruler (18:18-34) is contrasted with the blind man (18:35-43) and Zacchaeus (19:1-10). The fearful slave in the parable of the pounds is contrasted with the faithful slaves (19:11-27).

Separated from God by Goodness (18:9-14)

The parable of the Pharisee and the tax collector shows the three fatal flaws of self-righteousness: it is a pompous, unrealistic view of oneself; it is harshly judgmental of others; and it separates from God (vv. 9,14). The Pharisee's prayer was actually a critical review of the sins of others (v. 11) and a hymn of self-congratulation (v. 12). He fed his pride not only with the assurance that he was not a sinner but also with the recognition that he was better than most good people. The Law required only one fast a year, on the Day of Atonement, but he fasted twice a week. The Law required tithes of certain agricultural products, but he went beyond what was required (compare 11:42).

There is nothing wrong with going beyond what is required. To the contrary, this is a quality of true dedication. Unfortunately, the self-righteous person tends to credit himself, not the grace of God. The self-righteous person, therefore, often feels that God is in debt to him, not vice versa. He thinks he has accumulated extra merit by going beyond what was required; therefore, he feels he can draw on this extra merit to get special favors from God.

The tax collector brought to God only himself and his need. He did not look about and draw comparisons to others. He stood in the presence of God and saw himself as he was. His sins caused him deep anguish, but he also dared to believe that God might be merciful even to a sinner such as he (v. 13).

Only one of the two men emerged from the Temple in right relationship with God (v. 14). Only one had sought forgiveness and right standing with God. The Pharisee probably had not committed the same kinds of sins as the tax collector, but ironically his "goodness" became his own worst sin. It made him pompous and judgmental, and it separated him from God.

Receiving . . . Like a Child (18:15-17)

This incident is recorded in all three Synoptic Gospels. Luke's record of the incident makes explicit the theme of the larger passage—receiving the kingdom. The incident of Jesus and the children thus reinforces the point of the parable in 18:9-14 and prepares the way for the incidents that follow.

The disciples, with their false sense of adult importance, would have turned away the parents and their children (v. 15). They apparently had forgotten Jesus' earlier lesson about the importance of receiving children (9:46-48). Jesus used this occasion to teach a complementary lesson—the necessity of receiving the kingdom like a child. He did not explain what qualities of children he had in mind, but he probably meant those qualities seen in the actions of the tax collector (18:13), the blind man (18:35-63), and Zacchaeus (19:1-10). Children have less false pride and are quicker to make known their needs to God and others. They are less aware of difficulties and more persistent in their prayers of faith. They are quicker to respond to Christ's call and have less concern about what others may say and less awareness of the difficulties the future may bring. In short, they are the epitome of true faith with their openness and trust in the Heavenly Father.

The Peril of Prosperity (18:18-34)

The rich young ruler (vv. 18-23).—All three Synoptic Gospels tell us that this man was rich. Matthew tells us he was young (Matt. 19:22). Luke calls him a ruler (v. 18). His concern to "inherit eternal life" (v. 18) was another way to describe entering the kingdom (v. 25). Unfortunately, he seems to have regarded eternal life as something he could ensure by performing an act of generosity or goodness.

Jesus' words in verse 19 do not contradict the New Testament teaching of the sinlessness of Jesus. Rather Jesus was challenging the ruler's superficial view of goodness. He had the same kind of confidence in his goodness (vv. 20-21) that the Pharisee had in his (18:11-12).

The evangelist Charles Finney advocated pressing an un-saved person at the point of resistance to the gospel. This is what Jesus did with the rich ruler (v. 22). Jesus saw that the man's whole life was wrapped up in his prosperity. This was the source of his pride, the nourishment for his present enjoyment, and the basis for his future security. In other words, it was his religion, his god. Jesus saw that only a complete renunciation would free this man to follow Christ in the way of life abundant and eternal.

Riches and the kingdom (vv. 24-27).—The ruler's rejection of the gospel was the occasion for Jesus' statement about the difficulty of a rich man entering the kingdom (v. 24). The analogy in verse 25 was intended to be taken seriously.

The disciples were shocked by what Jesus said. The theology of the day interpreted wealth as a sign of God's favor. If a rich man could not be saved, who could?

Verse 27 states the heart of the issue of receiving the kingdom. From the human perspective, salvation is an impossibility not only for the rich man but for any person. Salvation means rescue or deliverance. The plight from which we need to be saved is one from which we cannot deliver ourselves. We cannot be righteous enough, religious enough, or rich enough to save ourselves individually or collectively. The evangelical interpretation of the Bible is that all of us are in a plight from which we can be saved only by the grace and power of God.

Forsaking all for the kingdom's sake (vv. 28-30).—Following the ruler's refusal to forsake all and follow Christ (18:23), Peter pointed out that he and the other disciples had done just that (v. 28). Jesus assured Peter and the others that any sacrifice for the sake of the kingdom would be more than repaid (vv. 29-30).

This does not mean that following Christ is like striking a bargain that assures greater returns or that the basic motivation in following Christ is "What will I get out of this?" It does mean that those who follow Christ gain far more than they ever give up (compare Phil. 3:7-8). Generally, this is something one sees only in retrospect or through the eyes of faith. If the rich ruler had seen this, he surely would not have clung to his possessions rather than follow Christ. In Matthew's account of this incident, Jesus followed up with a parable which teaches that rewards are gifts of grace, not occasions for pride (Matt. 20:1-16).

Jesus' willingness to forsake all (vv. 31-34).—Jesus followed up with another prediction of his coming rejection. In this context, verses 31-34 teach that discipleship is not motivated by self-seeking (whether for present enjoyment or future rewards) but by self-giving according to the will of God and for the good of others.

Jesus himself is the ultimate example of one who forsook all. This is the way of the cross he had chosen and to which he called others (Luke 9:22-23). Receiving the kingdom means receiving the King and following him in the way of the cross. Jesus explained this many times, but only later did his followers understand (v. 34).

Faith That Refuses to Give Up (18:35-43)

Mark 10:46 identifies the blind man's name as Bartimaeus. He was a striking contrast to the rich ruler. The ruler claimed to want eternal life, but he was unwilling to exercise faith by forsaking all in order to follow Christ. The blind man saw more clearly than the ruler that he had nothing to lose but his blindness; therefore, he refused to let anything keep him from Christ. Others tried to silence him, but he refused to be quiet. Jesus heard and answered his prayer, and verse 43 notes that the man not only received his sight but also followed Jesus.

The man called Jesus "Son of David" (vv. 38-39), a common Jewish title for the Messiah, the expected King. Ordinarily, Jesus was cautious about accepting such titles (see comments on Luke 9:18-22); however, he honored the blind man's prayer. Only later would even his closest followers come to understand what he had been trying to tell them—that he was the kind of King who had come to suffer and die on behalf of others.

Lost and Found (19:1-10)

Luke 19:1-10 has much in common with Jesus' parables in Luke 15. Zacchaeus was a lost person who was saved by the seeking love of God in spite of the hostility of self-righteous critics.

Lost.—Zacchaeus had some things in common with the rich ruler (18:18-23). Both were wealthy men, and both sought to see Jesus. In other ways they were very different. The rich ruler's wealth was viewed as a mark of the favor of God, whereas Zacchaeus' money was considered ill-gotten gain. Respectable Jewish society ostracized fellow Jews who collected taxes for Rome. It was bad enough to collaborate with the hated foreigners, but many tax collectors also were guilty of using their positions to extort extra money for themselves. Zacchaeus' position as chief tax collector (v. 2) probably means he administered tax collecting in an entire district.

His desire to see Jesus (v. 3) was based on more than curiosity. He went to great lengths to see Jesus (v. 4), and when Jesus spoke to him, Zacchaeus received him quickly and joyfully (v. 6). These are not the actions of a curious bystander. Like many people today Zacchaeus might not have used the word *lost* to describe himself; however, his actions show him to be a person who was aware that something was wrong and that his wealth could not set it right.

Sought.—Luke 19:10 is a clear statement of Jesus' mission. So far as Jesus was concerned, this was a mission on behalf of all people. Unfortunately, many excluded themselves from the category of the lost ones whom Christ came to save. True to his mission, Jesus saw the hungry look in Zacchaeus' eyes, called him by name, and went into his home (v. 5). As in so many earlier incidents, the so-called respectable people criticized Jesus for associating with such a notorious sinner (v. 7).

Found.—Neither Jesus nor Zacchaeus was deterred by the critics. The reality of Zacchaeus' conversion is seen in his words of verse 8. He gave half his goods to the poor, and he pledged fourfold restitution to anyone he had defrauded.

He had received the King and the kingdom. Jesus used different terminology to describe the same thing: "Today salvation has come to this house, since he also is a son of Abraham" (v. 9). The theology of that day tended to describe salvation primarily in future terms. They hoped to be declared righteous and acceptable to God at the time of the future judgment. The New Testament refers to salvation as a confident hope grounded in a present reality. Christians do not peer anxiously into the future, hoping against hope that all may be well. Rather we believe that God forgives our sins and sets us right with him when we trust Christ as Lord and Savior.

Zacchaeus was a true son of Abraham. Like Abraham he dared to entrust himself and his future completely into God's hands. This is part of the childlike faith Jesus referred to in Luke 18:17. Nothing is so hard for adults to believe as this: Life can begin anew! The people of Jericho didn't believe it, but Jesus and Zacchaeus did.

The Faithfulness Test (19:11-27)

His followers heard Jesus' words to Zacchaeus. The words about "today salvation has come" (v. 9) probably added to their expectation that the kingdom of God was about to appear. In spite of all Jesus had said and done, they still expected the trip to Jerusalem to result in a nationalistic kingdom with Jesus as king. Jesus told the parable of the pounds to correct this delusion (v. 11).

Jesus taught that there is a tension between the present reality and the future coming of the kingdom. An experience like Zacchaeus' marks the beginning of a pilgrimage of faith. His conversion was an exciting new beginning, but only a beginning. Receiving the kingdom involves commitment and faith, but life as a servant of the kingdom calls for patience and faithfulness over the long haul.

The disciples expected an immediate coming of the final kingdom, but Jesus taught that servants of the King must be faithful as they await the future coming of the King. When he returns, they will be called on to give account of their stewardship. A secondary theme is that of the rejected King (vv. 14,27), which served as a warning against the ultimate folly of totally rejecting the King.

The parable teaches some of the basic aspects of Christian stewardship:

All that we have actually belongs to God.—The faithful servants recognized this and referred to "your pound" in reporting to the king (vv. 16,18).

God's gifts are also trusts.—The nobleman instructed them to do business with his pounds while he was away (v. 13).

Faithfulness is the mark of good stewards.—This was the basis for the king's commendation of the two servants (v. 17).

Unfaithfulness is the result of lack of faith.—The unfaithful servant had not lost his pound, but he had not taken the risk of investing it in obedience to his master. His excuse was that he feared his master as a harsh taskmaster (vv. 20-21). Faithfulness involves taking risks, and only those who have faith in God's grace and help are willing to take such risks.

The rewards for faithfulness are opportunities and responsibilities consistent with the degree of faithfulness.—The servants were rewarded with a number of cities equal to the number of pounds they had gained (vv. 16-18).

Part of the punishment for unfaithfulness is the loss of responsibility and opportunity.—The pound of the unfaithful servant was taken from him and given to the servant with the ten pounds (v. 24). The bystanders were surprised by this (v. 25). Jesus stated the paradox of this principle in verse 26: using what we have enlarges our capacity for more; on the other hand, unused gifts wither away.

Final Ministry in Jerusalem
19:28 to 24:53

The last major section of Luke's Gospel tells of the culmination of Jesus' mission in Jerusalem. Much earlier Jesus had "set his face to go to Jerusalem" (Luke 9:51). The largest section of Luke's Gospel (9:51 to 19:27) frequently mentions that Jesus was journeying toward Jerusalem (13:22,33; 17:11; 18:31; 19:11). The last major section recounts what happened during his last days in and around Jerusalem.

Jesus' final ministry in Jerusalem is described in three blocks of material. Following his entry Jesus spent some time teaching in the Temple (19:28 to 21:38). The events connected with his crucifixion are described in 22:1 to 23:56. Chapter 24 focuses on Jesus' appearances after his resurrection.

The Prince of Peace (19:28-48)

These verses tell what happened as Jesus drew near to Jerusalem and entered the Temple. Thus in one sense 19:28-48 is the last part of the journey to Jerusalem and in another sense the beginning of the final ministry in the city.

Peace is a strong theme. Jesus approached the city as the prophesied King who would bring peace to the nations (Zech. 9:9-10). Peace was on the lips of those who welcomed him (v. 38). Jesus wept at the tragedy of Jerusalem's rejection of the way of peace he offered them (vv. 41-42).

The Coming of the King (19:28-40)

Preparing to enter Jerusalem (vv. 28-35).—Why did Jesus choose to enter Jerusalem as he did? During his ministry he had tried to avoid calling public attention to himself as the Messiah (see 9:20-21). Why then did he enter Jerusalem at the Passover season (22:1) when excitement about the Messiah was at its peak? And why did he make an entry that was bound to stir up this excitement?

Zechariah 9:9-10 points to the coming of the King riding on the colt of an ass and bringing peace to the nations. Jesus presented himself as the fulfillment of that prophecy (Matt. 21:5; John 12:15). He prepared to enter Jerusalem as the Messiah, but not as the Messiah many of his countrymen were seeking. They wanted a military strong man who would restore their fortunes as a nation; he came as the Prince of peace for all people.

Welcomed by some (vv. 36-38).—As Jesus approached Jerusalem, his following grew. He probably had a number of people with him as he came up from Jericho (v. 28). Very likely, word of his approach reached Jerusalem, and many pilgrims poured out of the city to join him. As the procession reached a point where the city came into view "the whole multitude of the disciples began to rejoice and praise God with a loud voice for all the mighty works that they had seen" (v. 37). This was the larger company of his followers, not just the twelve. They had witnessed many of his miracles; now they praised God for what they had seen.

Verse 38 quotes Psalm 118:26. This psalm, which celebrates the hope of God's deliverance, traditionally was sung as pilgrims approached the Temple for one of the great feasts. The disciples of Jesus used this psalm to praise God for Jesus, the King who had come to fulfill their hopes. The last part of Luke 19:38 sounds similar to the words of the angelic host in Luke 2:14. Peace is already a reality in the heavenly realm of the God of peace. This "Peace is heaven" (v. 38) is now offered in Jesus Christ.

Criticized by others (vv. 39-40).—The Pharisees called Jesus *teacher,* not *King.* This probably explains why they asked Jesus to rebuke his followers (v. 39). The Pharisees did not acknowledge Jesus as the promised Messiah-King.

Jesus' response in verse 40 sheds further light on why he entered Jerusalem as he did. If he had not been the Messiah, then he should have silenced his followers. On the other hand, since he was the Messiah, he was the fulfillment of the prophecies of centuries. His mission in Jerusalem was the decisive event in God's great plan of the ages. Someone must herald such a momentous event. If human voices had been silent, then nature itself would have found voices to praise God for what he was doing.

The Ultimate Tragedy (19:41-44)

Jesus had no illusions about the outcome of his final ministry in Jerusalem. He had predicted his rejection and death on more than one occasion (9:22,44; 13:33-34; 18:31-34). The acclamation by his followers as he approached Jerusalem did not change his mind. Others were shouting joyful words of praise, but Jesus was weeping (v. 41). Earlier he had described his desire to gather the people of Jerusalem as a hen gathers her chicks, but the people would not let him (Luke 13:34). Here he described the same ultimate tragedy in two other graphic ways: He had come as the Prince of peace, but their eyes failed to recognize him (v. 42). God had come to visit his blessings and salvation upon them, but they did not know it (compare Luke 1:68).

Verses 43-44 predict the judgment that came in AD 70 when the Romans destroyed Jerusalem and the Temple. Verse 43 describes the siege; and verse 44, the final ruin of Jerusalem (see also 21:5-7,20-24).

Robbers in the House of God (19:45-48)

Cleansing the Temple (vv. 45-46).—This was an act of prophetic symbolism, not a sudden outburst of righteous indignation. This statement does not mean that Jesus acted without emotion; it does mean that he had a larger purpose than driving out the people who were selling animals in the Temple. He was acting out the fulfill-ment of Malachi 3:1-2. He, not the priestly exploiters of the Temple, was the real Lord of the house of God.

The high priest and his cronies were the robbers of the poor, sincere worshipers who came to the house of God. The high priest claimed to be providing a service by selling animals for sacrifice. Animals had to be approved before they could be sacrificed, and the animals sold in the Temple court already had been inspected and approved. Thus a worshiper need not transport an animal a great distance and still run the risk that the animal might not be approved.

Jesus' words show that this "service" actually was used to exploit people. Since the high priest controlled the inspectors and the sellers of animals, he could charge fees for inspecting other animals and overcharge for his own animals.

The aftermath of the cleansing (vv. 47-48).—Jesus not only drove out the agents of the high priest; he proceeded to make the Temple court into the place for his daily teaching of the people. The high priest at this time was not a devoutly religious man; actually he had more in common with a corrupt political boss. From his point of view, Jesus' cleansing and occupation of the Temple was a brazen power play. The reaction of the high priest was predictable. No one was better at power plays than he; therefore, a powerful coalition began to make plans to destroy Jesus.

Questions and Answers (20:1 to 21:4)

The Temple was the setting for crucial events in the early days of Jesus' life (Luke 2:21-38); see also 1:8-23 and 2:46-49). The Temple was also the setting for important events of his last days. After cleansing the Temple (19:45-46), Jesus "was teaching daily in the temple" (19:47). Luke 20:1 and 21:38 records some of the teaching he did in the Temple. Luke 20:1 to 21:4 covers a variety of subjects; 21:5-38 tells about the coming destruction of the Temple.

Most of the teaching in 20:1 to 21:4 is in the form of questions and answers. The enemies of Jesus tried to trap him with a series of questions. He answered them, in some cases with questions of his own.

Who Gave You the Right? (20:1-8)

Jesus was not only teaching in the Temple; he also was preaching the good news to the people (v. 1). While he was doing this, the same groups mentioned in 19:47 asked him the source of authority for what he was doing (v. 2). This question was part of their plan to destroy him. They hoped his answer would get him in trouble with the Roman authorities. If Jesus claimed to be the Messiah, his enemies could accuse him of revolutionary activities.

Jesus didn't take the bait. Instead, he asked them a question, "Was the baptism of John from heaven or from men?" (v. 4). This put Jesus' questioners on the defensive. They faced a real dilemma. If they pleased the crowd by saying John was from God, the people would have asked them why they did not believe John when he was alive (v. 5). If they gave their honest opinions that John was not a true prophet, the people might have stoned them; for John was popular with the common people (v. 6). Therefore, these proud leaders of the people were forced into the embarrassing position of saying that they did not know whether John was from God (v. 7). Jesus then refused to answer their question (v. 8).

This refusal by Jesus was not just a ploy to avoid answering a loaded question. The people were aware of the close relationship between Jesus and John. Jesus had acclaimed John as a prophet sent by God to set in motion something Jesus would continue (see Luke 7:24-35). Jesus obviously believed that he and John acted with divine authority. By asking his critics about John, Jesus indirectly was answering their question about his own authority. When they refused to acknowledge the divine authority of John, they showed they were not willing to listen to an honest answer to their question.

Murdering the Son (20:9-18)

The parable of the wicked tenants (vv. 9-16).—Jesus told this parable to the people (v. 9), but the questioners of verse 1 probably also were listening. The parable amplifies two themes from verses 1-8: (1) Jesus showed the end result of refusal by the leaders to recognize the work of God in their midst. (2) Jesus claimed the authority of divine sonship.

This parable has the qualities of an allegory. The tenants represent the people of Israel. God is the owner of the vineyard who sends his servants the prophets. One after another the servants are mistreated and driven away. Finally the owner sends his son, but the wicked tenants murder the son. Jesus was saying that he had come from God as had the prophets, but that he was the divine Son. He also was saying that the people would reject him as their forefathers had rejected the prophets; in fact, they would treat him worse than the prophets had been treated.

The parable does not make clear why the tenants expected the inheritance would be theirs if they killed the heir. Perhaps they thought the father was dead or that he had transferred the property to his son; if so, they expected to be able to claim squatters' rights to the vineyard.

The three verbs in verse 16 show what the owner would do when he received word of his son's death. He would "come . . . destroy . . . give." The owner had sent servants and his son. Now he himself would come. His coming meant judgment for the wicked tenants, but it did not mean the end of the vineyard. The owner would give it to others.

All three Synoptic Gospels record this parable (Mark 12:1-12; Matt. 21:33-46), but only Luke records the response of Jesus' hearers, "God forbid!" (v. 16). They had understood the gist of Jesus' parable, but they were horrified at the ending. The common people were concerned because of the mention of the death of the son. The leaders, who were plotting Jesus' death, were disturbed at the thought that God would destroy their nation and give his vineyard to the Gentiles.

The rejected stone (vv. 17-18).—Verse 17 is a quotation from Psalm 118:22, which was considered a messianic psalm. Jesus is the stone rejected by the builders, but God will make him the key stone in a new building. Verse 18 uses the stone analogy to prophesy judgment on those who reject Christ. The rejection of Israel is tragic, but it does not stop the purposes of God. He builds a new Israel, with Christ as the cornerstone.

What About Taxes? (20:19-26)

The scribes and chief priests recognized that the parable was directed against them. They wanted to arrest Jesus on the spot, but he was too popular with the people (v. 19). So they sent spies to try to trap Jesus into saying something incriminating (v. 20). They tried to set the stage by flattering Jesus (v. 21). Then they asked, "Is it lawful for us to give tribute to Caesar, or not?" (v. 22).

They could have asked no more controversial question. When the

Romans first levied a poll tax in AD 6, the Jews were very unhappy and continued to chafe under the tax. One group of extremists, the Zealots, regarded paying this tax as infidelity to God. They advocated armed rebellion against Rome. Many of the people did not believe in armed rebellion, but they deeply resented the tax. Jesus' enemies hoped he would express sympathy with this popular feeling. This would give them an excuse "to deliver him up to the authority and jurisdiction of the governor" (v. 20). Later, when they did arrest Jesus, this was one of their false charges against him (Luke 23:2).

Jesus' response was a clear rejection of the Zealot position. He affirmed the right of government, even Caesar's government, to levy taxes. Someone in the crowd had a coin with Caesar's image on it. The traditional Jewish position was that the right to coin money carried with it the right to rule. If Caesar performed the God-given role of government, he had the right to levy taxes (see Rom. 13:1-7).

Jesus affirmed the ultimate claim of God on what is his. Just as Caesar's image was on the coin, God's image is on those who have been made in his image. We owe our taxes to the state. We owe ourselves to God. When a conflict arises between our allegiance to the state and our allegiance to God, we must be true to God.

What About the Resurrection? (20:27-40)

A question from the Sadducees (vv. 27-33).—The Sadducees are mentioned several times in the Book of Acts (4:1; 5:17; 23:6-8), but this is the only mention of their name in Luke's Gospel. The chief priests, however, are mentioned several times in the Gospel (19:47; 20:1,19), and the chief priests were Sadducees. Politically, they collaborated with Rome. Religiously, they differed in significant ways from the Pharisees. For example, the Pharisees believed in a resurrection, but the Sadducees did not (v. 27; see also Acts 23:6-8).

The Pharisees' concept of resurrection was stated in earthly terms. They expected a state of eternal bliss that was merely a heightening of normal human functions. The question posed for Jesus was probably one the Sadducees often had used to confound the Pharisees. The situation was based on the law about levirate marriage in Deuteronomy 25:5-10. *Levir* means brother, and a brother was commanded to marry the widow of his brother. No evidence exists that the practice was followed in Jesus' day or that the situation in verses 29-32 had ever happened. The Sadducees, however, hoped to make Jesus look as ridiculous as they had made the Pharisees look when they had tried to answer the question.

The nature of the afterlife (vv. 34-36).—The Sadducees had heard that Jesus believed in the future resurrection, but they were wrong to assume that he believed in the same kind of literalistic resurrection as the Pharisees. He affirmed a resurrection life, but he taught that it is a different mode of existence from life on earth. Since it is an existence from which death has been banished, there is no need for procreation. Therefore, the relationships in the resurrection life are on a different basis than that of husband and wife. Relationships in the resurrection life are like those of the angels, who have fellowship with God and one another, but not on a biological basis. (Compare Paul's description of the resurrection body in 1 Cor. 15:35-50.)

Life with God is eternal (vv. 37-38).—Jesus challenged the Sadducees with the implications of Exodus 3:6. The Lord told Moses, "I am . . . the God of Abraham, the God of Isaac, and the God of Jacob." The patriarchs had been dead for centuries, but God referred to himself and them in the present tense. Jesus drew from this the truth that "he is not the God of the dead, but of the living; for all live to him" (v. 38).

The Old Testament doctrine of life after death is not so clear-cut as the New Testament teaching; however, this truth is taught in both Testaments: fellowship with the eternal God is eternal. God made us for fellowship with him. If we walk with him now, we will continue to walk with him beyond death.

Questioners silenced (vv. 39-40).—The scribes, most of whom were Pharisees, found themselves in the strange position of commending Jesus for his skillful answer about the resurrection (v. 39). Jesus had successfully avoided the traps his enemies had set for him. His questioners had had the tables turned on them. As a result, none of them dared ask another question (v. 40).

What About the Messiah? (20:41-44)

After his critics decided not to ask Jesus any more questions,

Jesus asked them a question. His question challenged their concept of the Messiah. One of their favorite titles for the Messiah was *son of David*. This was an accurate title, for the Messiah was the anointed King of David's line who would establish God's eternal kingdom. Many of Jesus' contemporaries, however, used the title primarily to refer to one who would restore the ancient glories of Israel at the expense of the Gentiles. Jesus was the true son of David, but he rejected this nationalistic concept of his work.

He quoted Psalm 110:1 to show that David referred to the Messiah as *Lord*. Jesus Christ was the son of David, but he was much more than an earthly successor of David. He is the Lord.

False and True Religion (20:45 to 21:4)

The scribes' hypocrisy (20:45-47).—These verses describe religion at its worst. The scribes used their religion to advance their own personal ambitions and to feed their pride (v. 46). They went through the motions of long prayers, but only for the effect (v. 47).

Jesus also said they "devour widows' houses" (v. 47). Widows and orphans were the helpless members of ancient society. The Old Testament abounds in challenges to help and protect these groups (Ex. 22:22-23; Deut. 24:17,20; Ps. 146:9). The Book of James mentions this as one of the marks of genuine religion (1:27). As religious leaders, the scribes were in a position to take the lead in helping the widows of the community. Instead, however, they devoured widows' houses. Not only did they not help the widows, they actually preyed on them. They used their positions of trust to take advantage of the vulnerability of the helpless.

The poor widow's commitment (21:1-4).—The widow in the Temple was the epitome of true religion, just as the scribes were of false religion. Jesus praised her as profusely as he had condemned them. The scene was the court of the women, where offerings were made. The rich passed by and made their gifts, but Jesus called the attention of the disciples to a poor widow who had "put in more than all of them" (v. 3). The disciples must have been shocked by this statement, for Jesus went on to explain in verse 4. The amount of her gift was much less than theirs, but the big difference was in what was left after the gifts were made. The rich made large gifts, but they still were rich after they had left the Temple. They gave out of their abundance and, as a result, did not even miss it. By contrast, the widow gave all she had.

The Impact of the Future (21:5-38)

No passage in the Gospels is more difficult than Luke 21:5-36 and its parallels in Mark 13 and Matthew 24. Part of the problem is that these passages use apocalyptic language—the highly symbolic kind of language found in such Bible books as Ezekiel, Daniel, and Revelation. The main difficulty, however, is the intertwining of two events. Although Jesus focused on the destruction of the Temple, he projected this as a sign of his future coming. The two events are woven in and out of the fabric of the passage. As a result, it is difficult always to distinguish which verses refer exclusively to one or the other event.

In Jesus' day, both events were in the future. From our perspective, the Temple's destruction is long past. Jesus was describing to the disciples what appeared to them to be like a distant mountain range. From our perspective, however, we know that he was describing two mountain ranges with considerable distance between them.

We know what happened to Jerusalem and the Temple in the Jewish-Roman War of AD 66-70. The Jewish historian Flavius Josephus left a vivid account. By contrast, none of us has experienced what will take place at the Lord's future coming. Considerable agreement exists among Christians about the fact of the Lord's coming, but much disagreement exists about the particulars. These differences of opinion are reflected in what teachers say and commentators write about this passage.

A Startling Prediction (21:5-6)

As Jeremiah had prophesied the destruction of Solomon's Temple (Jer. 7), so Jesus foretold the destruction of Herod's Temple. Many people in Jeremiah's day and in Jesus' day assumed that God would never allow his Temple to be destroyed or his people judged.

The Babylonians destroyed Solomon's Temple in 587 BC. A second Temple was built by Zerubbabel about 515 BC. Herod the Great began a third Temple in 20-19 BC, and work on this magnificent structure was continuing in Jesus' day (see John 2:20). When the Roman armies besieged Jerusalem, the last fanatical defenders took refuge in the Temple. Even then, some of them expected God to come to their rescue; but the Romans eventually overwhelmed them. Then the Romans leveled the Temple, as Jesus had predicted.

Responses to the Future (21:7-19)

Signs and speculations (vv. 7-11).—The disciples' questions (v. 7) focused on how they could know *when* the Temple would be destroyed. This event was associated in their minds with the end of the old order and the establishment of God's final kingdom. Jesus had tried to teach that there was first to be a period of waiting and serving (Luke 12:35-40; 19:11-27), but his followers persisted in expecting Jesus to establish such a kingdom immediately (Luke 19:11). Even after his resurrection, they were speculating that God was about to restore the kingdom to Israel (Acts 1:6). Jesus warned against speculating about times and seasons (Acts 1:7); instead he called them to their real task of worldwide witness (Acts 1:8). Similarly in the passage before us, Luke 21:8-11 warns against speculating about signs, and Luke 21:12-19 calls to faithful witnessing.

The key to verses 8-11 is the last part of verse 9: "The end will not be at once." Jesus warned against the tendency to see every striking event as a sign of the end. Specifically he warned against those who would come in his name and announce that "The time is at hand!" (v. 8). Wars and unrest are not signs that the end is at hand (v. 9). Neither wars nor natural disasters are signs of an imminent end (vv. 10-11). Many such things took place in the years before AD 70, and many have taken place since then.

A time for faithful witnessing (vv. 12-19).—Jesus predicted a time of intense persecution before the Temple fell (vv. 12, 16-17). He challenged his followers to see hostility not as a threat but as an opportunity for bearing testimony (v. 13). They did not need to worry ahead of time about what they would say when they stood before their accusers; Christ promised to enable them to bear a powerful testimony (vv. 14-15; see comments on 12:11-12).

Verses 18-19 give further assurance and challenge. Verse 18 presents the same kind of assurance as Romans 8:35-39. Although some of them would be put to death (v. 16), they were safely in the hands of him who numbered the hairs on their head (Luke 12:7).

"Endurance" in verse 19 is another way to describe the faithfulness called for in verse 13. Some people are "survivors" who manage to come through all kinds of troubles; however, Jesus was not talking about survival but endurance. Endurance involves facing life with faith, courage, and love. This sometimes involves taking risks, even the risk of losing life itself. Christ does not promise survival; he promises life. Those who set out to save themselves may survive, but they will lose life; whereas those who lose their lives for Christ's sake find life (see Luke 9:24-25). Death itself cannot destroy this kind of life.

Judgment on Jerusalem (21:20-24)

These verses refer to the fall of Jerusalem, not the final coming of Christ. Notice the references to Jerusalem (vv. 20,24) and Judea (v. 21). The first part of verse 24 is a clear reference to what happened in AD 70.

The disciples had asked about the sign that the Temple was about to be destroyed (v. 7). Verse 20 is the answer. When the Roman armies began to encircle the city, its desolation was near. Jesus warned his followers to flee (v. 21). Jesus refused to be associated with the nationalistic groups whose main goal was to fight for independence from Rome. He did not want his followers to get involved in this; therefore, he told them to leave rather than stay and fight. The Christian historian Eusebius says that when the Romans came to Jerusalem, the followers of Christ moved to Pella across the Jordan River.

Jesus saw the fall of Jerusalem as a judgment on those who had rejected God's purpose (v. 23). The time of the old covenant had ended, and a new day had dawned. The real transition point was the life, death, and resurrection of Jesus Christ. When Jesus died, the Temple veil was torn in two (Luke 23:45). This signified the end of the old and the coming of the new, but the destruction of the Temple ended even the functioning of this central institution of the old covenant.

Under the old covenant Israel was commissioned as God's people in the world. God's plan always had been to broaden his commission to include all people of faith. The fall of Jerusalem was one sign that the new covenant had inaugurated "the times of the Gentiles" (v. 24). One of the themes of Luke-Acts is that the tragedy of rejection by many Jews did not end God's work; rather it opened the way for Gentiles as well as Jews to enter his kingdom and serve him (see Luke 13:22-30; 14:22; 20:16-18; Acts 13:26; 18:6). (Rom. 9—11 tells how God is at work to save as many as possible of both Gentiles and Jews through faith in Christ.)

In other words, "the times of the Gentiles" refers to the gospel age. The positive meaning of the phrase is that Gentiles have their opportunity to do God's work in the world. The negative connotation of the phrase is that pagan nations will continue to trample sacred things underfoot until the coming of Christ (Dan. 8:13-14; 12:7; Rev. 11:1-2,15). (The Greek word translated "Gentiles" twice in verse 24 is translated "nations" in the rest of the passage.)

Coming of the Son of Man (21:25-28)

Verses 20-24 point to Jerusalem's fall, but the setting of verses 25-27 is much broader. Jesus referred to the "distress of nations" (v. 25). The word *world* in verse 26 means the inhabited world. The setting, therefore, seems to be the events connected with Christ's coming. The judgment on Jerusalem in verse 23 was a sign of the judgment on all nations in verses 25-26.

The vivid apocalyptic language of verses 25-26 symbolized the giving way of the old order of creation to the new order of Christ's eternal kingdom. Jesus emphasized, however, not the signs themselves but the effect of these signs on humanity unprepared for Christ's coming.

Verse 27 refers to the fulfillment of Daniel 7:13-14,27. Jesus often referred to himself as the Son of man. Daniel described how God would give to the Son of man sovereignty over all things. In a sense this happened in connection with Jesus' life, death, and resurrection (Luke 22:69). In this sense the kingdom is already a reality (Luke 11:20; 17:21). In another sense, however, the present reality of the kingdom is recognized only through eyes of faith. At Christ's future coming, the domination of godless nations will end and all people will become aware of the sovereignty of the Son of man (see Phil. 2:9-11).

Verse 28 offers encouragement to God's people: "When these things begin to take place" (whether the things in verse 20 or verses 25-26), believers can take heart; redemption is drawing near. The Old Testament "day of the Lord" was described as a day of judgment on persistently sinful people and a day of redemption for the faithful people of God. The New Testament presents the same theme. The basic attitude of believers toward the future is confident hope in God and his gracious purpose.

Readiness for the Temple's Ruin (21:29-33)

This is the most controversial part of a difficult passage. The words *this generation* in verse 32 are the heart of the problem. This verse has been subjected to a wide variety of interpretations.

The most natural way to understand "this generation" is its obvious sense of the people alive then. This is its meaning elsewhere (Luke 7:31; 11:29-32). Some suggest the word here means "race," referring to the Jewish people; but this seems somewhat forced. It is an interpretation designed primarily to protect Jesus from what appears to be an error—mistakenly predicting his coming in that generation.

This problem disappears, however, if verse 32 referred to the Temple's destruction, not the Lord's coming. The main theme of the chapter is Jesus' explanation of his prediction about the Temple's ruin. Verses 5-24 deal with this. Verses 25-28 look beyond to Christ's coming, the final judgment and redemption which is prefigured by the fall of Jerusalem. It should not be surprising then if Jesus came back to the main theme in verse 32, actually verses 29-33.

The parable of the fig tree, therefore, may refer to the sign in verse 20. Jesus warned in verses 8-11 about seeing every striking event as a sign. However, Jesus did give one clear sign—verse 20 is the sign of Jerusalem's impending ruin. Therefore, the point of verses 29-31 may be this: the siege preparations of Roman armies about Jerusalem were as clear a sign of the Temple's coming ruin as a budding tree is of the coming summer.

What about the last part of verse 31? For one thing, keep in mind that Jesus often used similar language to refer to something other than his coming (Luke 10:11; 11:20; 17:20-21). And even if the words here refer to the final coming of the kingdom, this kind of language is used throughout the New Testament to heighten a sense of expectancy (1 Cor. 16:22; Phil. 4:5; Jas. 5:8-9; Rev. 22:20). The fall of Jerusalem signified that the new age had dawned in Christ. As a result, it increased rather than diminished the note of expectancy about the future.

Verse 33 stresses what abides in the midst of uncertainty and dissolution. Jerusalem and the Temple had been sources of stability and security for the Jewish people. Jesus knew that many of his followers, therefore, would be disturbed when these things passed away. One purpose of this passage was to help them distinguish between the temporal and the eternal. The real security of his Jewish followers was not bound up with the rituals of the past, but with the living, abiding word of God. Someday heaven and earth themselves will pass away, but our security is not rooted in these realities of our present existence.

Readiness for the Lord's Coming (21:34-38)

Watch and pray (vv. 34-36).—These verses, although addressed by Jesus to his followers, deal with the theme of preparedness for his coming. The people involved are not the inhabitants of Jerusalem, but "all who dwell upon the face of the whole earth" (v. 35). The mention of the "Son of man" (v. 36) also ties this to the earlier mention of the coming of the Son of man (v. 27).

In other words, Jesus predicted and explained the Temple's ruin in verses 5-24. Then he looked beyond to his future coming in verses 25-28. In verses 29-33 he spoke of preparedness for the former; and in verses 34-36, of readiness for the latter.

Although the judgment on that day will be primarily against persistent sinners, believers also must be ready to give account of their stewardship (see also Luke 12:41-48; 19:11-27; Rom. 14:12). Christians are children of light, not children of the world (Luke 16:8); therefore, we should not live like children of the world. Jesus warned against being weighed down not only with dissipation and drunkenness but also with the cares of this life (v. 34). This warning, especially the latter part, may be for many of us the most practical and personal verse in the passage. It expresses a persistent theme in Luke—the danger of preoccupation with material things (see Luke 12:13-34; 16).

Teaching in the Temple (vv. 37-38).—These verses remind us that the setting for this entire section of Luke—from 19:45 to 21:38—is the Temple.

In the Shadow of the Cross (22:1-53)

In Luke 22:1 the scene shifted from Jesus' teaching in the Temple to the events just prior to the trials and crucifixion of Jesus. With the exception of verses 1-6, the passage describes what happened on the day and night before his crucifixion: his Last Supper with the disciples (vv. 7-38), his prayer about the cup (vv. 39-46), and the arrest (vv. 47-53).

The Plot Against Jesus (22:1-6)

After Jesus' cleansing of the Temple, his enemies had sought a way to destroy Jesus, but they had been thwarted by his popularity with the people (see comments on 19:47-48; see also 20:19-20). Luke 22:2 says that although they were continuing to plot Jesus' death, they continued to fear what the people would do.

The account of this plot in the other Synoptic Gospels indicates that Jesus' enemies had decided to wait until the feast was over (Mark 14:2; Matt. 26:5). The Passover season was the most important time of the year in first-century Judaism. The feast began with the day of Passover on Nisan (their first month) 14 and included the seven-day Feast of Unleavened Bread, which began on Nisan 15 (v. 1; Num. 28:16-17). Jerusalem was crowded with pilgrims during the entire feast.

Then something happened that changed the conspirators' plan to wait. Acting on his own initiative, Judas came to them and offered to betray Jesus (v. 4). This solved their dilemma because Judas, as an insider, could lead them to Jesus at a time when the crowds were not around (v. 6).

Why Judas did this remains a mystery. Luke tells us that he opened his life to Satan (v. 3), but this does not explain what Satan used to draw Judas into this terrible deed. Some say that Judas was trying to force Jesus' hand by putting him in a position in which Jesus would have to declare himself and use his powers to set up his kingdom. As evidence, they point to Judas' later remorse (Matt. 27:3-10). Most of the biblical evidence, however, implies that Judas was a selfish man who was frustrated because following Jesus had not brought to Judas all that he had expected; he, therefore, determined to salvage something for himself out of this lost cause.

Sin is always irrational. It doesn't make sense even when we know the supposed reasons. This was true in the Garden of Eden; it was true of Judas; it is still true.

The Last Supper (22:7-38)

Preparation for the Passover meal (vv. 7-13).—The Passover lambs were slain during the afternoon of Nisan 14; and the meal was eaten in the evening, which was Nisan 15 for the Jews, whose days began at sundown. When that day arrived, Jesus sent Peter and John to prepare for the Passover meal (vv. 7-8).

Because Jesus was aware of Judas' plan to betray him, he kept secret the place of the meal. Even Peter and John did not know where it was to be until they got there (vv. 9-13). The sign was a man carrying a water jar, which was unusual since carrying water was considered women's work. The text does not say whether this man and the availability of the upper room were the result of arrangements Jesus had made earlier or of his use of supernatural knowledge.

The Last Supper and the Lord's Supper (vv. 14-20).—The Passover celebrated a past deliverance, God's deliverance of Israel from Egyptian bondage (Ex. 12), and over the centuries it also came to be an anticipation of God's coming kingdom. In connection with his last Passover meal with the apostles, Jesus instituted the Lord's Supper, which like the Passover commemorates a divine deliverance and looks forward to the future consummation of God's kingdom.

Jesus' words in verses 15-18 show that he saw this Passover meal as his last meal with his followers before his suffering and death. His words also look ahead to the future kingdom. Luke's Gospel contains several references to the future as a feast (13:29; 14:24; 22:30).

Luke's account of the Last Supper mentions two cups—verses

17-18 and verse 20. The other accounts mention only one. Some ancient manuscripts of Luke omit the reference to the second cup, possibly because an early scribe had trouble with the mention of two cups. Luke notes that the cup of verse 20 was taken "after supper." He may have used these words to set apart the institution of the Lord's Supper in verses 19-20 from the Passover meal itself. If so, the cup in verses 18-19 probably was one of four cups taken during the Passover meal.

Luke 22:19-20 and the other New Testament references to the institution of the Lord's Supper (Mark 14:12-26; Matt. 26:17-30; 1 Cor. 11:17-34) show why Christians observe the Lord's Supper rather than the Passover. The divine deliverance of Israel from Egypt foreshadowed the deliverance from sin and death made possible by the death and resurrection of Jesus Christ. The bread represents the body of Christ, given for us. The cup signifies his blood shed for us, which sealed the new covenant of God with his people.

A betrayer's hand (vv. 21-23).—Verse 22 shows two important aspects of the death of Jesus. From God's point of view, the death of Jesus was God's plan for human redemption; however, those who were responsible for his death are held accountable for what they did. Judas was not a helpless pawn in a divine drama; otherwise, Jesus would not have pronounced judgment on him for his betrayal.

A new definition of success (vv. 24-30).—The word *also* in verse 24 shows that the disciples moved from their discussion of who would betray Jesus (v. 23) to an argument about who deserved to be regarded as greatest. The fact that they would have such an argument at this time shows how out of touch they were with their Lord. Jesus' life and teachings had magnified the way of self-giving love for God and others. Within a few hours he would die in the same way; yet they were arguing about who was the greatest.

We marvel at the patience of Jesus. Verses 25-27 show how he explained again what he often had tried to teach them before. The "great" people of the world are those with the greatest power and honor (v. 25). In that day the youngest member of a family had the most menial work, but Jesus challenged his followers to take the initiative in choosing for themselves such service (v. 26). By the world's standards the person being served is greater than those who serve him, but the reverse is true by God's standards (v. 27).

The promise of future rewards in verses 28-30 needs to be viewed in light of verses 24-27. Jesus spoke words of assurance in verses 28-30. Because the apostles had continued with him in his trials, he assured them they would share in the joys of the coming kingdom; however, he did not place any of them in places of honor above the others. In the new Israel, the twelve will occupy places comparable to the places of the twelve tribes of ancient Israel.

Satan's sifting (vv. 31-34).—Earlier Satan had entered Judas (v. 3); now Jesus warned that Satan had asked to be able to sift the others as a farmer sifts wheat. (The word "you" in v. 31 is plural.) Verse 31 is reminiscent of the early chapters of Job where Satan sought permission to put Job to the test. Satan's purpose was to strike at Jesus through his followers. Satan intended to show that they were like useless chaff; God allowed the sifting that they might be shown to be like the wheat which survived the sifting.

The repetition of Simon's name in verse 31 and Jesus' words in verses 32 and 34 show that Jesus was aware of Peter's coming denial. Jesus' words in verse 32 were words of assurance that Peter would later remember and from which he would take heart. Although Peter would seem at first to have failed Satan's test, Jesus had prayed that his faith fail not. He called on Peter to strengthen his brothers after he was restored from his own failure. Unfortunately, at the moment Simon was too filled with self-confidence to heed Jesus' warning (v. 33).

The two swords (vv. 35-38).—This passage is another that shows how completely the disciples missed what Jesus was trying to teach them. He was trying to help them realize that they and he were about to face a crisis, the like of which they had never known. He, therefore, used symbolic language to encourage them to draw on all available resources as they girded for battle with Satan and the forces of darkness (see vv. 31,53). They took him literally when he said to sell their mantles and buy swords (v. 36). They held out two swords, possibly the butcher knives left over from preparing the Passover lamb (v. 38). Jesus said, "It is enough" (v. 38). He probably meant, "That's enough of that kind of talk."

A literal interpretation of Jesus' words in these verses would present real problems. It would go against everything else he did and taught (see, for example, Luke 6:27-29). More specifically, it would contradict his actions later that night (22:48-51).

Not My Will, But Thine (22:39-46)

In verses 35-38 Jesus had spoken symbolically about preparations for a struggle with Satan. Now he spoke plainly. Prayer is the believer's weapon against temptation. Earlier Jesus had promised to pray for Peter (v. 32); now he told them to pray for themselves (v. 40). Then he prayed as he faced his own crisis (vv. 41-44). Their response shows how little they were aware of the immediate crisis. When Jesus found them sleeping, he repeated his challenge to pray in the face of temptation (vv. 45-56).

Jesus' prayer reveals several things about his coming death: (1) It was the will of God. (2) The cross was not forced on Jesus, either by God or by his enemies; he voluntarily accepted it as God's will. (3) The cross involved terrible suffering for Jesus, and all his natural inclinations were to avoid it.

Although Satan is not explicitly mentioned in verses 39-46, he was still tempting Jesus to avoid the way of suffering and death. This was the purpose of Satan's earlier attacks, which Jesus had resisted (see comments on 4:1-13). The references in the larger passage to Satan (vv. 3,21) and the forces of darkness (v. 53), and the references in the immediate passage to "temptation" (vv. 40,46) support the view that Jesus was again wrestling with this temptation.

Many brave people have faced death without flinching. Why did Jesus shrink from it? It is not just that crucifixion was a horrible way to die. Martyrs have faced death—even slow, torturous death— without a word. Christians believe that the death of Jesus was much more than a martyr's death. The "cup" of verse 42 was the deep darkness into which Jesus descended as he died for the sins of the world. The depths of what he endured for others are far beyond our understanding and experience. All the Synoptics record Jesus' prayer (Mark 14:32-42; Matt. 26:36-46). Luke's account is the shortest, but he described more clearly than the others the agony Jesus endured as he faced the cross. Luke alone tells us "Being in an agony he prayed more earnestly; and his sweat became like great drops of blood falling down upon the ground" (v. 44).

Darkness Has Its Hour (22:47-53)

Jesus was not tracked down and seized against his will. He knew of the plot and of Judas' plan to betray him; yet he went to the Mount of Olives "as was his custom" (v. 39), knowing that Judas would lead his enemies there. He thus chose to drink the cup by turning himself over to the power of darkness. His enemies had been eager to seize Jesus for a long time, but they had feared the people's reaction (19:47-48; 20:19-20; 22:2). Now they came out to seize him under cover of night. This action, which had to be cloaked by the darkness of night, showed the moral and spiritual darkness portrayed by this act (vv. 52-53).

A Mockery of Justice (22:54 to 23:25)

Luke's account of the trials of Jesus is longer than his account of the crucifixion itself. The trials shed light on the meaning of Jesus' death. Luke tells how Jesus was denied by Peter (22:54-62), condemned by the Sanhedrin (22:63-71), and sentenced by Pilate (23:1-25). The Gospels show how the sinful self-interest of many people was involved. One of Jesus' own followers betrayed him; another denied him. Representatives of the best religious system and of the best judicial system sent the innocent Son of God to his death. These facts support the biblical teaching of the universality of sin.

The Tragedy of Denial (22:54-62)

When Jesus was arrested and taken to the high priest's house, "Peter followed at a distance" (v. 54), but at least he followed! All the other disciples except one had fled (Mark 14:50; Matt. 26:56; John 18:15). Peter knew that when revolutionary leaders were captured and executed, the authorities also sought to capture and execute their followers. Peter showed his loyalty by following Jesus right into the courtyard of the high priest.

Why then did Peter deny the Lord? Earlier that night Peter had told Jesus, "I am ready to go with you to prison and to death" (22:33). Peter no doubt meant what he said. At the time he thought Jesus was about to set up his kingdom, and Peter was ready to fight and die for him. When the armed mob came to arrest Jesus, Peter was the one who drew his sword and struck a blow (22:49-51; John 18:10-11). He did this even though he knew their two swords were no match for their foes.

Peter, however, was confused by Jesus' refusal to resist. Instead Jesus had meekly placed himself in the hands of his enemies. Peter was following, but he was a confused and disillusioned follower. He, therefore, was morally and spiritually unprepared for the three accusations in the courtyard. He was a brave man when he had a sword in his hand, but he was not willing to risk death for what seemed a lost cause.

Only Luke records that Jesus turned and looked at Peter as the cock crowed (v. 61). Jesus probably was being led from one part of the building to another. At any rate he was close enough for Peter to see the look in the Lord's eyes.

A Predetermined Verdict (22:63-71)

Mocked and humiliated (vv. 63-65).—When he was first arrested, Jesus was interrogated by Annas, the father-in-law of the high priest (John 18:12-24). Then Caiphas and the Sanhedrin conducted an informal hearing (Mark 14:53-65; Matt. 26:57-66). Jesus was kept under guard as they awaited morning, when the Sanhedrin was to conduct an official hearing. Meanwhile the high priest's men filled up the empty hours by mocking Jesus.

Condemned (vv. 66-71).—The "council" (v. 66) was the Sanhedrin, a Jewish court of seventy members plus the high priest. They exercised authority over the religious life of the Jewish people. They operated under the jurisdiction of the Roman authorities, but the Sanhedrin also managed to exercise considerable influence on the Romans from time to time. Roman procurators like Pontius Pilate were reluctant to resist a determined action by the Sanhedrin.

Luke does not record the earlier informal examinations of Jesus by this group. The morning meeting recorded by Luke (see also Mark 15:1; Matt. 27:1) was an attempt to legitimize what they already had decided to do. The Sanhedrin could not legally conduct a trial on a capital case at night.

They tried to get Jesus to admit that he was the Messiah (v. 67). This would then give them a basis for accusing him before Pilate.

Jesus' answer (vv. 67-68) was his way of telling them that he realized that they already had made up their minds. This was not a trial at which evidence was being considered. The verdict was predetermined. Jesus, therefore, refused to answer on their terms; rather he used the title "Son of man" (v. 69). His answer implied that whatever they did with him, he would live on in glory and would someday be their Judge. This answer, plus his admission to being the Son of God, was proof enough to them that he was guilty of blasphemy (vv. 70-71).

Sentenced to Die (23:1-25)

A false charge (vv. 1-5).—The entire Sanhedrin brought Jesus to Pilate. He was the chief Roman official in Judea from AD 26-36 (see 3:1). The Sanhedrin had condemned Jesus for the sin of blasphemy (Mark 14:64; Matt. 26:65); however, this was not a crime in the eyes of Rome. Therefore, the Sanhedrin accused Jesus of revolutionary activities. In addition to the general charge of perverting the people, they accused Jesus of forbidding the payment of taxes and claiming to be a king (v. 2). These were false charges. Jesus taught that people should pay their taxes (20:19-26), and he refused to be the kind of king who would have threatened Rome (John 6:15). This explains Jesus' ambiguous answer to Pilate's question in verse 3. He was the King of the Jews, but not in the sense that Pilate would have understood (see John 18:33-38). Pilate's verdict in verse 4 shows that he believed Jesus. This should have been his official verdict, and the charges then should have been dismissed; however, the enemies of Jesus were insistent (v. 5), and Pilate did not act decisively.

Mocked by Herod (vv. 6-12).—When Pilate learned Jesus was from Galilee, he tried to solve his dilemma by sending Jesus to Herod (vv. 6-7). This was Herod Antipas, the tetrarch of Galilee and Perea (3:1). He had imprisoned and killed John the Baptist, and for a long time he had felt a superstitious curiosity about Jesus (see comments on 3:18-20 and 9:7-9). Herod was thrilled at the prospect of seeing Jesus perform some sign (v. 8). Jesus refused to dignify him with any kind of a reply (v. 9). The evil ruler reacted by subjecting Jesus to a cruel and humiliating mockery (v. 11). He then sent Jesus back to Pilate without passing any kind of sentence on his guilt or innocence. Pilate interpreted this to mean that Herod found Jesus innocent (v. 15). Neither of these men, however, escaped guilt for their involvement in this shameful miscarriage of justice (see Acts 4:27).

Sentenced by Pilate (vv. 13-25).—Pilate then tried another way to avoid passing sentence on Jesus. He issued another strong statement about Jesus' innocence; then he offered to have him chastised and released (vv. 13-16). Roman law allowed for a prisoner to be beaten as a kind of warning for the future. Pilate hoped this compromise would satisfy Jesus' accusers.

Rather than satisfying them, this further inflamed them. They demanded that Pilate release Barabbas, an insurrectionist and murderer, and send Jesus to be crucified (vv. 18-21). Pilate repeated his innocent verdict and his offer to chastise Jesus, but they insisted that Jesus be crucified (vv. 22-23). Pilate, therefore, finally gave in to their demands (v. 24). Verse 25 is worded to show the irony of the innocent Jesus being condemned for the very crimes of which Barabbas was guilty.

Why did Pilate finally give in to their demand that Jesus be sentenced to death? Mark 15:15 says that he wanted to satisfy the crowd. John 19:12-13 says that the Jewish leaders threatened to report to Caesar that Pilate was not acting in behalf of Caesar. Jesus was the innocent victim of power politics. Pilate knew that the Sanhedrin was trying to use him to crucify an innocent man. He probably resisted not so much from his sense of justice as from his abhorrence at the idea of being controlled by the high priest. Pilate, however, knew that Tiberius Caesar was suspicious enough to believe an accusation against him, especially if it came from the highest Jewish court of the land. Therefore, he did what only he could do—he passed sentence on Jesus. The Sanhedrin had its guilt, but so did Pilate.

Dying for Sinners (23:26-56)

In the first century the cross was at the heart of the gospel message (1 Cor. 15:3-4), but the Christian witnesses encountered much prejudice against accepting a crucified person as the Savior of the world (1 Cor. 1:22-23). Luke wanted to show his readers that the crucifixion of Jesus was not what it appeared to be—a routine execution of a condemned revolutionary; rather, the death of Jesus was an act of divine love on behalf of sinners. On one hand, therefore, Luke stressed the fact that Jesus was completely innocent. This was the repeated verdict of Pilate (23:4,14-15,22). The penitent thief (23:41) and the centurion (23:47) recognized Jesus' innocence. Luke focused on the real meaning of the cross in the three sayings of Jesus (23:34,43,46). Even the mockery of Jesus' enemies points to the truth that Jesus refused to save himself in order to save others (23:35).

The Way to Golgotha (23:26-32)

Simon of Cyrene (v. 26).—Simon carried the cross "behind Jesus." Jesus was on his way to the cross, but he also had called others to follow him in the way of the cross (9:23). What Simon was forced to do by the Romans points to what Christ's followers are to do voluntarily. (Mark 15:22 implies that Simon became a follower.)

Women of Jerusalem (vv. 27-31).—This incident, recorded only by Luke, points to the judgment coming on Jerusalem. Rather than lamenting his death, Jesus called on the women of Jerusalem to weep about the coming ruin of their city (see comments on 19:41-44 and 21:20-24). A barren woman generally was viewed with pity; but during the death throes of Jerusalem, barren women would be glad they had no children to go through such suffering (v. 29). They would pray for the mountains to fall on them and put them out of their misery (v. 30). If the Romans would crucify Jesus, who was innocent of the charge of being a revolutionary, what would they do when they got their hands on some real Zealots? Jesus was like green wood compared to the dry wood of a Jerusalem that took up arms against Rome (v. 31).

Two criminals (v. 32).—The Suffering Servant "was numbered with the transgressors; yet he bore the sin of many" (Isa. 53:12).

Death of the Savior (23:33-49)

Prayer for sinners (vv. 33-34).—Crucifixion was a method of execution designed to torture and humiliate the victim. The Gospels do not focus on the torment Jesus endured, but on the significance of his death. The Gospels record seven sayings of Jesus on the cross:

one in Mark (15:34) and in Matthew (27:46), three in Luke (23:34, 43,46), and three in John (19:26-27,28,30).

Two of Luke's sayings are prayers. As Jesus was being crucified, he kept praying, "Father, forgive them; for they know not what they do" (v. 34). When men were crucified, they often screamed or cursed. Occasionally one prayed—for help or a quick death; but Jesus prayed for those responsible for his crucifixion. The prayer surely included the Roman soldiers; but judging from other New Testament references (Acts 3:17; 13:27; 1 Cor. 2:8), it also included rulers like Pilate and even the Sanhedrin. Since the purpose of his dying was redemptive, he prayed that all might have the opportunity to experience divine forgiveness, even those who crucified him.

Saving self or others? (vv. 35-38).—Luke recorded the responses of three groups: the people watched (v. 35*a*); the Jewish leaders scoffed (v. 35*b*); and the soldiers mocked (vv. 36-37). The intended ridicule by the rulers contained prophetic truth. Jesus could have saved himself, but he knew that he could not save others if he saved himself. He, therefore, refused to save himself. His enemies could not imagine God allowing his Chosen One to suffer such a fate, but the Christian good news is that "in Christ God was reconciling the world to himself" (2 Cor. 5:19).

"Today . . . in Paradise" (vv. 39-43).—The incident of the two thieves raises the question of why some people believe and some don't. The two thieves apparently had been exposed to the same sights and sounds; yet one joined in the mockery of Jesus, and the other believed. The penitent thief expressed an amazing faith. At the darkest hour when all seemed lost to Christ's closest followers, this man believed. He probably understood little of Jesus' mission; but he believed Jesus was the Messiah whose kingdom was coming, and he saw himself as a dying sinner.

The thief had asked to be remembered in Christ's coming kingdom. Jesus promised the thief that he would be with Jesus in Paradise on that very day. At death believers depart to be with Christ (Phil. 1:23; 2 Cor. 5:6-8). This does not contradict the biblical teaching of future resurrection. The dead in Christ share with the living this hope of the final consummation of God's redemptive purpose.

Darkness and death (vv. 44-49).—The eerie darkness of Jesus' final hours points to the cosmic significance of his dying. The cry recorded by Matthew (27:46) and Mark (15:34) shows that the forces of darkness did their worst to Jesus during that time (see comments on 22:42). The prayer in Luke 23:46, like "It is finished" in John 19:30, shows that Jesus had won the victory. At the time the disciples did not realize this, but after the resurrection they saw the cross in a totally new light.

The tearing of the Temple curtain (v. 45) signified that the death of Christ opened the way for all people into the presence of God. The Book of Hebrews tells how the Jewish sacrificial system was fulfilled in Jesus Christ.

The response of the Roman centurion is another ray of light in the darkness. He was convinced Jesus was innocent, and he also praised God (v. 47). Like Matthew (27:54) and Mark (15:39), Luke seems to have understood this as an expression of faith. This positive response by a Gentile pointed ahead to the time when the Jewish believers would preach the gospel freely to Gentiles.

Dead and Buried (23:50-56)

Joseph of Arimathea (vv. 50-53).—Joseph's act is a sign of hope. He was a member of the Sanhedrin, who opposed what that group had done. Now he acted with faith and courage to provide a tomb for the body of Jesus. Luke's description of Joseph as "looking for the kingdom of God" (v. 51) is reminiscent of the earlier descriptions of Simeon and Anna (2:26,38).

The women (vv. 54-56).—These verses bridge the gap between Luke's accounts of the crucifixion and resurrection of Jesus. These loyal women had ministered to him in life (8:3). They were determined to do what they could for him after he was dead.

"The Lord Has Risen Indeed" (24:1-53)

None of the Gospels records all the resurrection appearances of Jesus. Each evangelist told of the resurrection in light of his distinctive purpose. Luke emphasized the reality of the resurrection and the difference it made in the lives of the disciples. Although Jesus' followers had heard him predict his death and resurrection, they were not expecting him to be raised from the dead (vv. 1-12). They believed only after they had seen the risen Lord for themselves (vv. 33-43). The Lord helped them see the cross as a triumph, not a tragedy (vv. 13-32). He commissioned his followers to be his witnesses to all nations (vv. 44-49). Thus, although the disciples of Jesus had been in despair when he had left them earlier, they were able to live in confident joy after his ascension (vv. 50-53).

"An Idle Tale" (24:1-12)

Some skeptics try to explain away the resurrection of Jesus. One of their theories is that the disciples saw someone or something they mistook for Jesus. This assumes that the disciples were anxiously awaiting the resurrection. To the contrary, the New Testament shows that they were *not* expecting Jesus to be raised from the dead.

Luke 24:11 is clear evidence of this fact. The women had seen the empty tomb (vv. 1-3) and had heard the angels say that Jesus was alive (vv. 4-7). However, when they reported this to the apostles (vv. 8-10), "these words seemed to them an idle tale, and they did not believe them" (v. 11). Some of the men went to the tomb and found it empty (vv. 12,24), but they still were not convinced. Only later, when they saw Jesus for themselves, did they believe (vv. 33-43).

The angels reminded the women that Jesus had predicted his death and resurrection (vv. 6-7). How could the disciples have heard these predictions and not been expecting Jesus to be raised from the dead? They had heard what he said, but they had not understood (Mark 9:32; Luke 9:45; 18:34). They had their own expectations about what the Messiah was to be and to do; therefore, they heard only what they expected to hear (see comments on 9:22).

Suffering and Glory (24:13-32)

The cross as tragedy (vv. 13-24).—Only Luke records the appearance of Jesus to the two followers on the road to Emmaus. They spoke frankly to Jesus, but did not recognize him (v. 16). Their conversation reveals how Jesus' friends were feeling before they became aware of his resurrection. They had hoped that Jesus would deliver Israel (v. 21), but their hopes had been dashed by Jesus' condemnation and death (v. 20). They were aware of the report brought by the women (vv. 22-24), but they shared the view of the men in verse 11. Some of the men had gone to the tomb and found it empty, but they had not seen Jesus (v. 24). The implication of verse 24 is that if Jesus were alive, he surely would have shown himself to them.

They revealed their feelings not only by their words but also by how they looked. Luke says, "They stood still, looking sad" (v. 17).

The cross as triumph (vv. 25-27).—Many of the people of Jesus' day were diligent students of the Scriptures, but most missed the central message (John 5:39). They focused their attention on the passages that presented the Messiah as a glorious King, but they missed the passages that spoke of suffering as God's way of dealing with evil. The risen Lord, still unrecognized, proceeded to show the two Emmaus disciples how this theme runs through the Old Testament (v. 27). He showed them that the suffering of the cross was the way of triumph, not tragedy (v. 26).

He no doubt pointed them to specific passages, like Isaiah 53, but he also showed them that this theme underlies the entire history of Israel. God called his people not for privilege but for mission. This mission involved suffering, sometimes innocent suffering. The glorious King and the Suffering Servant are one and the same. Through redemptive suffering, the King fulfills the will of God and enters into his glory.

Jesus had tried to teach his followers that the way of self-giving love is the way of God (Luke 9:22-23), but the earth-bound disciples continued to measure success by worldly standards (Luke 22:24-27). When God raised Jesus from the dead, he showed that Jesus was right. The way of love is the way of life. Those who dare to live in the way of the cross can be assured of the power of the resurrection (see Rom. 6:3-4; Gal. 2:20; Col. 3:1-4).

Recognizing Jesus (vv. 28-32).—Why were they so slow to recognize Jesus? The same question comes up about Mary Magdalene in John 20:14. For one thing, they were not expecting to see him. Another factor may have been that his appearance was changed in some ways. The main factor, at least for these two, was that the mystery of this revelation was temporarily hidden from them (v. 16, 31). When they did recognize him, they were better able to understand some of their earlier feelings. During the time he was speaking to them, they were aware of strange feelings. Now in retrospect they understood why their hearts had burned within them (v. 32).

Seeing Is Believing (24:33-43)

Enthusiastic witnesses (vv. 33-35).—The day was almost over when the two disciples recognized Jesus (v. 29). A seven-mile journey at night was unusual in those days, but these two immediately returned to Jerusalem (v. 33). What a difference from standing still and looking sad (v. 17)!

Before the two Emmaus disciples could tell all their story, the Jerusalem disciples told good news of their own: "The Lord has risen indeed, and has appeared to Simon" (v. 34). Other than Paul's brief reference in 1 Corinthians 15:7, this is all we know of the appearance to Simon. With these two reports, the Jerusalem followers were beginning to dare to believe that Jesus was indeed alive.

Disbelieving for joy (vv. 36-43).—If the disciples believed that Jesus was risen (v. 34), why were they startled and frightened when Jesus appeared to them (v. 37)? Hearing Peter's testimony was one thing, but suddenly being confronted by the Lord was something else.

At first they thought he was a ghost; therefore, Jesus challenged them to look carefully and even to handle him (v. 40; compare 1 John 1:1). He even ate a piece of fish to show them he was not a ghost (vv. 41-43). The exact nature of his resurrection body remains a mystery. He was not with them all the time. He appeared here and there from time to time, usually suddenly. On the other hand, he had a body that could be seen and touched, and they recognized the body as Jesus' body. The resurrection of Jesus, therefore, means more than that Jesus' spirit survived death. The tomb was empty. His body was raised from death.

Even as Jesus spoke to them, they "still disbelieved for joy" (v. 41). What was happening was too good to be true; yet the growing sense of joyful excitement told them that it was true. Thomas was not the only doubter (John 20:24-29). None of them was expecting Jesus to be raised from the dead. They did not believe the first reports. Each had to see for himself; and even as they saw, they struggled with their natural doubt that such a miracle actually had taken place.

Commissioned As Witnesses (24:44-49)

Earlier Jesus had opened the Scriptures to the Emmaus followers in order to show that the way of the cross is the way of victory (vv. 25-27). Now he opened the Scriptures to the entire group (v. 44). He repeated the earlier lesson and added to it the message of repentance and forgiveness for all nations (vv. 45-47). In other words, Jesus taught that the key to understanding the Scriptures and the purpose of God is to recognize that God always has intended to declare the good news of divine salvation to all nations.

Luke's Gospel is the first part of a two-volume work. The Book of Acts shows how the Spirit led Christians to cross many barriers to take the gospel to all kinds of people. Luke's Gospel shows that this worldwide mission was inherent in all Jesus said and did. Luke 24:44-49 forms a kind of bridge between Luke's two books. Some of the themes of the last part of the Gospel are repeated in the early part of Acts. This is especially true of the commission to be worldwide witnesses (vv. 47-48; Acts 1:8) and the promise of power from on high (v. 49; Acts 1:4-5).

Sorrow Turned to Joy (24:50-53)

These verses are a short account of the ascension, which is described also in Acts 1:9-11. The striking part of Luke 24:50-53 is what happened after Jesus left them: "They returned to Jerusalem with great joy" (v. 52). Earlier, when Jesus had been taken from them by death, they were completely demoralized; but now, after being assured of his resurrection, they were able to rejoice even though he had parted from them. What could better show the difference made by their faith in the resurrection of Jesus Christ from the dead!

Bibliography

Caird, G. B. *The Gospel of St. Luke.* "The Pelican Gospel Testament Commentaries," edited by D. E. Nineham. New York: Pelican Books, 1977.

Conzelmann, Hans. *The Theology of St. Luke.* Translated by Geoffrey Buswell. New York: Harper and Row, 1960.

Danker, Frederick W. *Luke-Acts. Proclamation Commentaries,* edited by Gerhard Krodel. Philadelphia: Fortress Press, 1976.

Ellis, Earle E. *The Gospel of Luke. The Century Bible.* London: Marshall, Morgan and Scott, 1974.

Geldenhuys, J. Norval. *Commentary on Luke. The New International Commentary on the New Testament,* edited by N. B. Stonehouse. Grand Rapids, Michigan: Wm. B. Eerdmans Publishing Co., 1956.

Marshall, I. Howard. *The Gospel of Luke. The New International Greek Commentary.* Grand Rapids, Michigan: William B. Eerdmans Publishing Company, 1978.

Miller, Donald G. *Luke.* Vol. 18, *The Layman's Bible Commentary,* edited by Balmer H. Kelly. Atlanta: John Knox Press, 1959.

Morris, Leon. *The Gospel According to St. Luke. Tyndale New Testament Commentaries.* Grand Rapids, Michigan: William B. Eerdmans Publishing Company, 1976.

Plummer, Alfred. *The Gospel According to St. Luke. The International Critical Commentary,* 5th ed. Edinburgh: T. and T. Clark, 1953.

Summers, Ray. *Commentary on Luke.* Waco, Texas: Word Books, 1972.

Talbot, Malcolm O. *Luke.* Vol. 9, *The Broadman Bible Commentary,* edited by Clifton J. Allen. Nashville: Broadman Press, 1970.

Tinsley, E. J. *The Gospel According to Luke. The Cambridge Bible Commentary.* Cambridge: At the University Press, 1965.

March 16, 1993

May the Lord bless you
and keep you —
while we are absent
one from the other.
Your 8:30 A. M. Tuesday
Prayer Partners,

Lennie Wascoms
Riley Cable
Ruth P. Keen
Dorothy Gunn
Opal Rae Wild

Layman's Bible Book Commentary
Hebrews, James, 1 & 2 Peter

LAYMAN'S BIBLE BOOK COMMENTARY

L B B C

HEBREWS, JAMES, 1 & 2 PETER

VOLUME 23

Foy Valentine

BROADMAN PRESS
Nashville, Tennessee

4211-93

ISBN: 0-8054-1193-3

Dewey Decimal Classification: 227.87

Subject Headings: BIBLE. N. T. HEBREWS//BIBLE. N. T. JAMES//
BIBLE. N. T. PETER

Library of Congress Catalog Card Number: 79-56863
Printed in the United States of America

Dedication

This volume is respectfully dedicated to three professors and friends who taught during my years of graduate theological study, 1944-1949, at The Southwestern Baptist Theological Seminary:

Doctor T. B. Maston, who was my teacher in Christian Ethics;

Doctor Ray Summers, who was my teacher in New Testament Interpretation; and

Doctor R. T. Daniel, now deceased, who was my teacher in Old Testament Theology.

Foreword

The *Layman's Bible Book Commentary* in twenty-four volumes was planned as a practical exposition of the whole Bible for lay readers and students. It is based on the conviction that the Bible speaks to every generation of believers but needs occasional reinterpretation in the light of changing language and modern experience. Following the guidance of God's Spirit, the believer finds in it the authoritative word for faith and life.

To meet the needs of lay readers, the *Commentary* is written in a popular style, and each Bible book is clearly outlined to reveal its major emphases. Although the writers are competent scholars and reverent interpreters, they have avoided critical problems and the use of original languages except where they were essential for explaining the text. They recognize the variety of literary forms in the Bible, but they have not followed documentary trails or become preoccupied with literary concerns. Their primary purpose was to show what each Bible book meant for its time and what it says to our own generation.

The Revised Standard Version of the Bible is the basic text of the *Commentary*, but writers were free to use other translations to clarify an occasional passage or sharpen its effect. To provide as much interpretation as possible in such concise books, the Bible text was not printed along with the comment.

Of the twenty-four volumes of the *Commentary*, fourteen deal with Old Testament books and ten with those in the New Testament. The volumes range in pages from 140 to 168. Four major books in the Old Testament and five in the New are treated in one volume each. Others appear in various combinations. Although the allotted space varies, each Bible book is treated as a whole to reveal its basic message with some passages getting special attention. Whatever plan of Bible study the reader may follow, this *Commentary* will be a valuable companion.

Despite the best-seller reputation of the Bible, the average survey of Bible knowledge reveals a good deal of ignorance about it and its primary meaning. Many adult church members seem to think that its study is intended for children and preachers. But some of the newer translations have been making the Bible more readable for all ages. Bible study has branched out from Sunday into other days of the week, and into neighborhoods rather than just in churches. This *Commentary* wants to meet the growing need for insight into all that the Bible has to say about God and his world and about Christ and his fellowship.

BROADMAN PRESS

Contents

HEBREWS

JAMES

2 PETER

HEBREWS

Introduction

Hebrews is a perfect treasure of God's Word in man's language. It is a masterpiece of religious thought, spiritual authority, and practical value. It is one of the major books of the Bible. Its doctrinal depth, its high moral standards, its lofty themes, its exquisite language, its great style and dignity, its reverent tone, its soaring heights of inspiration, and its universal appeal long ago assured it a place in the Bible canon. Some of the best known passages in the Bible are found in Hebrews. The texts for some of Christian history's greatest sermons are found in Hebrews. Some of the most convincing support for the deity of Christ and some of the most persuasive pleading for disciplined obedience to him in the Christian life are found in Hebrews. Hebrews, moreover, is said by competent scholars to contain the purest and best Greek of the entire New Testament.

What we sometimes call the book of Hebrews is more generally called the letter to the Hebrews. Only once, however, is there any reference that would identify this work as a letter, and that is at the very end where the author says, "I have written to you briefly" (13:22).

There are some indications that this work may originally have been a sermon. It sounds like a sermon. Its eloquence and cadences would befit a sermon. Such references as "we are speaking" (2:5), "we speak" (6:9), "we cannot now speak" (9:5), and "I say" (11:32) would properly be used in a sermon. It would have been a fairly long sermon, of course, but a very powerful one to which Christians of Hebrew origin in the first century would have been strongly attracted and by which they would have been greatly impressed. The entire work can be read aloud in about forty minutes, which could indicate its sermonic character.

The inclusion of Hebrews as a "book" of the Bible and its general acceptance by Christians through the centuries as the major "general epistle" in the New Testament are justification enough for its consideration throughout this commentary, however, primarily as a letter.

13

The Author

Hebrews is anonymous, and any attempt to establish its authorship is conjecture. The author of the work is not mentioned anywhere in the entire thirteen chapters. It is not possible to speak with certainty or credibility, therefore, about who was humanly responsible for it. Though it was known in the first few centuries by the early Christians and was frequently quoted from, no person was at first identified widely as its author. Gradually the sentiment grew, at first among Eastern Christians, especially those at Alexandria, and then among Western Christians, especially those at Rome, that Paul wrote Hebrews. That tradition has been maintained by many with a considerable amount of fervor since about the fifth century AD. Clement of Alexandria contended that Paul originally wrote the letter in Hebrew and that Luke then translated it into Greek. Tertullian thought Barnabas wrote it. Luther ascribed it to Apollos. Some scholars have suggested that Aquila and Priscilla were the coauthors. Many other possible authors, including Luke, James, John, Philip, Sylvanus, and Clement of Rome have been suggested as possible authors by responsible scholars. Early in the third century AD Origen said, "As to who wrote this Epistle, God alone knows the truth," and Origen's observation still stands.

Whoever the author of Hebrews was, it seems clear that the person was of Jewish extraction, a masterful interpreter of the Hebrew scriptures, immersed in the tradition that God is one and that he is righteous, completely at home with Greek thought and philosophy, and possibly an itinerant preacher given to frequent travel. Although the church has never been able positively to identify the human author of Hebrews, this in no way has diminished the letter's great value to Christians through the ages, and it in no way lessens its worth to the people of God today.

Date and Place of Writing

Like the author, the date of Hebrews is not known. It seems likely to have been written in a time of limited persecution of the Christian recipients who are said not yet to have resisted to the point of actually shedding their blood (12:4). Since Clement of Rome quoted from Hebrews in a letter to the Christians at Corinth thought to have been written about AD 85 or possibly as late as AD 95, Hebrews must have been written before then. If Paul is considered to be the author,

Hebrews would have to be dated before AD 64, when Paul is thought to have been martyred. Jerusalem fell in AD 70, and since no mention is made of that great and historic event, it is convincingly argued that Hebrews was likely written before then. Many date Hebrews at about AD 80, but others make a strong case for its having been written between AD 60 and AD 70. The place of writing is not mentioned, although more scholars surmise Italy as the geographic origin of the letter than any other single place, since Italy is mentioned at the conclusion (13:24) in such a way as to make possible such an interpretation.

Recipients

No title, "Hebrews" or "To Hebrews" or "To the Hebrews" or "The Letter to the Hebrews," is a part of the work itself. Since the letter never went by any other name, however, it seems clear that even though the title was not original, it must have been employed quite early. The letter seems to have been intended for a specific community of Christians who give evidence of having been born and reared in the Jewish heritage. It must be admitted that the entire book can be read in vain, however, for a specific reference of address to Hebrew Christians. Nevertheless, the recipients were obviously Christians with special knowledge of, and interest in, the Jewish system.

Since all Christians of every age find the headwaters of our faith in God's Old Testament revelation of himself to the Jews, the book of Hebrews has never ceased to be a fascinating and spiritually profitable study for all Christians. The Gospel according to Matthew provides a very special focus on the Jewish foundations of Christianity, and what Matthew is to the four Gospels, the letter of Hebrews is to the rest of the New Testament. Hebrews focuses on our special spiritual kinship to the Jews, who were called by the Lord God—first out of Ur of the Chaldees, then out of Egypt, and then out of Babylon—to be his people and to prepare the way for the Messiah to do his redemptive work in the world. The original recipients of this communication were a fellowship of faithful followers of Christ. We share that good fortune as we carefully read and reverently study Hebrews today.

Occasion

The writer of Hebrews used this letter to call the readers to understand the deep meaning of their faith and to accept the full responsibility of their Christian experience of grace. We are especially challenged to be faithful, obedient, disciplined, principled, and unfailingly committed to living the Christian life.

To read Hebrews through quickly at one sitting is to be impressed with its unmistakably practical purpose. A survey of some of the dozens of commentaries available on Hebrews, however, reveals how easy it is to major on minors, to accentuate the relatively inconsequential, to focus on secondary concerns, and scrupulously to avoid the ethical imperatives of this important portion of God's holy Word.

Hebrews is not a treatise about Jewish traditions. It is not solely about the person and priesthood of Jesus Christ. Neither is it a book of speculative philosophy or abstract theology. Its main thrust is pastoral. The very heart of the letter is the recurring call to practice the Christian faith in daily life. To that end, the author skillfully interpreted the Scriptures, magnified the Lord Jesus Christ, made his points, bent his arguments, and rested his case. Teaching, inspiring, encouraging, challenging, warning, and exhorting, he put together a powerful, practically irresistible, appeal for constancy in the Christian life.

Christ's Superiority Demands Superior Faithfulness, Obedience, and Service
1:1 to 4:13

Introductory Statement Concerning the Superiority of Christ (1:1-4)

Without any small talk and even without any salutation, the letter of Hebrews is launched. From the very first sentence, there is a powerful proclamation of the good news of God through Jesus Christ the Son. This introduction is intensely concise. At the same time, it is astoundingly broad in its sweep and scope.

The reference, "God spoke of old to our fathers by the prophets" (v. 1), leaves the clear impression that those originally addressed were of Jewish origin. The Hebrew prophets were God's spokesmen who uniquely brought the word of the Lord's judgment and the word of the Lord's loving-kindness to his chosen people.

Hebrew theology was built on the conviction that God is, that he is one, and that he has spoken. The prophetic tradition was a forward-looking tradition of religious fervor, spiritual depth, and ethical passion. In that tradition, plain people, men like Amos and Micah and women like Miriam (Ex. 15:20) and Anna (Luke 2:36), were caught up by God's Spirit and compelled to proclaim his Word in a language that could be clearly understood by the common people. As Amos said, "The lion has roared; who will not fear?/The Lord God has spoken; who can but prophesy?" (Amos 3:8). The prophets' "thus saith the Lord" was the standard by which Israel moved forward from Ur of the Chaldees to Bethlehem of Judea. That forward movement was dynamic progression toward the Messiah. The prophets "of old" were both seers of the messianic hope and speakers for God concerning the revelation of redemption that was more and more drawing near.

Now, however, "in these last days" God "has spoken to us" not through another prophet, as high and holy an office as that is. Instead, he has spoken to us directly by his "Son, whom he appointed the heir of all things, through whom also he created the world" (v. 2). No longer must we get God's message relayed through the prophets as middle men. It has now come to us through the Son, by whom the world was created, who "reflects the glory of God and bears the very stamp of his nature," and who upholds "the universe by his word of power" (v. 3). We are reminded of John's insight that "all things were made through him, and without him was not anything made that was made" (John 1:3), and of Paul's profound word that "by him all things consist" (Col. 1:17, KJV), that in Christ all the great star systems of the universe and every last atomic particle in all creation hold together.

When the Son's redemptive work on earth was done and "he had made purification for sins, he sat down at the right hand of the Majesty on high, having become as much superior to angels as the name he has obtained is more excellent than theirs" (vv. 3-4). This powerful statement reminds us of Christ's virgin birth, his matchless works, his sinless life, his sacrificial death, his victorious resurrection, and his final ascension into heaven. Christians are redeemed by a mighty Savior and a wonderful Lord whose name is above every name.

Seldom has so much strong doctrine been compressed into such a small space. These four verses have been called the most beautiful passage in the New Testament. The preacher of Hebrews has plunged without idle talk into gloriously deep water, and there is more, much more, ahead.

In the supercharged atmosphere created by these thrillingly inspired words, the author of Hebrews has begun to weave his preacher's spell. He has commanded our attention. He has stirred our imagination. He has rooted us in our spiritual heritage. He has reminded us of our cleansing. He has pointed us to our destiny. Now he moves into his message.

The Witness of the Scriptures to the Superiority of Christ in Obtaining Salvation for the Faithful (1:5 to 2:18)

The Son of God is not presented here in these first two chapters of Hebrews, nor elsewhere in the Bible for that matter, as an object to be adored. He is presented, rather, as a person to be trusted for salvation and to be obeyed on the living out of the Christian life.

It has already been declared that he is superior to the angels and that his name is more excellent than theirs (v. 4). The witness of the Scriptures is now brought to bear in support of that declaration. Quoting from the Septuagint, the Greek translation of Psalm 2:7 and 2 Samuel 7:14, the author states that the superiority of Jesus Christ to angels is demonstrated by the fact that of none of them did God ever say, "Thou art my Son, today I have begotten thee" or "I will be to him a father, and he shall be to me a son" (v. 5). Later, "when he brings the first-born into the world" (v. 6), the Scriptures (Deut. 32:43 and Ps. 97:7) demand, "Let all God's angels worship him" (v. 6). The witness of Psalm 104:4 is then marshaled: the angels are God's messengers, God's servants, his winds to blow where he wills and his flames of fire to brighten and to burn according to his purposes (v. 7). Psalm 45:6-7 is quoted to magnify God's moral uprightness, "the righteous scepter is the scepter of thy kingdom. Thou hast loved righteousness and hated lawlessness," and to demonstrate how God "anointed" the Son "with the oil of gladness beyond" others (vv. 8-9). Quotations from Psalm 102:25-27 and from Psalm 110:1 are given to illustrate God's permanence and the Son's exaltation at God's "right hand," together with his ultimate victory over all his spiritual and moral enemies (vv. 10-13).

The angels, according to the Scriptures with which the author of Hebrews is intimately acquainted and which he has faithfully hidden in his heart and made a lamp to his feet, are "all ministering spirits sent forth to serve, for the sake of those who are to obtain salvation" (v. 14).

In the light of all this redemptive activity on the part of God, his angelic messengers, and his Son, "we must pay the closer attention to what we have heard, lest we drift away from it" (2:1). In the brief first chapter of Hebrews, God's grace has been remembered, his Son has been magnified, and his Word has been preached so as to call people to pay careful attention to the gospel which has been proclaimed. It is our nature to "drift away" from the truth, to weigh anchor without cause, to be forgetful hearers. As eternal vigilance is the price of liberty, so everlasting watchfulness is the price of stability in the Christian life.

God's messengers, the angels, have faithfully declared his "valid" message (v. 2). We may be completely sure that our righteous God who has always made certain that "every transgression or disobedience received a just retribution" will not allow anyone to escape his judgment who neglects "such a great salvation" (vv. 2-3).

Verse 3 contains one of the truly towering texts of the entire Bible, "How shall we escape if we neglect such a great salvation?" While the text in recent times has most often been used as the basis for an evangelistic call to come to Christ in the initial commitment of life to him, it is actually a word directly addressed to Christians. Read in this light, it calls us to moral alertness and spiritual watchfulness. It keeps us on our toes. It warns us against laziness. It reminds us as believers not to neglect the salvation which God has given, is giving, and will give to those who trust and obey him.

That great salvation "was declared at first by the Lord" (v. 3) himself. He declared the good news by his preaching, by his teaching, by his good works, by his virgin birth, by his sinless life, by his personal example, by his sacrificial death, and by his powerful resurrection. Moreover, that great salvation "was attested to us by those who heard him" (v. 3). We have heard and we now believe because the first witnesses shared Christ whom they had seen and his good news which they had heard. That great salvation is the gift of God himself who "also bore witness by signs and wonders and various miracles and by gifts of the Holy Spirit distributed according to his own will" (v. 4) to sign it and to seal it, to acknowledge it and to authenticate it.

God has not put everything in the world under subjection to the angels (v. 5). It is his purpose, rather, to put everything in the world under subjection to humanity made in his image and after his likeness, leaving nothing outside man's control (vv. 6-7). That purpose, however, is not yet fully realized (v. 8). "But we see Jesus, who for a little while was made lower than the angels" (v. 9), as the One who brings God's purposes for humanity to glorious fulfillment. As God's perfect man, Jesus was "crowned with glory and honor because of the suffering of death, so that by the grace of God he might taste death for every one" (v. 9). As the "pioneer" of our salvation, the Son has been made "perfect through suffering" (v. 10). The word here translated "pioneer" may be translated "author" or "leader" or "originator." As such, and on our behalf, our Lord Jesus Christ has gone where no other could go, and his redemptive work has been finally completed, or made perfect, in the suffering and death which he endured. As the pioneer of our salvation, his work was fully perfected. Moreover, his life was morally perfect, a quality required of one who was to bring salvation to sinners and lead the way to "glory." That glory toward which the people of God are moving is not only the prospect of glory in heaven but also the assurance of triumph over temptation on earth. It is the assurance of deliverance from the enslaving power of sin in this world. And it is the assurance of victory in living the Christian life here and now.

As Christians, our *roots* are established fully and firmly in God's Son, who is the pioneer of our great salvation and the true source of our entire being. Our *fruits* are nurtured by God's indwelling Spirit. It is the Spirit who is the source of the believer's productivity. If we are rightly rooted in the source, fruit bearing will appropriately come, and if we are truly fruitful it is because our life and work have him as our spiritual source. He has made us and not we ourselves.

Both Jesus "who sanctifies and those who are sanctified have all one origin" (v. 11). As God is our Father, so Jesus is our Elder Brother. He is not ashamed to identify with us as members of his own family. In God's gracious providence, we are his kin. Christ who sets Christians apart in salvation and authentic holiness of life and the ones who are so set apart have the same source. God has emptied himself in the incarnation of Christ by which he became fully human. At the same time, humanity has come to itself, found its name, and become somebody in the man Jesus Christ (vv. 12-13).

By sharing the identical human nature which we have, Jesus became subject to human death "that through death he might destroy him who has the power of death, that is, the devil, and deliver all those who through fear of death were subject to lifelong bondage" (vv. 14-15). Adam and Eve disobeyed God and ate the forbidden fruit of which God had said, "In the day that you eat of it you shall die" (Gen. 2:17). Then, just as God had said, the moment they willfully disobeyed him they began to die, and the human race has been dying ever since. In our fallen and sinful condition, we are enslaved to death. We are now by nature terrified by death. It is our last great enemy. This last great enemy, however, Jesus conquered in the resurrection. In the resurrection, he took the sting out of death and the victory out of the grave; and now death is swallowed up in life (v. 15). Jesus identified not with angels (v. 16) but with us "so that he might become a merciful and faithful high priest in the service of God, to make expiation for the sins of the people" (v. 17).

In the Jewish system, the sins of the people were forgiven as the priests made prescribed sacrifices on behalf of sinners. Atonement of some kind is at the heart of every religion. That is, religion universally offers some way for sinners to get rid of their sin. In most religious systems, human acts are required to banish sin and bridge the chasm between humanity and deity. In Christianity, however, it is Jesus Christ himself, the "faithful high priest," whose divine act of self-sacrifice on the cross has banished our sin and bridged the gap. He is our Bridge Man.

Jesus Christ knew human life and its suffering and temptation personally, from the inside, and it is for this reason that "he is able to help those who are tempted" (v. 18). God's intention in the incarnation, by which he actually became human and was tempted and suffered and finally died, was not to devise a plan of salvation but to save us. It was his concern to help hurting human beings who are tempted, who suffer, and who are destined to die. His purpose was not to "make expiation for the sins of the people" in some religious system but "to help those who are tempted" (v. 18), who are weak, who are poor, who are in need, who are lost, and who are dead in their trespasses and sins. Our divine Redeemer is our helper in our times of human need. Our glorious Savior is our deliverer from the inglorious temptation which dogs our feet. Our

High Priest is himself our sacrifice. Our Pioneer is the trailblazer of our way to glory. "He is able" (v. 18). What an incomparable affirmation about our Lord and Savior.

Jesus' Superior Faithfulness Challenges Christians to Faithful Endurance (3:1-19)

"Therefore," in the light of the superiority of Christ in providing salvation to those who are willing to receive it, Christians are called to "consider Jesus" further (v. 1). The first recipients of the letter are addressed and identified here for the first time. They are called "holy brethren." That is, they are understood to be brothers and sisters together with the writer in the family of God, and they are "holy" in the sense that they are separated to God in their entire life and conduct.

This is a powerful reminder that the church must never draw its net of evangelism so loosely and so irresponsibly as to count its membership as anything other than a holy brotherhood closely related to our holy God. Our relationship to him should show up in every relationship of every member to every other member under every circumstance.

Christians "share in a heavenly call" (v. 1). This is a marvelous reality in our experience of grace: God has called us all to salvation. We have many gifts. Some are chosen for one office and some for another, but God has called from heaven to bid us all alike to come to life and light through the gospel. "Consider Jesus," we are told, "the apostle and high priest of our confession" (v. 1). This is a unique challenge. Nowhere else in the entire Bible is there anything that compares precisely to it. To "consider Jesus" is to look at him, bring the mind to bear upon him, observe him so as to understand his profound significance, perceive him in all his fullness, concentrate on him so as to discern the true meaning of his life and work. As "the apostle," Jesus is God's special messenger and authoritative spokesman concerning his new covenant of grace made with his believing and behaving people. As the "high priest," he is the special enabler and mediator of "our confession" (v. 1). As God's special apostle, Jesus has come from God to us, and as high priest he has gone to God for us. He has done, once for all, the work of going between "the Judge of all the earth" (Gen. 18:25) and us. "Our confession" which Christians universally make is that Jesus Christ, God's apostle and our High Priest, is our Lord. No formula, no creed, no set of doctrines, no human document can ever be the proper object of the believer's confession. We confess Christ. With our minds and hearts we believe "unto righteousness" and with our lives and mouths "confession is made unto salvation" (Rom. 10:10, KJV).

We are to "consider Jesus" because of his faithfulness (v. 2). Jesus was "faithful" to the Father "who appointed him" or commissioned him as Moses had been "faithful in God's house" (v. 2). This reference to Moses picks up the statement attributed to the Lord in Numbers 12:7, "My servant Moses . . . is faithful in all mine house" (KJV) and acknowledges the special respect or even veneration paid by the Jews to Moses, and great deliverer from their Egyptian bondage. The house of God is God's entire household or family, and the term is meant to include all God's redeemed people, delivered from the bondage of sin by his grace. Jesus is more worthy of glory than Moses, just as the builder of a house is worthy of more honor than the house he has built (v. 3). "The builder of all things," it is observed parenthetically, "is God" (v. 4). Moses was faithful as a steward, "but Christ was faithful . . . as a son" (vv. 5-6).

A word of caution is sounded then, however, to keep us from turning aside from our commitment to God: "We are his house if we hold fast our confidence and pride in our hope" (v. 6). Christians have always been prone to sing, " 'Tis done—the great transaction's done" ("O Happy Day That Fixed My Choice," by Philip Doddridge), to relax in their spiritual discipline, to drift, to grow lukewarm, to let go of their first love. This word is an antidote for the poison of such carelessness. We are the family in God's own household *if* we hold fast to him as he holds fast to us. We are his chosen people *if* we cling in "confidence" to him as he clings in love to us. We are in his loving care and under his never-failing protection *if* we proudly hold to our hope in him, remaining steadfast to the end, as he will surely remain steadfast in his care for us.

The next passage, Hebrews 3:7-11, is a quotation of Psalm 95:7-11. The preacher of Hebrews loved the Bible. He quoted it freely and lengthily. He skillfully appropriated it to make particularly important points. Here he called it to mind with special attribution, "As the Holy Spirit says" (v. 7). It was God's Spirit who warned the Jews in the psalmist's time, and it is his Spirit who warns Christians in our own time not to harden their hearts in rebellion, not to put Almighty God to the test, not to provoke him to anger, not to go astray, not to refuse to know his ways, not to precipitate his righteous wrath (vv. 7-11).

Sometimes it is more effective to quote such an inspired and well-known masterpiece of a statement than it is to state the same truth in less familiar words. The author of Hebrews appropriately used this psalm to remind his readers to keep on hearing God's voice, to keep on walking in God's ways, and to keep on holding fast to the hope of entering into the eternal rest which God is preparing for his faithful people. The psalmist here linked together two dramatic events from Israel's experience of Exodus from Egypt. The first reference is to their murmuring anxiety over the apparent lack of water in the wilderness. The second reference is to the pessimistic report of the apprehensive spies who caused the people to shrink back from the immediate conquest of the Promised Land which God intended. Both incidents illustrated their lack of faith. This passage in Hebrews deals with that same kind of complaining and fearful unbelief in the lives of Christians.

"Take care, brethren" (v. 12) is a solemn warning. Caution in the presence of aggressive evil is appropriate. Humility is in order. Let any who thinks he is standing "take heed lest he fall" (1 Cor. 10:12). This particularly forceful warning to take heed, to look to it, to beware is issued "lest there be in any of you an evil, unbelieving heart, leading you to fall away from the living God" (v. 12). The emphasis here is on "you" "brethren," as opposed to the Hebrew children. We are urged to take care so as to avoid the fate of that unhappy company who wandered in the wilderness for forty years and who finally died because they would not put faith to work in the task for which the Lord had delivered them out of their Egyptian bondage.

When the heart harbors unbelief, that unbelief leads to separation from God (v. 12), "the deceitfulness of sin" (v. 13), hardness of heart and rebellion (v. 15), disobedience (v. 18), and final inability to enter into God's rest (v. 19). Unbelief leads to disobedience, disobedience issues in sin, and sin brings punishment. God's oath of exclusion (v. 11) is a solemn warning for us to bear in mind against the great judgment day.

To the end that such a fate may be avoided, Christians are advised, "Exhort one another every day, as long as it is called 'today' " (v. 13). It is a part of our continuing responsibility as Christians to prop up one another. In the community of obedient and active faith we are to cultivate an everlastingly vigilant concern for each other. The entire letter of Hebrews is characterized by this pastoral care about the well-being of the church. It is hard to understand how there could be those who find in Hebrews hardly anything but angels, teachings about Moses, Joshua, Melchizedek, and Abraham, and doctrines related to Christ's high priesthood. Some seem unable to see or accept this fundamental and recurring theme in Hebrews related to endurance and faithfulness in living the Christian life. By daily exhortation of one another we avoid the deceitfulness of sin. By mutual admonishment of each other church members share the warnings and cautions, the affirmations and encouragements, the edification and nourishment which are required for Christians to be sustained, to grow in grace and the knowledge of Christ, and to avoid apostasy, or falling "away from the living God" (vv. 12-13). "Today" is the time when opportunity is still knocking, when hope is still beckoning, when God is still speaking, and when the Spirit is still calling.

By God's mercy "we share in Christ," partaking of abundant life, "if only we hold our first confidence firm to the end" (v. 14). No wonder some early Christians, some of the Reformers, and some Christians in our own day have sought to discount, discredit, or discard the book of Hebrews. The author is so unrelentingly persistent in calling Christians to live the Christian life that he simply will not let the people of God relax and be at ease in Zion with never-ending Bible study and an irresponsible preoccupation with the future rewards and joys of heaven. He refused just to go on and on about the doctrine of God. He would not be stopped short of calling believers to hold firmly to their original confidence in Christ and to maintain steadfast commitment to him, "firm to the end" (v. 14). The idea is exquisitely, emphatically put: we keep on enjoying Christ as we keep on enduring. We keep on being delivered from disobedience, rebellion, callousness of spirit, sin, and death as we keep on believing. Though the unbelieving Hebrew children "were unable to enter" the Promised Land "because of unbelief" (v. 19), we who maintain our faith and endure to the end are assured of entering God's rest.

This chapter begins with a compelling presentation of Jesus' superiority and ends with a ringing challenge for Christians to endure.

True Rest Will Come to Obedient Believers (4:1-13)

The prospect of ultimate victory is still out in front of us. "While the promise of entering his rest remains" open, Christians are called to moral alertness "lest any of you be judged to have failed to reach it" (v. 1). "Let us fear" is not an admonition to nurture a spirit of fear or to tolerate a debilitating anxiety. Instead it is a call for God's people to cultivate a healthy fear of the awful consequences of failing to reach God's rest. Those with a creative fear of the Lord need suffer from no crippling earthly fear. We must keep pressing toward the mark to avoid the possibility of missing it. Again, the pastoral concern of the author of Hebrews is coming through here, loud and clear. This is not only his concern. It is also the everlasting concern of the church, God's caring community. "The promise . . . remains" may serve to remind us that more attention is given to the promises of God in Hebrews than in any other New Testament book.

As good news came from Moses to the Israelites while they were yet in bondage in Egypt, so through Jesus Christ "good news came to us" (v. 2) when we were yet in bondage to sin. The message they heard from Moses did not benefit them because it did not meet with personal faith on their part (v. 2). The gospel we have received from Christ, however, benefits us; and "we who have believed enter that rest" (v. 3). Salvation is an accomplished fact, for when we hear the good news proclaimed through the Son we hear God's clearest word, and when we make the commitment of ourselves to Christ, then without delay we "enter that rest."

Salvation is a present experience too, and this passage may properly be translated, "We are entering into the rest, we who believe," meaning that it is our faith which is carrying us into the promised rest.

Moreover, the entire context of this presentation makes it clear that salvation is also a future experience for which we persevere, toward which we work, and by which hope we endure. God's wonderful "works were finished from the foundation of the world" (v. 3), in the sense that God's intention of something absolutely assures its realization. God's rest has been ready from the beginning. No works on the part of the Creator-Redeemer remain to be done, for God himself "rested on the seventh day from all his works" (v. 4). His rest was denied to the disobedient Hebrew children (v. 5); "it remains for some to enter it" (v. 6) who choose to turn to God through faith in Jesus Christ; and he has set today as the "certain day" of salvation (v. 7). Joshua, it is interjected, was not able to deliver rest to the people of God (v. 8). "So then, there remains a sabbath rest for the people of God" (v. 9) when the blessed repose and perfect peace which he has promised will actually be ours.

This is a thumbnail sketch of the interaction of God and mankind in history. With this in mind, readers are now issued yet another strong challenge: "Let us therefore strive to enter that rest, that no one fall by the same sort of disobedience" (v. 11). We need not stumble in disobedience; we need not drift in disbelief; we need not fall away in apostasy, because "the word of God is living and active, sharper than any two-edged sword, piercing to the division of soul and spirit, of joints and marrow, and discerning the thoughts and intentions of the heart" (v. 12). Here again is one of those familiar and wonderfully significant texts which the church knows by heart. The "word of God" here is the Son of God. He is alive. He is active. He is all-discerning. "And before him no creature is hidden, but all are open and laid bare to the eyes of him with whom we have to do" (v. 13).

Sinners love darkness rather than light because their deeds are evil (John 3:19). Like Adam and Eve attempting to hide from God after their rebellious disobedience, sinful humans through all the ages have sought to avoid the eyes of God. We are called here to the realization that every day and every moment God sees every act, hears every word, knows every motive, numbers every heartbeat, counts every hair. Because our lives are utterly open to him, our obedience must never lessen and our striving to move forward in the Christian life must never cease.

Christ's Special Priesthood Requires Special Perseverance
4:14 to 10:18

The Christian Confession Is to Be Held Fast (4:14-16)

In view of the fact that "we have a great high priest who has passed through the heavens, Jesus, the Son of God" (v. 14), the pastoral plea for Christians to endure is restated. "Let us," we are urged, "hold fast our confession" (v. 14). We do not have in Jesus a high priest who is untouched with the feeling of our infirmities but one who is able "to sympathize with our weaknesses" and "who in every respect has been tempted as we are, yet without sin" (v. 15). God's ideal high priest

knows our frame, remembers that we are dust, understands our humanity, and has experienced the same temptations we have. He therefore
has compassion on us in our weakness and identifies with us in our great
need. No single sentence in the Bible more profoundly and yet simply
and helpfully states what God has done for us in the incarnation of
himself in Jesus Christ.

Human priests under the Jewish system were involved in complex
ceremonies that had very special meaning to sinners of those times.
Priests were human ministers chosen by God to do sacred things. They
performed the prescribed functions which were required to draw the
people near to God and then to keep them there. They represented God
to the people and the people to God. They offered sacrifices. They made
intercession. They pressed the claims of God on the people. They
pressed the claims of the people on God. They were the source of religious knowledge. They bridged the gap between righteous God and
stumbling sinners. Their work was of profound importance in God's
ancient scheme of things.

In this Levitical priesthood, the high priest went once each year, on
the great Day of Atonement, through the curtain into the innermost
and holiest place to make special sacrifice for his own sins and for the
sins of all the people. Sprinkling the blood of the sin offering seven times
before and on the mercy seat, he symbolically covered the sins of the
people from the eyes of the Lord. Now Jesus, our great High Priest, has
passed, once for all, not through the inner curtain of a tabernacle made
with human hands, but "through the heavens" (v. 14) to God himself to
make atonement for all our sins.

Atonement is accomplished. The great transaction is done. Pardon is
perfected. Mediation is fully consummated. Salvation may be appropriated by anyone who wants it. "Whosoever will" may now come to God.
This High Priest's work will never have to be repeated. We do not have
to look forward to a Day of Atonement next year and the year after and
the year after that, because God's great and final Day of Atonement has
already come at Calvary.

In the light of all this, we can "then with confidence draw near to the
throne of grace, that we may receive mercy and find grace to help in
time of need" (v. 16). This text is another of those brilliant gems from
the treasure box of Hebrews. The writer of Hebrews could be tough,
but he could also be tender. He could be prophetic, but he could also be

pastoral. The tender and pastoral note is sounded here. God has opened his heart of grace and love to us. It is possible for us now to draw near to him. "Let us then" (v. 16) do it.

The "throne of grace" (v. 16) speaks both of God's sovereignty and of his compassion. As King of kings, he is enthroned by his very nature. His throne, however, is not one from which harsh and capricious judgments are thundered out. Rulings from God's throne are never arbitrary, never prejudiced, never biased, never merciless. On the contrary, those rulings are gracious. The presence of God is here characterized as "the throne of grace." Nowhere else in the entire Bible does this beautiful description appear. Yet this concept is universally known and generally used throughout Christendom because it uniquely draws together vitally important insights about the nature and character of God. The most frequent use of *grace* in Old Testament times had to do with finding favor in the sight of God or some human authority like an earthly ruler. Now through Christ all believers draw near to God and there find his unmerited favor. God is not against us. He is for us. He is not willing that any should perish but that all should come to life. "I have no pleasure in the death of any one, says the Lord God; so turn, and live" (Ezek. 18:32). It is in Christ that we come to the throne of grace, respond to this prophetic call to turn or to repent, and receive from God his great gift of life eternal and life abundant.

In Jesus Christ, God has shown us his face. In Jesus Christ, God has bared to us his very heart. In his loving presence, we "receive mercy and find grace to help in time of need" (v. 16). Everybody is hurting or is about to hurt. Our need is limitless. Our time of need is always. Thank God for his grace which supplies every need we have according to his riches in glory through Christ Jesus (Phil. 4:19). He is never-failingly eager to supply our need. "Let us then with confidence draw near" (v. 16) to him.

The Work of Christ in Obtaining Salvation for All Who Obey Him (5:1-10)

The statement just completed (4:15-16) has declared that as we hold fast our confession we may with confidence draw near to God's throne of grace. Then through the special ministry of Jesus Christ, our great high priest, we may receive mercy and find grace to help in time of need. The message in chapter 5 continues along this line: "Every high priest chosen from among men is appointed to act on behalf of men in relation to God, to offer gifts and sacrifices for sins" (v. 1).

The office of the high priest is filled by one who is chosen. He does not take the office on his own initiative, nor is he chosen by the people in some elective process or contest that might determine the most popular prospect. The office is established by God, and the person occupying the office "does not take the honor upon himself, but is called by God, just as Aaron was" (v. 4). To be especially chosen, appointed, or ordained is to be especially entrusted with special responsibility by the one choosing, appointing, or ordaining. Aaron is mentioned because the priestly line began with him. He is said to have been "called by God," and Aaron served with special prominence and distinction as the first one to be particularly consecrated or set apart for what God called "my priesthood" (Ex. 28:1-3).

Only those who are sure that they have neither called themselves nor assumed their roles of religious leadership in obedience to human direction can expect to work in full liberty and love to do God's will as it is revealed. If anyone assumes the work of ministry for himself, he may tire and give up. If any assumes the work of ministry in response to the call of others, he may become disappointed or grow disgruntled and drop out. If anyone works directly for God, however, the conviction of divine call is a never-failing source of strength and energy, a never-failing divine mandate that wards off undue disappointment in others or personal despair over failures, large or small.

Under special appointment from God "to act on behalf of men in relation to God," the high priest offered "gifts and sacrifices for sins" (v. 1). Our sins cannot be taken lightly. Most church people may approve of a polite condemnation, in a well-modulated tone of voice, of those sins of which we are not guilty and which we are too refined, too scared, too tired, too old, or too lazy to commit. The Bible is concerned, however, about much more serious matters regarding our sins. There is a sense in which every Christian begins the pilgrimage of faith with Isaiah's lament, "Woe is me" (Isa. 6:5, KJV) and cries, "God, be merciful to me a sinner" (Luke 18:13). The high priest's offering was not merely a bit of impressive ritual perfunctorily done. It was "for sins" of rebellion against God, of willful disobedience, of intentional mark-missing, of perversity, of transgression, of trespass, of evil, of violence, of injustice, of unrighteousness. While the actual word for missing the mark is used for sins here, the broadest possible interpretation of the concept is justified in this instance. There is no effort here, or elsewhere in the Bible, to argue about the existence of sin or to establish its reality. It is an awful reality in our kind of world, and a righteous God dealing with a morally responsible human race requires that sin be taken seriously and that it be dealt with seriously.

Sören Kierkegaard's observation that Christianity begins with the doctrine of sin makes sense, and G. K. Chesterton who became a Christian and joined the church in his mature years "to get rid of my sin" did what every human on earth in his better moments wants to do. Sin is serious.

The high priest under the Levitical system could "deal gently with the ignorant and wayward, since he himself is beset with weakness" and is therefore "bound to offer sacrifice for his own sins as well as for those of the people" (vv. 2-3).

Even Jesus Christ, our great High Priest under God's new covenant consummated on the cross, did not call himself. He was called by the Father. He did not appoint himself. God appointed him. He did not exalt himself to do the high priestly work. The Father exalted him (v. 5). He is not only God's Son, of whom the Father said, "Today have I begotten thee" (v. 5), but his special ordination from God is, "Thou art a priest for ever, after the order of Melchizedek" (v. 6). This is the first reference in Hebrews to Melchizedek, but eight other references are to follow—one other in chapter 5, verse 10; one in chapter 6, verse 20; and six in chapter 7, verses 1, 10, 11, 15, 17, and 21. Since Melchizedek is about to occupy this much of our attention, we do well to take a careful look at him.

Who was Melchizedek? He is identified in Genesis 14:18 as "king of Salem" and as "the priest of the most high God" (KJV). To him Abraham, the father of the faithful, gave "tithes of all" (Gen. 14:20, KJV). The only other Old Testament reference to Melchizedek is in Psalm 110:4, which the author of Hebrews has here (5:6) quoted, "Thou art a priest for ever after the order of Melchizedek."

Combining the high priesthood of Aaron and the unique high priesthood of Melchizedek, Jesus, "in the days of his flesh," prayed and made earnest supplication to God "with loud cries and tears, to him who was able to save him from death" (v. 7). In his complete identification with humanity, Jesus prayed as we pray. He petitioned and entreated God as we do. He cried aloud as we do in times of personal crisis. He wept as we sometimes do. As with all who truly trust God, Jesus "was heard for his godly fear" (v. 7).

Although Jesus was God's only begotten Son, yet "he learned obedience through what he suffered" (v. 8). Here the author of Hebrews returned to a theme that was particularly important to him and that should therefore be of special interest to us, the suffering of the Savior. It was the creative pain of suffering that taught Jesus obedience to the Father and subjection to his will. Designated or ordained "by God a high priest after the order of Melchizedek" (v. 10), Jesus, being "made perfect," "became the source of eternal salvation to all who obey him" (v. 9). The treasure chest of Hebrews is open again, and another priceless jewel is flashing here in 5:8-9. The perfection which Jesus achieved was accomplished through his movement from Bethlehem through Galilee and Samaria and Jerusalem to Calvary and the open tomb of Joseph of Arimathea. This was the end for which he came. God appointed him, and he responded with absolute faith, complete obedience, and redemptive suffering. His obedience was not a conditioned response to external stimuli. It was rather a supremely moral, absolutely responsible response to the Father's leadership. Though Jesus was God's Son, his humanity was so total that he actually "learned" obedience through the things that he suffered along life's way—such painful experiences as the great temptation, Lazarus' death, Jerusalem's refusal to know the things that make for peace, the disciples' petty jealousies, Peter's denial, Pilate's harsh sentence, and the agony of crucifixion. What harsh things our Lord suffered! What deep lessons he learned! What matchless perfection characterized his human pilgrimage!

The "eternal salvation" which Jesus authored, or of which he is the source (v. 9), is not poured indiscriminately on believers and unbelievers, on the obedient and the disobedient. The eternal salvation which has Jesus as its source is given "to all who obey him" (v. 9). The divine imperative is for us to *obey* him. There is no other way out of the dark valley of sin and death except the high and narrow way of obedience to him. He is our apostle and high priest, and as such he has made the ultimate sacrifice for our sins. That sacrifice which he made on the cross is not appropriated, however, by something we think or by something we say but by something we do. Salvation is laid hold of in the lives actually lived and in the things actually done by "all who obey him" (v. 9).

Counsel to Keep Moving Toward Maturity (5:11 to 6:12)

About God's call to maturity, the preacher of Hebrews declared, "we have much to say" (v. 11). The many things that ought to be said about Jesus and about obedience to him in the Christian life are "hard to explain, since you have become dull of hearing" (v. 11). This chastisement for the recipients of the letter who earlier were called "holy brethren" (3:1) was laid on them in love, but frankly and without equivocation. They had once heard the word of the gospel with keenly attentive ears. Familiarity with the good news, however, seems gradually to have hardened their hearing. "By this time" they ought to have so disciplined themselves in the faith and so developed in their own Christian experience that they could "be teachers" (v. 12), bringing others to the knowledge of Christ and obedience to him in daily life.

Without able teachers and serious teaching any church is in deep trouble. Where there is no real learning, there can be no committed disciples, and discipleship is at the heart of all authentic church life. The author of Hebrews addressed all the recipients of this letter when he declared that "by this time you ought to be teachers" (v. 12). Every member of the body of Christ has some teaching responsibility. Some of that teaching can be done and should be done when the church is gathered together in regular assembly, and some of it can be done and should be done when the church is scattered into the community and into the world. Some of the teaching should be to the lost and unchurched, while some of it should be to one another in the covenant community where Jesus Christ is Lord.

Though by this time, it is reasoned, "you ought to be teachers," actually the sad truth is that "you need some one to teach you again the first principles of God's word" (v. 12). These dull-of-hearing Christians not only had not moved into the deeper spiritual things with which they ought by then to have been concerned, but they actually had allowed even the most basic and elementary teachings to become clouded in their minds. Instead of being steady, they were drifting. Instead of being attentive, they were drowsy. Instead of being alert teachers, they had even ceased to be responsible learners of Christ and his way.

The chastisement continues: "You need milk, not solid food" (v. 12). They ought to have been ashamed. They were behaving like babies. Like immature children, "unskilled in the word of righteousness" (v.

13), the readers are challenged to realize that "solid food is for the mature, for those who have their faculties trained by practice to distinguish good from evil" (v. 14).

Virtue, as John Milton observed, can never be a fugitive and cloistered thing but must move out into the dust and heat of battle to demonstrate its authenticity. It is by practice that we are able to tell the difference between right and wrong. Formal teaching has its place, but the real proof that the lesson has been truly learned is when it is put into practice. When our "faculties"—our minds, spirits, hearts, and wills—which demonstrate our personhood, are "trained" or disciplined to discern between good and evil, and we then consistently choose the right and reject the wrong, then we are moving responsibly toward maturity in Christ.

There is powerful moral meaning in this passage. The mature adult is distinguished from the immature child by the commitment to be morally responsible, to be morally discriminating, and to make consistent moral judgments. Christian maturity is related to the development of skill in the use of "the word of righteousness" (v. 13). This phrase is a reference to moral truth. It has to do with the glue that holds civilization together. Without "the word of righteousness" both religious institutions and civil structures would crumble and fall apart. First-century Christians were likely familiar with many earnest seekers for moral truth, particularly among the Greek thinkers and teachers. They had no reason to deride anyone who in any way earnestly sought to find moral truth and to do it. They understood, however, that ultimate and final moral truth had come to the world from Jesus Christ, the great high priest of God who was himself the living "word of righteousness." They trusted him implicitly and preached him faithfully as the way, the truth, and the life.

The most spiritually profitable passage in Hebrews for many is this marvelous word: "Therefore let us leave the elementary doctrines of Christ and go on to maturity, not laying again a foundation of repentance from dead works and of faith toward God, with instruction about ablutions, the laying on of hands, the resurrection of the dead, and eternal judgment. And this we will do if God permits" (6:1-3).

Christians are not to abandon the basics, but to build on them. A foundation is absolutely necessary, but it is no substitute for a superstructure.

No word in the letter to the Hebrews is more needed by the churches today than this one. None would be more productive of genuine revival in our time. None could be more completely appropriate, more timely, more relevant to our own day and age than this.

The elementary doctrines of Christ are fundamentally important, and they are not to be forgotten. They are to be built upon as God's obedient people heed his call to "go on to maturity" (6:1). The elementary doctrines or first principles themselves deserve careful attention.

"Repentance from dead works" is mentioned first. Repentance is a keynote in the New Testament message. Its great prominence in the early church is reason enough for its being mentioned first in this passage. Repentance is godly sorrow for sin and intentional turning away from sin. For those who had trusted in works to make them right with God, it was necessary that repentance should come in order that the work of the great High Priest, Jesus Christ, could take effect. The term "dead works" does not refer to Hebrew ceremonialism but to activities and interests and sensate pleasures that pertain to spiritual death. They are moral offenses from which a person must break away in order to become a Christian. Dead works are like a sheepskin over a wolf. He is still a wolf even though he may be in a sheep's clothing. In conversion, we Christians learn to trust Christ for new hearts while distrusting the former covering of dead works which once occupied his energies.

"Faith toward God" is the saving faith that is directed to the Lord when we first believe. It is closely connected to repentance. This is not merely the belief that there is a God. It is not just faith in God's existence. It is trust in him as Redeemer, Savior, and Lord.

"Ablutions" is translated "baptisms" in the King James Version. The reference is not clear. Since it is in a list of things that pertain to the elementary doctrines of the Christian faith, it could be better understood if it were singular instead of plural. Some believe the reference is to immersions such as those practiced by some of the Jewish cults for initiates, proselytes, and regular gatherings of the faithful. Many ancient religions utilized all kinds of purification rites connected with water. The distinctively Christian use of water for believer's baptism, therefore, had to be carefully taught to early Christians, who needed to distinguish between baptism, similar rites practiced by non-Christians, and ablutions or washings, which at least some very early Christian converts carried over as a custom connected with such things as blessing, rededication, and ordination in the church.

"The laying on of hands" was the early church's recognition of special need for the Holy Spirit's indwelling and empowering if any Christian mission or task was to be successfully carried out. Ordination in any highly formal sense for a special class of ministers like preachers, teachers, deacons, or missionaries is apparently not here intended.

"The resurrection of the dead" is obviously not something that the recipients of this letter would have already experienced. The reference is to the doctrine of the resurrection of the dead. Because the resurrection of Christ is the keystone in the superstructure of Christian doctrine, his resurrection is the guarantee of our own resurrection from the dead at the last day.

"Eternal judgment" is likewise a vital doctrine which they needed to understand, as we do. Human beings do not die as dogs die with no hope for eternity. On the contrary, we will all experience God's righteous judgment on the great judgment day. Then for eternity each will live with the choices made in life as a free moral agent.

The writer apparently did not intend to mention each and every elementary doctrine embraced by Christians. He drew out these, under the Holy Spirit's leadership, as illustrative of primary points with which Christian converts would be familiar. Churches today would do well to make sure every single convert gains a working knowledge of these basic concepts.

Though we are admonished to leave these doctrines, we are not to lose them. We are not to banish them but to build on them. We are not to erase them but to add to them. We are not to forget them but to fulfill them.

"And this we will do if God permits" (v. 3) is a way of saying that forward movement in the Christian life is wholly dependent on the grace of God. Our doing must be by his mercy.

Hebrews 6:4-8 is one of the most difficult passages in the entire letter. At the same time, it is a passage capable of yielding exceptionally helpful spiritual insights. It must therefore be examined cautiously, soberly, and yet hopefully.

In the Christian pilgrimage, believers are beset by dangers on every hand. If, as God permits, we develop and keep moving forward toward maturity (vv. 1-3), we do well. If, on the other hand, any should ever stop, there would be the direst of consequences. If we will not move forward, we are bound to slip back, for we cannot stand still. In this passage, the writer did not say that among the "holy brethren" to whom the letter was originally sent there actually were apostates. Neither did he say that he was afraid apostasy was actually about to break out among them. On the contrary, in the passage immediately preceding and in the one immediately following, a note of strong affirmation and encouragement is sounded. This reference then must be seen as a spur to make Christians press forward. It must be understood as a caution, a warning, or a shock treatment, like a genuine scare for a child not yet unafraid to play in the street. It is not provided so that we may judge others but so that we may check ourselves and make sure we keep moving toward Christian maturity.

It has already been noted that repentance is a powerful theme in Hebrews, and it is with this important doctrine of repentance that this statement is introduced: "It is impossible to restore again to repentance those who have once been enlightened, who have tasted the heavenly gift, and have become partakers of the Holy Spirit, and have tasted the goodness of the Word of God and the powers of the age to come, if they then commit apostasy, since they crucify the Son of God on their own account and hold him up to contempt" (vv. 4-6). The phrase here translated "commit apostasy" is better translated as "shall fall away" in both the King James and American Standard versions.

Repentance is used here as it is in 2 Peter 3:9, and as faith is often used in the New Testament, as a kind of shorthand for the entire experience of salvation in which the eyes of the spirit have been opened, God's good gift of new life has been tasted, and the Holy Spirit has been received. It would be impossible to bring again to salvation any who would intentionally and contemptuously "crucify the Son of God on their own account" (v. 6). Jesus would be useless and dead to any who would sever all connection with him, to any who would utterly banish him from their lives. The sin against the Holy Spirit of which Jesus spoke (Matt. 12:31), the sin unto death of which John spoke (1 John 5:16), and this sin of falling away of which the writer of Hebrews here spoke would seem to be the same sin of deliberately, willfully, intentionally rejecting God. If a person should be so committed to his own destruction that he deliberately rejected God's great gift of salvation through Jesus Christ, that he intentionally trampled underfoot the Holy Spirit with his tender wooing and compassionate pleading, that he

called good evil and evil good, and that he rejected light and chose
darkness, then that person would be damned. He would be damned
because he would have rejected life and would have chosen death.

It is a useless exercise for us to argue that if a person really is a Christian he will not fall away and that if he falls away he never really was a
Christian. Hebrews 6:4-8 does not teach that Christians can fall from
grace; it warns that if Christian salvation should ever be abandoned, it
could not ever be recovered.

The danger of misinterpreting this passage is that if we do not rightly
divide the word of truth, some eternity-bound sinner might be kept
back from repentance and from everlasting salvation. Instead of theor-
izing, debating, and arguing about precisely where the point of sinning
too much is, Christians should see how close we can draw to Christ and
how much distance we can put between us and the devil. Sin is serious,
but Christ Jesus came into the world to save sinners (1 Tim. 1:15). If we
say we have not sinned against God, we "make him a liar, and his word
is not in us" (1 John 1:10). We are instructed by Jesus to forgive each
other's sins not seven times but seventy times seven (Matt. 18:22). Peter
was forgiven by our Lord in spite of the fact that he cursed and denied
Christ three times in the time of trauma and travail preceding the crucifixion, and Peter's restoration came because he truly repented and kept
on truly believing in the unfolding experiences of his life and work.
Though he denied Christ and swore, he went out and wept bitterly.
Though he sinned, he quickly found a place for repentance. Because he
had truly received Christ as his Savior, Peter could not live a life which
would deny that Jesus Christ is Lord. This passage supposes a condition
contrary to fact in order to keep Christians moving toward spiritual
maturity.

Illustration of this teaching is furnished by the reminder that land
which produces good crops "receives a blessing from God" (v. 7), but
that land which bears nothing but weeds and brush is worthless and
that "its end is to be burned" (v. 8).

After this stern and somber warning about falling away, the author
of Hebrews turned immediately to a pastoral expression of affection and
encouragement. The focus is turned specifically to the things that pertain to salvation. The first recipients of the letter would be assured that
they would not fall away. They would be affirmed by this encouraging

word. The King James Version is to be preferred here, "But, beloved, we are persuaded better things of you, and things that accompany salvation" (v. 9). The word translated "beloved" here is rendered "dear friends" by Tyndale. They were people to whom the writer was apparently close and for whom he felt special warmth. The term "beloved" is used only here in the entire letter. The word translated "accompany" or "belong to" is the word from which we get our word "echo." What are the things that echo salvation across all the valleys and through the hills of life? They are the things that God enables his people to do. They are the things Christians want to do. They are undistorted reflections of God's mind and heart, purpose and will. They are the things that make for righteousness. They are the fruit of the Spirit: love, joy, peace, patience, kindness, goodness, faithfulness, gentleness, and self-control (Gal. 5:22).

Salvation is not just a theological transaction, a psychological phenomenon, or an emotional experience. It is a marvelous reality. It echoes ways of integrity, words of wisdom, and works of righteousness. It issues in Christian character, unbending honesty, and uncompromising morality. It is marked by self-sacrifice, giving, discipline, obedience, and faithfulness. It has to do with sharing, ministry, and witness. It is distinguished by just balances, fair dealings, and good works.

Our labors are not in vain. Our works and ministries are all known to the Lord. "God is not so unjust as to overlook" our service to "the saints" and our other works of love which Christians have done and "still do" (v. 10). Each one is to show spiritual earnestness and confident hope "until the end" (v. 11). Christians must avoid sluggishness (v. 12), realizing that enthusiasm and excitement in the work of the Lord are winsomely contagious. The counsel to be "imitators of those who through faith and patience inherit the promises" (v. 12) is advice to follow the example of those who worked faithfully and patiently and who always found God absolutely trustworthy.

Believers Have a New Covenant and a Sure and Steadfast Anchor in Christ (6:13 to 9:28)

The letter now moves on with a fairly long and involved discussion of God's new covenant by which believers experience complete security in Christ. When God makes a covenant, that covenant will be kept. His promises are sure. His dealings with Abraham (vv. 13-15) appropriately illustrate "the unchangeable character of his purpose" (v. 17) and show how "it is impossible that God should prove false" (v. 18). God's promise was that he would bless Abraham and multiply him (v. 14). It was the continuing purpose of God that "the heirs of the promise" (v. 17) maintain absolute confidence in him. The human part of the covenant, however, is not to be ignored, for it must be remembered that it was only when faithful Abraham "patiently endured" that he "obtained the promise" (v. 15).

Christians, as latter day heirs of God's promise to Abraham, the father of the faithful, have "fled for refuge" to Jesus with "strong encouragement to seize the hope set before us" (v. 18). When all about us the storms of life are raging, there is refuge in him for the faithful. When the tides of adversity are sweeping over us, there is encouragement in him for the faithful. When the battles of life are going against us, there is hope in him for the faithful. He will never leave us or forsake us. "We have this as a sure and steadfast anchor of the soul, a hope that enters into the inner shrine behind the curtain, where Jesus has gone as a forerunner on our behalf" (vv. 19-20). The promise-keeping God of Abraham has kept his promise in Jesus Christ. The covenant-making God of Abraham has renewed his covenant in Jesus Christ. And the God who worked the miracles of birth through the lives of Abraham and Sarah in their old age is now working a greater and far more universal miracle of new birth through Jesus Christ whose converted people are commissioned to be his witnesses "unto the uttermost part of the earth" (Acts 1:8, KJV).

Jesus, "as a forerunner on our behalf" became, we are told again, "a high priest for ever after the order of Melchizedek" (v. 20). Like a preacher repeating a text over and over again in order that his hearers will have its truth etched indelibly in their memories, the preacher of Hebrews repeated this favorite text of his and then proceeded again to expound on it (7:1-10).

Melchizedek, was, by translation of that name, "king of righteousness" (v. 2). As king of Salem, he was, by translation of the place name of Salem, the "king of peace" (v. 2). As "priest of the Most High God" (v. 1), he received Abraham's tithes (v. 4) and, symbolically through Abraham, the tithes of all the Levitical priesthood (vv. 5-10). As a person "without father or mother or genealogy" (v. 3), that is, without any historical reference whatsoever as to his human origins or his human descendants, Melchizedek "continues a priest for ever" (v. 3). The eternal Christ is here referred to when it is said not that Jesus resembles Melchizedek but that Melchizedek resembles "the Son of God" (v. 3). As God's peculiarly ordained priest, he both received Abraham's tithes and "blessed him who had the promises" (v. 6). Who is "superior" and has the power to bless "the inferior" (v. 7) except one who is especially set apart by "The Most High God"?

This impressive line of reasoning now moves forward. Perfection was not possible under the Levitical priesthood, so it was necessary for God to raise up the truly ultimate High Priest not from the tribe of Levi at all but from the tribe of Judah (vv. 11-14).

Jesus was God's great High Priest not according to the Jewish "legal requirement concerning bodily descent," therefore, "but by the power of an indestructible life" (v. 16). This inspired and memorable reference to "the power of an indestructible life" is translated "the power of an endless life" in the King James Version and "the power of an indissoluble life" by Moffatt and others. Through the centuries other high priests had come and gone, receiving their office by inheritance and relinquishing it at death. Jesus knew no such limitation, for as God's Son he both *has* life indestructible and *is* life eternal. In him Christians have life, life abundant and life everlasting.

The "former commandment," or regulation concerning the Levitical priesthood, now "is set aside because of its weakness and uselessness" (v. 18). In Jesus Christ, "a better hope is introduced, through which we draw near to God" (v. 19). No longer is a human mediator needed to go to God for us, to part the curtain, and to enter the holiest place on our behalf. God has given us, and the world, a better hope. By this "better hope" every believer, through Christ, personally draws near to God. Nowhere in the Bible is the profoundly important Christian doctrine of the priesthood of the believer so beautifully stated and so clearly explained as in this passage in Hebrews.

That Jesus is "the surety of a better covenant" (v. 22) means that God's Son is the certain guarantee of God's agreement to save and to bless. The covenant is still God's covenant with faithful people like Abraham, of whom God said, "I have chosen him, that he may charge his children and his household after him to keep the way of the Lord by doing righteousness and justice" (Gen. 18:19). The commitment from

God is unconditional. Any covenant, by definition, is an agreement between two parties. However, the human part of the covenant to walk in the way of the Lord and to do righteousness must be kept in order for the divine part of the covenant to be in effect. In this sense, the covenant between God and his people has not changed. The moral demands of the gospel are the same moral demands God made on Abraham. The new covenant is "better," however, in the sense that his high priestly work is fully completed, absolutely permanent, and utterly effective (v. 24). Jesus "is able for all time to save those who draw near to God through him, since he always lives to make intercession for them" (v. 25).

Walking from spiritual mountain peak to spiritual mountain peak, the author of Hebrews here scales a new height. Jesus is able. He is able to save. He is able to save for all time. Because "he always lives," he is able "to make intercession" for "those who draw near to God through him" (v. 25). This drawing near to God through Jesus is a repetition of a vital point already made, but it is not a broken record playing over and over exactly the same thing. This is a further unfolding of all that the Father has done, is doing, and will do for humanity through the Son.

The resurrection of Christ and his ascension to be with the Father, "exalted above the heavens," is completely appropriate or "fitting" since our great High Priest is "holy, blameless, unstained, separated from sinners" (v. 26). "Once for all," Jesus "offered up himself" (v. 27), a perfect high priest and a perfect sin offering. This is God's "Son who has been made perfect for ever" (v. 28).

The point is that Christians have in Jesus a mediator who now "is seated at the right hand of the throne of the Majesty in heaven, a minister in the sanctuary and the true tent which is set up not by man but by the Lord" (8:1-2). Priests on earth, offering "gifts according to the law," have always worked in a tent made with human hands according to the divine pattern given by God to Moses. The earthly sanctuary is but "a copy and shadow of the heavenly sanctuary" (8:5). The old covenant was incomplete and therefore flawed. The new covenant mediated by Jesus, the Son of God himself, "is better, since it is enacted on better promises" (8:6). Likewise his ministry is "much more excellent" than the ministry of the priests under the old covenant (8:6), a ministry of incarnational involvement, self-denial, suffering, and final self-sacrifice.

Turning to Jeremiah 31:31-34, the longest passage directly quoted in the entire letter, the author of Hebrews called on one of the major Old Testament prophets to illustrate his point that the old covenant was inadequate and that a new covenant was therefore mandated by the Lord. With prophetic vision, Jeremiah had foreseen the day when God would establish a new covenant with his people (8:8) not like the one originally made when he first took them by the hand and led them out of bondage (8:9). "They did not continue in my covenant," God said, "so I paid no heed to them" (8:9).

In Jesus, the promised new covenant with God's people has come to glorious realization: "I will put my laws into their minds, and write them on their hearts, and I will be their God, and they shall be my people. And they shall not teach everyone his fellow or every one his brother, saying 'Know the Lord,' for all shall know me, from the least of them to the greatest. For I will be merciful toward their iniquities, and I will remember their sins no more" (8:10-12). The author of Hebrews then commented that Jeremiah's reference to a new covenant treated the old covenant even then as already essentially obsolete. He concluded this lesson with the observation that "what is becoming obsolete and growing old is ready to vanish away" (8:13).

Under the first covenant there were regulations for formal "worship and an earthly sanctuary" (9:1). A very concise but adequate description is then given of the outer tent, called the Holy Place, and the inner tent, called the Holy of Holies, together with the deeply important symbols reminding the Jews of God's mighty acts of redemption which he had done and of his grace and mercy which he ever wills for his people. "Of these things," however, "we cannot now speak in detail" (9:5), it is said.

Into the outer tabernacle or tent the priests continually went for the performance of their ritual duties (9:6), and into the inner tent the high priest went once a year on the great Day of Atonement to make a blood offering for his own sins and for the sins of the people (9:7). "By this," the author of Hebrews said, "the Holy Spirit indicates that the way into the sanctuary is not yet opened as long as the outer tent is still standing" (9:8). This inability of the priests to go beyond the Holy Place and into the Holy of Holies was a symbol or figure of that time (9:9). The old Jewish system simply could not bring about a spiritual approach to God, a vital union with him, and continuing fellowship with him. According to the old arrangement, sacrifices were made for sins, but those sacrifices could not "perfect the conscience of the worshiper" (9:9). Instead they dealt only with regulations imposed "until the time of reformation" (9:10), washings for the body but not for the heart, gifts for time but not for eternity, sacrifices for sins but not a perfect sacrifice for all sin. In Jesus, the time of reformation came and God's great drama of redemption was perfected.

When Christ came to do his great high priestly work, "he entered once for all into the Holy Place, taking not the blood of goats and calves but his own blood" (9:12). As the animal blood represented the lives of the sacrificial beasts, so the reference here to the "blood" of Jesus is a reference to his supreme sacrifice of his very own life. That life was given on our behalf and in obedience to the heavenly Father's will. Sprinkling sinners with the blood of goats and bulls and with the ashes of a heifer provided "purification of the flesh" (9:13) under the old covenant. "How much more shall the blood of Christ, who through the eternal Spirit offered himself without blemish to God, purify your conscience from dead works to serve the living God" (9:14). The eternal redemption (9:12) provided by God through Christ comes as repenting and believing persons draw near to God through Christ to have the conscience purified, the heart cleansed, and the mind renewed. The purification is provided in order for the redeemed "to serve the living God" (9:14).

The "dead works" of 9:14 may possibly mean works of ceremony and ritual, woodenly performed, thus representing the inadequacy of that whole legal system and, possibly, the futility of going through the motions when the heart is not in something. The reference, on the other hand, may mean works or practices that bring moral and spiritual defilement, that pollute the life, and that spoil the spirit. Whatever dead works may have characterized the Christian's past life, Christ has cleansed us from them and has redeemed us for a better work, "to serve the living God" (9:14).

Christ, through the Spirit, "offered himself without blemish to God" (9:14). It was an ideal offering, absolutely perfect beyond human ability to conceive. It somehow met all the requirements in the mind of God and all the requirements to cover the sin of mankind. It was God's final response to sin's challenge. Christ's sacrifice, as James Denney has said in his profound and classic book *The Death of Christ*, "was rational and voluntary, an intelligent and loving response to the holy and gracious will of God, and to the terrible situation of man."[1] There are many theories of the atonement, but all of them together cannot tell the whole story of how Christ makes the sinner right with God. The author of Hebrews has combined the concept of the high priest with that of the blood offering to explain how Jesus both did the high priestly work and made himself the offering. Jesus did not walk away from suffering. He walked through suffering and death to break sin's dominion over all who want salvation's glorious freedom. This brief passage, 9:11-14, contains the theological heart of the letter to the Hebrews.

In the light of the majestic truth that we are cleansed by the blood of Christ "to serve the living God" (9:14), it is important to consider the service that God expects. The matter will come up later, but at this point it should be observed that the intention of "service" here is not formal worship. The recurring emphasis on obedience, growth, maturity, and the things that accompany salvation argue for assigning a meaning to "service" which would encompass the doing of truth, righteousness, justice, and peace. When questioned about what reasonable service to God might have as its absolute minimum, Jesus answered that we are to love God with our entire being and our neighbors as ourselves (Matt. 22:34-40).

The death of Christ redeems us from the sins, or transgressions, which would have left us dead under the old covenant (9:15). In so dying, Jesus became the mediator of the new covenant "so that those who are called may receive the promised eternal inheritance" (9:15). This careful line of reasoning is continued by the author of Hebrews: where a will is involved, the death of the one who made it must be verified (9:16); a will takes effect only at the death of the one making it (9:17); and the first covenant was not ratified except by the life blood which signified life given (9:18). Then, "when every commandment of the law had been declared by Moses," he took the blood of the sacrificial animals and sprinkled the book of the law, the people, the tent, and the vessels used in the formal ceremony of worship (9:19-21). Moses' words "This is the blood of the covenant which God commanded you" (9:20) are a reminder to the author of Hebrews that "under the law almost everything is purified with blood, and without shedding of blood there is no forgiveness of sins" (9:22).

This profound theological insight is not one that today's churches may properly ignore. A theology that steers around this insight is sadly anemic. A hymnologist who cuts out all gospel songs about the blood of Christ is unbiblically squeamish. A ministry that will not preach or teach about the deep meaning of sacrificed life as symbolized in the blood and stated here in Hebrews 9:22 is too politely proper to communicate the gospel of God in Christ. Incidentally, there are twelve references to blood in the ninth chapter of Hebrews, more than are found in any other entire book of the New Testament with the exception of Revelation, though the same number (twelve) may be found in Acts. This major emphasis on blood represents a major concern for the life of the people of God by the sacrifice of the life of God's Son.

In what could easily be perceived as an effective preaching style, the author of Hebrews proceeded. Under the old covenant it was necessary for both the tabernacle and the things in it to be purified through prescribed rites (9:21). "The heavenly things" (9:23), the things of heaven itself, are somehow purified and given special glory and honor in the presence of the crucified and risen and ascended Lamb of God whose "better" sacrifice transforms not only earth but also heaven itself. He entered not into an earthly tent of sanctuary but "into heaven itself, now to appear in the presence of God on our behalf" (9:23-24). Christ does not offer himself repeatedly but "once for all at the end of the age to put away sin by the sacrifice of himself" (9:25-26).

Here is another of the great texts of Hebrews: "It is appointed for men to die once, and after that comes judgment," or as the more familiar King James Version puts it, "It is appointed unto men once to die, but after this the judgment" (9:27). The word translated "judgment" is the word which is transliterated, transferred letter by letter, to make our word *crisis*. The crisis of final determination of the everlasting fate of every person will come after death at the time of judgment. The Judge's determination, according to Jesus' own words as recorded in Matthew 25:31-46, will be on the basis of what we have done in life.

In the normal course of human events people die, and they are not then allowed to come back to life in this world to start all over again (9:27). So Christ came and gave his life once. As judgment follows death in the normal course of human events, so Christ's sinless life and sacrificial death will not be repeated. However, "he will appear a second time, not to deal with sin" as he did on the cross, "but to save those who are eagerly waiting for him" (9:28). For Christians there is to be no fearful, apprehensive, anguished waiting for the judgment of the Lord.

Instead, we joyfully anticipate the second coming when there will be a final consummation in eternity of our salvation that has begun in time.

Christ Conquered Sin and Perfected for Us a New and Living Way (10:1-18)

The exhaustive statement about Abraham, Moses, Melchizedek, the tabernacle, the Levitical priesthood, the high priests, and the sin offerings is about to be brought to a close. The law and the sacrifices are but shadows of the true redemption achieved through Christ's sacrifice (vv. 1-9). Having come to earth to do the Father's will, he abolished the old order and established a new order (v. 10). According to the will of God himself "we have been sanctified through the offering of the body of Jesus Christ once for all" (v. 10). All Christians are "sanctified" by Christ who brings us pure, spotlessly cleansed by his own blood, before the Father.

When Christ's great high priestly work was finished, "he sat down at the right hand of God, then to wait until his enemies should be made a stool for his feet" (v. 13). By his single offering of himself, he "perfected for all time those who are sanctified" (v. 14), putting his laws in their hearts and writing them on their minds (v. 16), and remembering their sins no more (v. 17). Where such forgiveness is fully given by God in Christ and fully received through personal repentance for sin and personal faith in the Lord Jesus, there need be "no longer any offering for sin" (v. 18).

The author of Hebrews has carefully shared his mind and heart about these immensely important matters. No more about them needs to be said. The sermon has been preached, and the exhortation is about to begin.

Advice for Practical Christian Living
10:19 to 13:19

Counsel to Draw Near to God and to Encourage One Another (10:19-25)

God has done great things for us. By his grace, Christians can come boldly to him. We are endowed with "confidence to enter the sanctuary by the blood of Jesus" (v. 19). We are enabled to live a new life, to walk in "the new and living way" (v. 20). Since we have in Christ "a great priest" (v. 21), we are called to "draw near with a true heart in full assurance of faith" (v. 22). The concept of drawing near to God is a prominent one in this letter, and its use again in this context is particularly important. Repenting sinners draw near to him for conversion, and needy believers draw near to him for renewal, for strength, for comfort, for help, and for guidance.

It is only with a "true heart" (v. 22) that anyone can draw near to God. The lost sinner must bring a certain integrity of heart and will to God in the first place in order to experience God's saving grace, and the Christian who continues to seek a closer walk with him, who sincerely and prayerfully strives to draw near to the heart of God, must keep approaching God in honest commitment of mind, soul, and will. Only those with fundamental genuineness are able to worship God in spirit and in truth in line with the will of the Father who ever seeks such true-hearted people to worship him (John 4:23). Those who want to draw near to God must do so in sincerity of spirit. None may do so with a false, pretending, hypocritical heart.

In drawing near to God our first concern is faith. As Christians draw near to God with a true heart, we are to do so "in full assurance of faith" (v. 22). A primary aim of the writer of Hebrews was to bring his readers to this full assurance of faith, to complete confidence in God, to positive certainty about him to whom we have committed everything for time and eternity. To know whom we have believed (2 Tim. 1:12) is to have this full assurance of faith.

The second concern, as we draw near to God with cleansed hearts and purified bodies, is hope. We are urged, "Let us hold fast the confession of our hope without wavering" (v. 23). Christians throughout history have shared the hope of spending eternity with the Lord and all of his redeemed people. It is in hope that we endure trials, conquer temptations, bear witness, follow righteousness, do the things that make for peace, and await the return of our Lord. It is rightly said that hope springs eternal in the human breast, and it does so by virtue of the spark's having been kindled by the Spirit of God. That spark is fanned into flame in the Christian's confession of Christ. Such confession is born in hope, is now being nurtured in hope, and will go on to glory in hope.

The third concern in drawing near to God is love. "Let us consider how to stir up one another to love" (v. 24). Love is not something you think or say or feel. Love is something you do. As important as love is, it cannot be assumed to be such an inevitable quality of the Christian life that it can be taken for granted. It must be stirred up, aroused, fanned into flame, nurtured, cultivated, encouraged.

The word translated "consider" here is translated "vie with one another" in the *Twentieth Century New Testament* and "see how each of us may best arouse others" in the *New English Bible*. It could be translated "Let us rival one another" or "Let us outdo one another."

The author of Hebrews did not ask his first readers calmly and mildly to contemplate some possible ways to encourage each other to love. Instead, he called them to a constructive outdoing of one another in outgoing, self-giving love. An eager aggressiveness is called for in stirring up one another to love, lest we miss the full blessing of love which God intends for us to experience.

A fourth concern in drawing near to God is "good works" (v. 24). The subject of good works is treated here in the closest linkage with love. Christian love and good works belong together. Authentic Christian love is, in fact, inseparable from good works. Christians are to strive to outdo each other in good works. Instead, most Christians seem ready to spend their time and energies in arguing about how good works cannot save us. Granted. Salvation is through Christ. Christians know that. The author of Hebrews hammered away at it with such persistence that his message can hardly be missed. Nevertheless, he urges us to vie with one another in doing good works. Not in order to be cleansed, but because we have been cleansed, we are to stimulate one another to do the gospel. It is the nature of authentic Christian faith, authentic Christian hope, and authentic Christian love to do good without ceasing. Faith, hope, and love find both validation and fruition in good works.

Moreover, Christians are not to neglect meeting together (v. 25). "Not forsaking the assembling of ourselves together, as the manner of some is" in the King James Version is the more familiar translation of this immensely important word of pastoral counsel. There are grave dangers, spiritual and ethical, in the excessive individualism which fancies itself above and beyond the need for the Christian fellowship experienced in the general meetings of the church. The first function of a New Testament church is fellowship. No human being can be born

alone, and none can successfully live alone. God has made humanity for
community. Moreover, he has especially designed the church as a spiritual family in which the members will spiritually "brother" and "sister"
each other. Christians were never intended by the heavenly Father to
be pious particles apart from God's family of faith. Since the church is a
support community, individuals who cut themselves off from its meetings cut themselves off from its undergirding and care. The good advice
given here is for Christians to avoid those problems.

Mutual undergirding and reciprocal encouragement to live the Christian life are important "all the more as you see the Day drawing near"
(v. 25). That Day is the day of Christ's return. The second coming was
viewed by the church then, as it is today, as imminent. It could take
place this very day. Great moral power is inherent in this doctrine. It
denies us the worldly luxury of moral relaxation. It prods us to readiness. It wards off weariness. It is a powerful incentive to right living. It
compels us to keep our lamps trimmed and burning as the wise virgins
in the parable of Jesus did who were ready for the bridegroom's coming
(Matt. 25:1-13). For the lost, that day is the day of awful judgment. For
Christians, however, that day is the day of celebration, joy, and victory
when the great Judge himself will receive the faithful into everlasting
bliss.

Judgment to Fall on the Disobedient (10:26-39)

Since Christians can "see the Day drawing near" (v. 25), we must be
vigilant to avoid deliberate sin (v. 26). We must also be careful not to
spurn the Son of God (v. 29), profane the blood of the covenant (v. 29),
throw away our confidence (v. 35), or shrink back from our commitment (v. 39). The author of the letter to the Hebrews returns in this
passage to the haunting terror with which he had previously dealt
(6:4-8), that of apostasy. Perhaps an evil spirit of apostasy was actually
working among the particular Christians to whom this letter was originally sent. Or perhaps here, as earlier, he meant to sound the note of
grave warning which would keep them decisively turned away from
lukewarmness, coldness, and subsequent apostasy.

The deliberate sin mentioned in 10:26 is willful, intentional aban-
donment of Christ after "receiving the knowledge of the truth" (v. 26).
If such a thing should be, then "there no longer remains a sacrifice for
sins" (v. 26). Instead there would be "a fearful prospect of judgment,

and a fury of fire which will consume the adversaries" (v. 27) of God.

Under the Mosaic law, the death penalty had been prescribed for some twenty-five offenses when guilt was confirmed "at the testimony of two or three witnesses" (v. 28). Such a death was awful; but "how much worse punishment do you think will be deserved by the man who has spurned the Son of God, and profaned the blood of the covenant by which he was sanctified, and outraged the Spirit of grace?" (v. 29).

The vengeance and judgment of God (v. 30) are in mind when this solemn warning is issued, "It is a fearful thing to fall into the hands of the living God" (v. 31). With that tremendous text, Jonathan Edwards called multitudes to repentance in early American revivals. With it, we ourselves do well to cultivate a continuing spirit of personal repentance and personal faith. The warning of Hebrews 10:26-31 is that any who would presumptuously spurn Christ after receiving "the knowledge of the truth" must certainly expect to be consumed by the burning wrath of the Almighty.

This is strong medicine. It must be remembered, however, that God is not an indulgent granddaddy and that the gospel of God in Christ is not a soft and shallow thing. It is a solemn matter which has to do with birth and death, blood and fire, heaven and hell, time and eternity. Here is a corrective for the bumper sticker piety and T-shirt theology which has beset us in this time of doctrinal flabbiness. A morally frivolous age, bent on pasting up posters that insist we are all OK and that confound the faith, confuse the faithful, and comfort the faithless, would do well to hear this prophetic warning, "It is a fearful thing to fall into the hands of the living God" (v. 31). There is in life and in the very nature of reality an element of unremitting judgment. God's promises of judgment are as certain as his promises of grace, and we had better not forget it.

The original recipients of this letter were reminded next of their struggles and sufferings in the time of persecution through which they had passed. They had been able to endure because they knew they 'had a better possession and an abiding one" (v. 34). Those who "do not throw away" their "confidence" are assured of "great reward" (v. 35). We are not to go off into apostasy, but we are to endure to "do the will of God and receive what is promised" (v. 36). Habbakuk 2:3-4 is quoted to call attention to the fact that the just, or righteous, shall live by faith, but that God can have no pleasure in anyone who shrinks back (vv.

37-38). Christians, however, "are not of those who shrink back and are destroyed, but of those who have faith and keep their souls" (v. 39).

Faith in Action: the Roll Call (11:1-40)

The eleventh chapter of Hebrews is magnificent. It is not only the best known chapter in this letter but is also one of the best known and best loved chapters in the whole Bible. It is not just a chapter about faith. It is a chapter about faith in action. It is about faith at work, faith that does not shrink from battle, faith that does not flee from confrontation, faith that does not bend under pressure, faith that does not wither under the heat of persecution. With almost incomparable beauty and excellence, the author has painted a masterpiece of a word picture that has left the church through the centuries breathless, thrilled, and inspired.

What is faith? "Now faith is the assurance of things hoped for, the conviction of things not seen" or, as the more familiar translation puts it, "Now faith is the substance of things hoped for, the evidence of things not seen" (v. 1, KJV).

Faith is the foundation of hope, standing under hope, providing the ground on which hope is built. And what does faith do? It is the evidence, proof, or conviction which enables us to perceive unseen things just as if they were seen, to sense spiritual realities just as truly as we sense things by seeing and smelling, hearing and touching. Faith claims the future in the present. It gives things that are yet to come all the certainty of things that already are. Through faith, unseen things take on substance, and future things take on present reality. Faith transcends the time-space framework in which this present life has to be lived. It transports its holders to the high places where eternity can be seen beyond all present boundaries and barriers. By faith we hold clear title to the property of salvation. With faith in our possession, history becomes filled with meaning, life's present puzzle is no longer an insoluble mystery, and the unseen future comes into plain view in clear focus. Faith is not the gift of seeing something that is not there but the gift of seeing through all the haze of doubt and the pollution of sin to the distant city of God set on the mountain of eternity. Faith is not believing something in spite of the evidence. It is living life for the Lord God in scorn of all earthly consequence.

Great beauty and majesty characterize the older translation of the eleventh chapter of Hebrews, but the newer one is more accurate in communicating the true meaning of what the inspired writer of the letter to the Hebrews originally said. Faith is not actually the "substance" of salvation but the "assurance" that there is substance to the hope given us by the God of all grace. And faith is not actually to be understood so much as the "evidence" itself of "things not seen" as it is our "conviction" that God is absolutely trustworthy and that his promises are completely sure. It is not faith itself that is great and good and gracious, but God, and it is God in Christ toward whom we are pointed in the roll call of the faithful which immediately follows.

By faith, our spiritual forebears "received divine approval" (v. 2). As they demonstrated their trust in God, he affirmed them and blessed them. "By faith we understand that the world was created by the word of God" (v. 3). Scientists have kept coming forward with new theories about the *when* of creation and have recently moved their guesses backward some three or four billion years. The *how* of creation, however, is a theological perception to which the author of Hebrews has spoken with profound insight. By faith we understand that whenever it was done, creation was done "by the word of God," that he made the material out of the immaterial, "that what is seen was made out of things which do not appear" (v. 3).

We are now ready for the thrilling journey back through the history of revealed religion. The purpose of the trip is to let us see illustrations of how faith has been put into action by men and women like ourselves. Those illustrations are windows. Like the parables of Jesus, when appropriately used these illustrations provide earthly examples with heavenly meanings. It is heavenly meaning, not the details of history, with which the writer is primarily concerned. This chapter has been called the Westminster Abbey of the Old Testament, for as the great London cathedral contains the graves and appropriate markers for most of the famous men and women of the British Empire, so this passage contains appropriate markers for many of the great men and women who are the spiritual giants of the Bible.

Abel comes first (v. 4). By faith Abel offered a better sacrifice than Cain, "through which he received approval as righteous, God bearing witness" to the validity of his acting faith "by accepting his gifts" (v. 4). It was not the right words that Abel said which caused him to receive God's approval as righteous. Instead, it was the right deed, his offering to God of the better or more acceptable sacrifice. In spite of the fact that Abel died, "through his faith he is still speaking" (v. 4). Through his own act by which he demonstrated his faith, Abel still speaks to us concerning the importance of obedient and active faith.

Enoch is next in line (vv. 5-6). Enoch "walked with God" (Gen. 5:24), and by faith he "was taken up so that he should not see death" (v. 5). Enoch's communion with God was so complete that his journey from time to eternity was not interrupted by the detour of death. His faith, in line with Jesus' teaching that by faith we can move mountains (Matt. 17:20), simply removed the mountain of death. In active faith Enoch walked with the Lord and by so doing "pleased God" (v. 5). Then, in special consequence, God delivered Enoch from death. Without such faith "it is impossible" so to "please" God (v. 6). Indeed, "whoever would draw near to God must believe that he exists and that he rewards those who seek him" (v. 6). Anyone who draws near to God must believe first that God is and then that God is just and righteous to reward, or to be found by, those who sincerely seek him. The devils believe that God exists (Jas. 2:19), but they do not respond to his righteous character which insists that we cease to do evil and learn to do well (Isa. 1:16-18). Whoever comes to God in faith for salvation must use the mind so as to understand both God's existence and his justice in rewarding those who seek his face. Faith expects great things from God and attempts great things for God.

If we were making up our own roll call of people who put faith into action, we might possibly omit Abel or Enoch, but we certainly would not omit Noah. Of Noah there is something especially important to be said (v. 7). After being warned by God of the flood to come, by faith he "took heed," or really listened, "and constructed an ark for the saving of his household" (v. 7). By so doing "he condemned the world" which perished in the deluge "and became an heir of the righteousness which comes by faith" (v. 7). It was Noah's active faith that actually built the ark and made him "an heir of the righteousness." By such a working faith comes such righteousness for us that we do not perish in the floods of adversity but float above them in the perfect safety of God's grace.

Abraham, the father of the faithful, has the unquestioned place of greatest prominence in this list (vv. 8-12,17-19). The Genesis account says that Abraham "believed the Lord; and he reckoned it to him as righteousness" (Gen. 15:6). This passage in Hebrews says, "By faith

Abraham obeyed when he was called to go" (v. 8). "By faith he so-
journed in the land of promise" (v. 9) as "he looked forward to the city
which has foundations, whose builder and maker is God" (v. 10). "By
faith Abraham, when he was tested, offered up Isaac" (v. 17) because
by faith he believed "that God was able to raise men even from the
dead" (v. 19).

As a heroine of the faith, Sarah receives special attention. "By faith
Sarah herself received power to conceive, even when she was past the
age" (v. 11). Conception, birth, and child rearing require a desperate
concentration of strength, energy, nerve, heart, and will. Sarah's faith
was active faith that reckoned God "faithful who had promised" (v. 11)
to enable her even in old age to achieve such concentration and blessing.

The writer of the letter did not want his readers to forget the main
point that was being made with all these illustrations. Therefore he
paused a moment to remind them of his purpose before proceeding (vv.
13-16). All of these, Abel, Enoch, Noah, Abraham, and Sarah, "died
in faith" without having received the complete realization of the promises of God. With eyes of faith, they saw "from afar" the distant promise
of God's redemption and "greeted it," remaining essentially "strangers
and exiles on the earth" (v. 13). They spoke and lived in such a way as to
"make it clear" that they were "seeking a homeland" (v. 14), that their
hope had not been realized on earth and in time. They could have returned to the lands and occupations and ways of life from which God
had called them (v. 15). Instead, they set their hearts on "a better
country, that is, a heavenly one" and because of their active and obedient faith "God is not ashamed to be called their God, for he has prepared for them a city" (v. 16). With this review, we are reminded not to
set our own minds to things on earth. We are not to forget that we, too,
are sojourners on our way to a better country. We are to maintain an
orientation to God's unfolding future. We are to cling in faith to righteousness and a sense of unchanged and unchanging moral values.

The roll call continues then with a reference to Isaac, of whom it is
said, "By faith Isaac invoked future blessings on Jacob and Esau" (v.
20). Like his father Abraham, Isaac believed God and manifested that
faith by passing on his blessing to Jacob and Esau and, through that
blessing, to succeeding generations. In this way he showed faith that his
own death would not cancel out the promises of God.

Likewise, "By faith Jacob, when dying, blessed each of the sons of Joseph" (v. 21) as a sign that he, like Isaac, was looking to the future for the fulfillment of the promises of God. Although famine had forced him and his family to emigrate to Egypt, his ties to the Land of Promise were not severed and his confidence in the promises of God was not shaken. This is evident in the fact that God had said to Jacob, "I will go down with you to Egypt, and I will also bring you up again" (Gen. 46:4), and in the fact that Jacob said to Joseph, "I am about to die, but God will be with you, and will bring you again to the land of your fathers" (Gen. 48:21).

Then by faith Joseph is said to have spoken at the end of his life "of the exodus of the Israelites" and to have given instructions for them to take his bones back for burial in the Land of Promise when they themselves returned.

By faith Moses' parents hid him to save his life (v. 23). By faith Moses identified with the Israelites, refusing to be called the son of Pharaoh's daughter, "choosing rather to share ill-treatment with the people of God than to enjoy the fleeting pleasures of sin" (v. 25). He considered "abuse suffered for the Christ greater wealth than the treasures of Egypt" because he was looking ahead to the reward that God had promised (v. 26). By faith, Moses left Egypt, endured (v. 27), kept the Passover, "and sprinkled the blood, so that the Destroyer of the first-born might not touch them" (v. 28).

By faith, the people of God passed miraculously through the Red Sea though the pursuing Egyptians, when they tried to do the same thing, were drowned (v. 29).

By faith, the walls of Jericho fell after the armies of Israel had obediently followed God's instructions to get ready for that mighty miracle (v. 30).

By faith, the life of Rahab the harlot was spared, and she did not perish with the disobedient "because she had given friendly welcome to the spies" (v. 31), thus proving herself to be not faithless but believing.

There was simply not time, the writer of Hebrews said as he drew to the end of his roll call, to tell of Gideon (who destroyed Baal's altar and led his select band of soldiers to a brilliantly successful midnight victory over the Midianites), of Barak (who utterly routed the Canaanites in the plain of Jezreel), of Samson (a Nazirite of incredible strength who saved Israel out of the hand of the Philistines and who slew a thousand of them with the jawbone of an ass), of Jephthah (who as a bold and successful military leader threw the yoke of Ammon off the necks of the people of Israel), of David (who was Israel's greatest king, who led Israel to some of her finest hours, and who was called a man after God's own heart), of Samuel and the prophets (who warned against idolatry, judged with equity, and prophesied with indomitable courage). All of these were people "who through faith conquered kingdoms, enforced justice, received promises, stopped the mouths of lions, quenched raging fire, escaped the edge of the sword, won strength out of weakness, became mighty in war, put foreign armies to flight" (vv. 33-34).

This is a superb piece of concise writing which underscores the active nature of living faith. Furthermore, he continued, "Women received their dead by resurrection. Some were tortured" (v. 35) and killed. Still "others suffered mocking and scourging, and even chains and imprisonment. They were stoned, they were sawn in two, they were killed with the sword; they went about in skins of sheep and goats, destitute, afflicted . . . wandering over deserts and mountains, and in dens and caves of the earth" (vv. 36-38). Of these it is clear that the world was not worthy (v. 38).

The great chapter is concluded with these summary words: "And all of these, though well attested by their faith, did not receive what was promised, since God had foreseen something better for us, that apart from us they should not be made perfect" (vv. 39-40). They lived in faith, worked in faith, and died in faith. Faith for them was nothing ultimate. God was. He did great things for them under the old covenant promise, and he has done and is doing something far better for us under the new covenant through Christ.

Admonition to Put Faith to Work (12:1-13)

Since Christians are surrounded by this great "cloud of witnesses," we ourselves are called to action (v. 1). We are to "lay aside every weight, and sin which clings so closely" in order that our working faith will not be frustrated. Our God-given freedom guarantees that we may choose to run with handicaps, that we may pet the sin which dogs our feet, but we will do well to lay aside every hindering weight and shun every distracting and hobbling sin. The purpose of this personal initiative to reject sin is that we may "run with perseverance" or patience "the race that is set before us" (v. 1). Christian salvation is not just a finished transaction. It is not just a past psychological experience. It is not just an apprehended prize. It is a race to be run, a life to be lived, a work to be accomplished. God has set the race before us, and we are chosen by him and enabled by him not to drop out of it but to run it. As we do so, we are to keep "looking to Jesus" (v. 2), because if we take our eyes off him and lose our concentration on him who has redeemed us and called us and whom we are to honor and serve with our lives, then we cannot possibly run well. He is the Christian's coach in the race of life, "the pioneer and perfecter of our faith" (v. 2), the author or initiator of our new life and the one who will perfect or finish the good work begun in us. "For the joy that was set before him" (v. 2) he endured the cross and despised its shame, counting the suffering and even death itself as *means* to be endured in order that the *end* of doing the will of the Father might be realized (v. 3). Now in "joy" he "is seated at the right hand of the throne of God" (v. 2), already having run his special race, already having finished it victoriously and gloriously.

"Consider him," (v. 3) we are admonished. Keep him in sight. Think about him. Make him the focus of life. Bear in mind Jesus "who endured from sinners such hostility against himself, so that you may not grow weary or fainthearted" (v. 3). Jesus is our example of patience in the face of opposition. As he did not grow weary or fainthearted, so are we to endure in our own struggle. Jesus endured the cross in his cosmic conquest of sin, but the first recipients of this letter were reminded that in their own "struggle against sin" they had not yet resisted to the point of losing their lives (v. 4).

Persecution and hostility can be extremely debilitating. They can sap the juices of life. They can steal joy and squelch enthusiasm. They can bring on weariness and faintheartedness (v. 3). The exhortation in which the father addresses his son in Proverbs 3:11-12 is called to mind: do not disregard the Lord's discipline nor be discouraged by his punishment because the Lord disciplines those whom he loves and chastises those whom he receives (vv. 5-6). "It is for discipline that you have to endure" (v. 7) means that for Christians suffering endured is meant to be discipline experienced. The discipline of suffering reminds us that God loves us. As we respect "earthly fathers" who care enough for us to discipline us, so we respect the heavenly Father who loves us enough to discipline "us for our good, that we may share his holiness" (vv. 8-10). Christians are, in all things, to "be subject to the Father of spirits and live" (v. 9). By obedience in suffering and through trials, by patient endurance of hostility and even open persecution, Christians are to demonstrate subjection to God, "the Father of spirits"; and in so doing, we "live" (v. 9). The end result of such endurance is "the peaceful fruit of righteousness to those who have been trained by it" (v. 11).

"Therefore lift your drooping hands" (v. 12) to praise God and serve others; "strengthen your weak knees" (v. 12) for the heavy loads to be lifted and the hard tasks to be undertaken; "make straight paths for your feet" (v. 13). It is not God's intention that Christians should march into spiritual battle with "lame feet" but with the members of the body fully healed, fully healthy, and fully well (v. 13). The concern here is for spiritual health and vibrant faith. The door to God has opened through Jesus Christ, and we are to walk confidently through that door and in his way. The reference to weak hands and feeble knees is from Isaiah 35:3, where the prophet was encouraging the people to endure with the assurance that God would come and save them. Christians now are encouraged to endure in the full knowledge that Christ himself will return to save us.

The Beauty of Holiness (12:14-17)

Hebrews 12:14 is one of the uniquely powerful ethical texts in the Bible. It is a clarion call for holiness. Just a couple of sentences before, Christians have been reminded of how discipline from the Lord comes in order "that we may share in his holiness" (v. 10). Here we are told, "Follow peace with all men, and holiness, without which no man shall see the Lord" (v. 14, KJV). The word *follow* in the King James Version is better translated "strive" in the newer versions. "The peace with all men" for which we are to strive is a normal derivative of peace with God. Such peace does not come simply and routinely, however. It must be worked for by toiling Christians determined to reflect a right relationship with God in right relationships with others. True peace with others is achieved as we work faithfully for the things that make for peace: justice and righteousness, honesty and fairness, selflessness and kindness, mercy and love. "Holiness" (RSV), however, is a better translation of that for which we are to strive than "consecration," which was used in the earliest editions of the Revised Standard Version, or "purity" (TCNT), or "sanctification" (ASV).

Holiness is a drawing near to God with a cleansed conscience. We need holiness because God commands it: "Be ye holy; for I am holy" (Lev. 20:7 and 1 Peter 1:16, KJV). We need holiness because our natures are such that we can never be at rest until we are at rest in God who is holy. We need holiness because, in the last analysis, holiness in the lives of believers is the only thing to which the lost world has ever paid attention and is the only thing in the world which will authenticate our faith to the lost multitudes. Holiness is available to those who come to Christ in faith and who then strive for it with all their hearts. Holiness is never laid on Christians like a heavy harness on an unwilling beast of burden. It is taken on like a yoke by those who are willing to be identified as people of wholeness, integrity, righteousness, morality, uprightness, holiness.

It is a particularly striking, even shocking, thing to realize that without holiness "no one will see the Lord" (v. 14). Holiness is not a frequently used word in our modern Christian vocabularies, but its recovery will have to be made a matter of paramount importance if we are to find our way out of the debilitating moral compromise which characterizes our age and robs the church of power and credibility.

Next, a three-dimensioned admonition is issued: "See to it that no one fail to obtain the grace of God; that no 'root of bitterness' spring up and cause trouble, and by it the many become defiled; that no one be immoral or irreligious like Esau, who sold his birthright for a single meal" (vv. 15-16). This passage calls us all to be careful for ourselves and watchful for others in avoiding defection. To "see to it that no one fail" means that we are to be careful to leave no one behind in the pilgrimage of faith, that we are to be watchfully solicitous about others in the Christian fellowship. Our concern is to be that "no one fail to obtain the grace of God" (v. 15). Here the concern seems to be for those not yet in the family of faith as Christians seek to reach out in caring compassion to all lest any fail to lay hold of the blessings offered by God's grace.

The "root of bitterness" is a reference from Deuteronomy 29:18 which warned against turning away from the Lord. As tares could choke out the wheat in Bible times and as Johnson grass can ruin a crop in our times, so we are to "see to it" that noxious weeds of evil doctrine or evil doing are not allowed to grow in the garden of faith, lest trouble and defilement prevail.

We also are to "see to it . . . that no one be immoral or irreligious" (vv. 15-16). The King James Version here renders these two words "fornicator" and "profane." The first reference seems to be to sexual immorality. The word used is the one from which our word *pornography* is derived. The word is generally taken to mean sexual vice and is most frequently translated "fornication." The second warning against being irreligious or profane is bolstered by a stern reminder of the awful fate of Esau who so despised the heritage which should have been his in line with the promises of God that he sold it all "for a single meal" (v. 16). Christians are to be everlastingly vigilant to "see to it" that none be sexually immoral or profanely irreligious. Those qualities are outward signs of inner chaos.

God's Great Salvation Requires Grateful Service (12:18-28)

Christians have not come to Mount Sinai with its terrifying manifestations of the awful presence of the Almighty (vv. 18-21) but "to Mount Zion and to the city of the living God, the heavenly Jerusalem, and to innumerable angels in festal gathering, and to the assembly of the firstborn who are enrolled in heaven, and to a judge who is God of all, and to the spirits of just men made perfect, and to Jesus, the mediator of a new covenant, and to the sprinkled blood that speaks more graciously than the blood of Abel" (vv. 22-24). With this breathtakingly inspirational statement of the meaning of God's great salvation, the writer prepared to press once more for grateful service.

"See that you do not refuse him who is speaking" (v. 25) is a reference to Christ who has spoken God's redemptive word to all mankind. Under the old covenant there was no escape for those who ignored the warnings of God to turn from sin and flee from the wrath to come. "Much less shall we escape if we reject him who warns from heaven" (v. 25). God has made it clear that he is sovereign, that he will not allow sin to go unpunished, and that he will not allow righteousness to go unrewarded so "he has promised, 'Yet once more I will shake not only the earth but also the heaven' " (v. 26). Christians are called, therefore, to "be grateful for receiving a kingdom that cannot be shaken" (v. 28). As a consequence, and never forgetting that "our God is a consuming fire" (v. 29), we are to "offer to God acceptable worship" (v. 28).

How to Live While Moving Toward the City of God (13:1-19)

The letter of Hebrews is profoundly theological, and its emphasis on the great high priestly work of Christ is unsurpassed in the Bible. It is also deeply ethical, however, from its beginning to its ending. In the last chapter of the book, ethical issues of great importance are raised and dealt with by the writer in the knowledge that Christians need help in knowing how to live while seeking the city of God. The writer did not conclude the letter with chapter 12. Instead, he climaxed it with chapter 13 and some immensely important moral teachings.

The first moral challenge is, "Let brotherly love continue" (v. 1). Where the Spirit of Christ is, there is brotherly love; wherever the church is found, there is brotherly love. John Calvin believed that people could not be Christians without also being brethren. Christians are not to let brotherly love cool off or fade away. Instead, we are to be diligent to "continue" it and to cultivate it.

"Do not neglect to show hospitality to strangers" (v. 2) shows how important hospitality, as an expression of brotherly love among the early Christians, was considered to be. By showing such hospitality, many, through the centuries, have entertained "angels," the very messengers of God himself, "unawares." It is true that some risks are taken when strangers are entertained, but living the Christian life was never meant to be a risk-free adventure. The moral ministry of hospitality, therefore, is not to be neglected.

"Remember those who are in prison . . . and those who are ill-treated" (v. 3) is a reminder that Christians are to maintain a deeply genuine concern for the common, poor, powerless, and downtrodden people of the world. It is not to be claimed that most prisoners are innocent, but it is known that they are all needy, lonely, and frustrated by their self-made shackles inside their society-made walls. We are to remember them as if we were there with them, in the knowledge that inasmuch as we render moral ministries to them and to needy people like them in Jesus' name we actually serve our Lord himself (Matt. 25:31-46).

"Let marriage be held in honor among all, and let the marriage bed be undefiled" (v. 4) is the clearest statement related to marriage and sexual ethics in the book of Hebrews. "God will judge the immoral and adulterous" (v. 4), but Christians are assured of escaping that judgment because God has called us not to sexual immorality but to purity. "The marriage bed" or sexual union, is extremely important to individuals, families, churches, nations, and society at large. Only as its sacredness is preserved can the institution of marriage be "held in honor" and properly be preserved. There are not many things on earth more important for Christians to do than this.

"Keep your life free from love of money" (v. 5), for greed is a sickness of the soul, a malignancy in the spirit, a bottomless pit which Christians are to steer away from at all costs. The love of money is the root of all kinds of evil (1 Tim. 6:10) because it is a kind of addictive idolatry. The more the greedy person gets the more he wants, like the rich farmer in Jesus' parable who so lusted for increased possessions that he determined to tear down adequate barns in order to build even bigger ones. Pagans are not the only ones who need this ethical advice. Christians need it too. The reason that Christians, of all people, should be content with what they have is that God has promised, "I will never fail you nor forsake you" (v. 5), a quotation found in Deuteronomy 31:6 and in Joshua 1:5. Christians need not be anxious about money since the Lord is our helper. We need not be afraid, for what can man do to us if we have in fact drawn near to God?

"Remember your leaders" (v. 7) is an admonition to honor and imitate "those who spoke the word of God" by which faith came. They are gone, but by their precept and example, they have left us firmly anchored to "Jesus Christ" who "is the same yesterday and today and for ever" (v. 8).

"Do not be led away by diverse and strange teachings" that have to do with "foods," but let "the heart be strengthened by grace" (v. 9). This is a warning against any new religious fad which would foolishly focus on foods while turning away from faith in God whose grace is uniquely mediated through Christ. Bread can succor the body, but only grace can sustain the heart. The sacrifice which Christ made as he "suffered outside the gate in order to sanctify the people through his own blood" (v. 12) does not require or involve or even allow any special meal. It is faith in him alone on which the Christian's right relationship to God depends.

"Let us go forth to him outside the camp," bearing abuse for him (v. 13), is an appeal for Christians not to be at home where Jesus was homeless, not to get all settled down when Jesus had no place to lay his head, not to seek the world's praise when it has heaped abuse on our Lord, and not to cling so selfishly to life inside the camp that we will not risk life outside the camp for him who loved us and gave himself for us. Christians are to live always with the realization that "here we have no lasting city" and that when we have our proper bearings we will always be a people who "seek the city which is to come" (v. 14).

"Through him then let us continually offer up a sacrifice of praise to God" (v. 15) with "lips that acknowledge his name" (v. 15). Such an acceptable sacrifice of praise to God might also include, however, mouths that preach his gospel and lives that demonstrate his love. The "fruit of lips that acknowledge his name" has always been the fruit of more believers, inasmuch as God's Word never returns to him void.

"Do not neglect to do good and to share what you have" (v. 16) is a powerful reminder that those who rail out against do-gooders are not on God's side. The alternatives to doing good are to do evil or to do nothing. Christians of every age do well to heed this call "to do good" and "to share" what we have. Such self-sacrifice is the authentication of the genuineness of the words of profession and confession which we have uttered with our mouths.

"Obey your leaders and submit to them" (v. 17) was advice providing unqualified endorsement of the leaders in the particular fellowship of Christians to whom the letter was originally sent. The advice was also intended to provide encouragement for the members to obey the teachings and to submit to the spiritual leadership of those who were called to keep watch over their souls "as men who will have to give account" (v. 17) to God.

There is a timelessness, however, about this advice. God-called leaders are universally and everlastingly concerned for the highest interests of all the Christians to whom they are related. They provide spiritual direction for the community of faith. They rightly divide the word of truth. They preach God's Word in season and out of season. They are "apt to teach" (2 Tim. 2:24, KJV). They press the claims of Christ on both unbelievers who need to come to him and on believers who need to come closer to him. As the shepherd sleeplessly keeps watch over his flocks by night or as the soldier remains wakefully vigilant through the long watches of the night, so the spiritual leader is spiritually alert to discharge his pastoral responsibilities.

To "do this joyfully" (v. 17) is the special responsibility of church leaders. If they should do their work "sadly" or groaningly or complainingly, their grim reluctance would plainly show that their hearts would not be in their labors. When such a spirit prevails, those in their spiritual charge cannot be helped, comforted, reproved, or strengthened.

Only those who labor for the Lord in joy and with contagious enthusiasm can lead effectively.

Because the writer of the letter had a clear conscience in knowing that he had desired "to act honorably in all things" (v. 18) toward the recipients to whom the message was first sent, he besought them, "Pray for us" (v. 18). Using the first person for the first time, he wrote, "I urge you the more earnestly to do this in order that I may be restored to you the sooner" (v. 19), that is, that he might quickly be with them again.

Conclusion
13:20-25

A final appeal is made at the very end of the letter for the readers to "bear with my word of exhortation, for I have written to you briefly" (v. 22). The good news "that our brother Timothy has been released" is shared, as is the writer's intention to see them, with Timothy, providing "he comes soon" (v. 23). They are to greet all their leaders and "all the saints" on behalf of the writer. "Those who come from Italy," he added, "send you greetings" (v. 24). Then with this beautifully simple word the letter is concluded, "Grace be with all of you. Amen" (v. 25).

Since the most majestic and memorable benediction in the whole Bible is recorded in Hebrews 13:20-21, it is fitting that it should be the benediction for this study:

> Now may the God of peace who brought again from the dead our Lord Jesus, the great shepherd of the sheep, by the blood of the eternal covenant, equip you with everything good that you may do his will, working in you that which is pleasing in his sight, through Jesus Christ; to whom be glory for ever and ever. Amen.

Note

1. James Denney, *The Death of Christ* (Downers Grove, Illinois: Inter-Varsity Press), p. 228.

JAMES

Introduction

James is a powerful affirmation of relevant religion. It reflects the stringent moral demands of Jesus' Sermon on the Mount. It is a storehouse of practical wisdom. It is shockingly candid. It presents an abrasively critical view of the rich establishment. It identifies with the poor, the powerless, and oppressed. It sympathizes with the sick. It knows works as the proof of faith. It understands sin and takes it seriously. It sees that religion and life belong together. It is characterized by unbending integrity. It calls a spade a spade. It tells it like it is. It is a tract for our own times. It is the New Testament's Magna Charta of practical Christianity.

Martin Luther called James "a right strawy epistle" and omitted it from the first edition of his German translation of the New Testament published in Wittenberg in September of 1522. Nevertheless he included James, along with Hebrews, Jude, and Revelation, at the end of the 1534 edition of his complete German Bible because, he grudgingly admitted, "there is many a good saying in it."[1] Luther's irresponsible treatment of James has been all too influential among Christians for hundreds of years. His view deserves to be rejected, and the letter of James deserves to occupy its rightful place of honor and respect among all the other books of God's holy Word.

The book of James is hardly a book at all in the sense that the word is generally used. An ordinary book today contains about fifty thousand words, while James consists of only about twenty-three hundred. It can be read aloud, as the church historian Eusebius said it frequently was in the early churches, in about fifteen minutes. There is still something positively electrifying about being together with a great company of believers when it is so read or preached today.

James is a sermon in the form of a letter. Vivid illustrations from farming and seafaring, compelling figures of speech, gripping thoughts tersely put, striking expressions, pressing questions, fierce attacks, and comforting assurances are all packed into this brief letter-sermon. With the exception of the utterance of Jesus Christ himself, the forcefulness of the language of James is without parallel in early Christian literature. J. B. Mayor, an eminent Greek scholar and the author of the most definitive book written about the letter of James, said that he was "inclined to rate the Greek of this epistle as approaching more nearly to the standard of classical purity than that of any other book in the New Testament with the exception perhaps of the Epistle to the Hebrews."[2]

The letter of James often pulls together various proverbs and wise observations with little apparent concern for order and then addresses them to a particular class or group. This style is called a paranesis, a style often used for teaching ethics in the Greek world of the first century. The epistle also employs another literary form called the diatribe, which uses the style of a debater engaged in a spirited exchange with an opponent who, to prove a point on an ethical issue, presents an argument, quotes his opponent, refutes him, addresses him directly in extraordinarily harsh terms, and then appeals for the hearers or readers to agree with him. The letter of James uses paranesis and diatribe to make an impact on the hearer or reader in support of living the Christian life, not to present a finely honed philosophical approach to religion as a speculative system of thought.

The Occasion of the Letter

Addressed "to the twelve tribes in the Dispersion" (1:1), the letter is pastoral in purpose. It encourages those beseiged by trials. It rebukes the prejudiced. It condemns an idle faith that will not work. It instructs with regard to the tongue. It explains the nature of pure religion. The letter counsels concerning ministries to the sick. It shows concern for evangelism. It comforts the distressed. And it demands the doing of God's Word and work in the world. In a book on James written in 1915, the great Greek scholar A. T. Robertson chose for his title *Practical and Social Aspects of Christianity*. That title appropriately picks up the theme of this particularly powerful epistle.

The Author

Three men named James are prominent in the New Testament. One James, son of Zebedee and brother of John, was chosen by Jesus as one of the twelve apostles and was killed by King Herod (Acts 12:2) as one of the earliest Christian martyrs. Another James, the son of Alphaeus, was also one of the twelve, and is listed in Matthew 10:3; Mark 3:18; Luke 6:15; and Acts 1:13. Still another James, the Lord's brother, is mentioned twice in the Gospels, in Matthew 13:55 and in Mark 6:3, and then much more frequently and prominently in the rest of the New Testament (1 Cor. 15:7; Gal. 1:19; Acts 12:17; Acts 15:13-21; Gal. 2:9-12; and Acts 21:18).

It is James, the Lord's brother, to whom this letter has been most generally attributed on the basis of convincing evidence. It includes many references that seem to come from a common background with Jesus. It contains significant coincidences of expression with the address of James, the Lord's brother, at the Jerusalem conference as recorded in Acts 15:23-29. It reflects the qualities of character and life ascribed to James, the Lord's brother, both in the New Testament and in tradition: authority, righteousness, justice, wisdom, prayer, and moral integrity. It is Jewish in nature and tone, as might have been particularly expected from James, the Lord's brother and the leader of the Jerusalem church. It refuses to seek any special hearing, possibly out of the author's confidence that he had no need to argue his authority or prestige. It appears to contain in 1:2-8 and 1:17 certain parallels with the writings of the Qumran community which could best be accounted for if the author were indeed James, the Lord's brother, whose leadership of the Jerusalem church would have placed him in close proximity to the Qumran people. Moreover the letter displays an uncompromising commitment to the ethical imperative of the Judeo-Christian tradition of revealed religion. It completely avoids the essentially Greek heresy of dividing faith and works. In this way a strong argument is made for its authorship by one who was personally close to Jesus and whose faith had not been fragmented by the deadly doctrine of dualism. That doctrine, which artificially separates mind from matter and religion from life, has done more to paralyze and discredit the church of Jesus Christ than any other false doctrine in the history of Christianity. The letter of James is a perfect antidote for this pernicious poison of dualism.

The Date and Place of Writing

The letter of James is thought by some scholars to be the earliest of the New Testament writings. It reflects a confident expectation of Christ's early return. Instead of using the term *ecclesia* which would be translated as "church," it uses the term *synagogue* which is translated "assembly" in 2:2. This usage is an early carry-over of Jewish terminology into the Christian vocabulary. The letter mentions the elders of the church in 5:14 without any reference to deacons or pastors, which could be an indication of an early period in the life of the church before the offices of the church were generally systematized. The date of writing could be placed prior to AD 50 when the Jerusalem council was held to consider the status of Gentile believers. Or it could be placed as late as AD 62 when James is thought to have been martyred.

Salutation
1:1

The author of this letter identifies himself only as "James, a servant of God and of the Lord Jesus Christ." The name James is an English form of Jacob, still a highly popular name around the world wherever the Judeo-Christian influence has permeated. As a servant of God, James acknowledged God's only begotten Son, Jesus Christ, as his Lord. By so doing he established the only credentials really necessary for what he was about to write to others of like faith in God and commitment to Jesus Christ as Lord.

The greeting is given "to the twelve tribes in the Dispersion." "The twelve tribes" was a term commonly used to refer to Israel, God's chosen people, as a whole. James could have been meaning to send this letter to all Jews. Or he could have meant the letter for a specialized category of Christians of Jewish origin with whom he felt a special relationship by virtue of his own Jewish background and position of leadership in the Jerusalem church. Most of the very earliest churches, of course, were made up of faithful Jews who accepted Jesus as the promised Messiah. Or he could have meant to send this letter to all believers, whom Christians, early in the Christian era, came to consider the true Israel (Rom. 2:28-29; 9:4-13). Christians today easily find ourselves in this greeting, for we readily recognize that God is speaking powerfully and compellingly to us through this portion of his holy Word.

Advice for Living the Christian Life
1:2-15

Move Through Trials to Maturity (1:2-4)

"Count it all joy, my brethren, when you meet various trials" (v. 2) is the advice with which James began his letter. The first recipients of the letter, in their dispersion, were likely experiencing serious adversities. Loneliness, grief, suffering, hardship, rejection, frustration, homesickness, social isolation, language barriers, and culture shock all tend to beset exiles and pilgrims. Actual persecution could have already begun.

Because all things, including trials, are working together for good for those who love God and who are called according to his purpose, Christians are not to thrash around in frustration or in fury at the troubles to come. On the contrary, Christians are to rejoice when such trials are encountered because they can be God's gift for helping his people move forward in the Christian life to maturity and victory. "The testing of your faith produces steadfastness," (v. 3) and steadfastness leads to maturity.

To "be perfect and complete, lacking in nothing" (v. 4) is not James's advice for Christians to achieve an obviously impossible sinless perfection. It is, rather, a powerful reminder that God's people must not surrender to trouble. On the contrary, we must faithfully endure trials and stand steady through the storms of life. When such steadfastness has "its full effect," then God's faithful people will be "complete, lacking in nothing" (v. 4).

Salvation is here understood to be wholeness. Christians who have not yet endured such "trials" and "testing" have not yet come to maturity or complete wholeness in the Lord. Those who have so endured are God's finest trophies of grace. Therefore trials and tribulations are not to be considered as hard luck. Neither are they necessarily to be thought of as punishment for sins. Trials and testings are meant by our heavenly Father not to be stumbling blocks but stepping-stones for Christian pilgrims moving toward maturity. In God's providence, trials are the occasion for spiritual growth which Christians are to "count it all joy" to meet.

Seek Wisdom Through Prayer (1:5-8)

The letter of James might appropriately be entitled "The Wisdom of James." A quick reading of the entire letter reveals the author's deep concern for wisdom. At a very early point in the letter, therefore, James introduced this topic of very special importance.

Wisdom is the attainment of worthy ends by the use of worthy means. As used by James, wisdom is right understanding, moral discernment, spiritual insight, responsible words, and worthy deeds. *Wisdom* is a word not often encountered by moderns in our daily reading of newspapers, listening to radio, watching television, or conversing with families and friends. Too preoccupied with facts, too harried to look up, too hurried to be still and know God, modern men and women keep stumbling past the gate of wisdom. James knew a more excellent way, however, and wrote, "If any of you lacks wisdom, let him ask God who gives to all men generously and without reproaching, and it will be given him" (v. 5). Facts can be gathered by inquisitive minds, and scientific data can be accumulated by careful observers of nature's phenomena; but widom is the special provision of God. To pray to God for wisdom is to recognize God's omniscience and to acknowledge his providence. The God of all grace delights in giving his great gift of wisdom, without reproach, to those who "ask in faith, with no doubting" (v. 6). Solomon prayed to God for wisdom and found his prayer answered beyond anything he might have dared to ask or think. Likewise every believer who searches his inner self and finds a lack of understanding and then asks God to supply his want will receive "from the Lord" (vv. 7-8) the gift of wisdom. The wisdom for which Christians are admonished to pray has deep roots in the soil of faith. Such wisdom sought through prayer is a fundamental characteristic of the believer's good life in Christ.

Experience the Leveling Power of a Common Faith (1:9-11)

"Let the lowly brother boast in his exaltation, and the rich in his humiliation" (v. 9) was the advice of James for early Christians beset by inferiority complexes on the one hand and by superiority complexes on the other hand. The poor, the plain, and the weak are to rejoice that the Lord has lifted them up to make his strength perfect in their weakness. The rich, the beautiful, and the strong are to rejoice that the Lord has helped them down from their dizzying, dangerous, and rickety ladders of self-love. The ground at the foot of the cross is wonderfully level.

The full force of James's prophetic indignation against the injustices perpetrated by the rich against the poor begins now to be expressed. "Like the flower of the grass" the rich "will pass away . . . . So will the rich man fade away in the midst of his pursuits" (vv. 10-11).

The church has nearly always been reluctant to hear the word of God about wealth. The words of Jesus at this point are all too often glossed over. The message of the prophets regarding riches is thought by many to be particularly obnoxious. The teaching of James in this regard is considered especially offensive by many. Why? This is true because it is a hard doctrine, and hard doctrines are much more easily ignored than confronted. They are much more easily discounted than accepted. They are much more easily explained away than obeyed. It was not the disposition of James, however, to mince words, so he shared his spiritual insight at this important point. Wealth is a great danger to the spiritual life. Human beings need a little but are choked by a lot. Riches may buy special status in this world's clubs but in the church, bought by the blood of Jesus Christ, everybody is somebody.

In this letter James returned again and again to the subject of riches.

Endure Trials and Resist Temptations (1:12-15)

Turning again to the subject of trials, James next employed the only beatitude of the entire letter, "Blessed is the man who endures trial, for when he has stood the test he will receive the crown of life which God has promised to those who love him" (v. 12). This statement is in complete agreement with the recurring word of Jesus to the effect that "he who endures to the end will be saved" (Matt. 10:22; 24:13; Mark 13:13). The trials and tribulations of life in this kind of world are not to be endured out of a dull indifference to pleasure or pain. Rather, they are to be endured in a hopeful and loving faith in God through Jesus Christ who will see his people safely through.

Temptations are different from trials. Trials beset us from without and are an inevitable part of living in a fallen, sin-cursed world. Temptations, however, spring up from within when a person "is lured and enticed by his own desire" (v. 14). This kind of temptation never comes from God, "for God cannot be tempted with evil and he himself tempts no one" (v. 13). Inordinate desire or lust has many facets, all of which are ugly. Lust may have reference to sexual appetite in its basest, most manipulative, self-gratifying form. Or it may have reference to material goods or money or fame or position or influence or prestige or power or even comfort. It is to be resisted because such lust or inordinate "desire when it has conceived gives birth to sin; and sin when it is full-grown brings forth death" (v. 15).

Pure Religion
1:16 to 2:26

The Good Gifts of God (1:16-18)

The statement, "Do not be deceived, my beloved brethren" (v. 16), may be taken as referring to those just mentioned who deceive themselves with the notion that God has tempted them with evil desire. The most obvious interpretation, however, is that this statement is intended to relate to the point that follows concerning God as the source of "every good endowment and every perfect gift" (v. 17). Christians are to maintain spiritual perspective and not err in recognizing that every such blessing "is from above, coming down from the Father of lights" (v. 17).

Faithful Jews prayed daily, "Blessed art thou, O Lord, creator of the luminaries" or "Blessed be the Lord our God who hath formed the lights." Out of this Jewish heritage, James made a natural reference to God as "the Father of lights with whom there is no variation or shadow due to change" (v. 17). The sun and the moon and the stars are constantly moving and are periodically concealed. The Father of lights, however, who made them all and directs them in their courses, is constant, steady, and unchanging. No shadow comes from him, and "in him is no darkness at all" (1 John 1:5).

God's good and perfect gift of salvation is contemplated next, "Of his own will he brought us forth by the word of truth that we should be a kind of first fruits of his creatures" (v. 18). Intentionally parented by God the Father, Christians are "begotten" (KJV) or brought forth by the gospel. We are to be fully dedicated to him just as the firstfruits of the fields were to be dedicated (Lev. 23:10; Deut. 18:4; 26:1-11) in the special service of God. The supreme gift of salvation, new birth through God's good news in Christ, is no chance development but is the result of the heavenly Father's divine intention.

Develop Maturity of Character (1:19-21)

As pure religion begins with the good gifts of God, so it continues with the development of Christian character. "Know this" (v. 19) could be either an admonition to know or an acknowledgment that the "beloved brethren" who share membership in the church family where God is Father and Jesus Christ is Elder Brother already know what is about to follow. "Let every man be quick to hear, slow to speak" (v. 19) is James's first reference to talk and the tongue. This is a major theme in the letter.

Christians, of all people, are to cultivate the grace of ready and sympathetic listening on the one hand, while we are to practice the wisdom of careful and deliberate speaking on the other hand. Also, we are to be "slow to anger" (v. 19). We are not to indulge in temper tantrums because human orgies of wrath do not bring about divine justice, or, as James has put it, "the anger of man does not work the righteousness of God" (v. 20).

The reference to "filthiness and rank growth of wickedness" which Christians are to "put away" (v. 21) speaks of the evil which lurks in our lives, to "the sin which doth so easily beset us" (Heb. 12:1, KJV). God's people do not have this practice of sinning forcefully jerked out of our hands by an impatient parent. Rather, we are to exercise spiritual discipline in personally ferreting it out and in personally putting it away. As we do so, we are to "receive with meekness" or a spirit of teachableness and true repentance "the implanted word" (v. 21). God's great word of grace in the gospel first takes root in the lives of believers when life is initially committed to the lordship of Jesus Christ. That word then continues to grow and mature as Christians continue to be, in daily life, committed to his lordship. Such acceptance of the word of the gospel "is able to save your souls" (v. 21). That is, it is able to make our lives sound and keep them perfectly safe for time and eternity. What good news! What a Savior! What a Lord! And what a victorious and abundant life God means for Christians to live!

Put Faith to Work (1:22-27)

Pure religion is practical religion. In one of his most impassioned utterances, James here recorded the essence of his inspired message to Christians of all time. Those who only hear the word of the gospel and do not do it deceive themselves. "Doers of the word" (v. 22) do not glance into a cloudy mirror and then promptly forget what they have seen (vv. 23-25). Instead, the believer "looks into the perfect law, the law of liberty, and perseveres, being no hearer that forgets but a doer that acts" so that he is consequently "blessed in his doing" (v. 25).

Twice, here in 1:25 and later in 2:12, the seemingly paradoxical term, "law of liberty," is used. The term is not found elsewhere in the Bible. It is an immensely enlightening and helpful concept, however, deserving careful attention. Christians live not under compulsion from without but under constraint from within. We are both bound to Christ and liberated to the abundant life. Believers living under the law of God are free, and unbelievers living under the control of their own passions are slaves, the servants of sin and death. The "law of liberty" represents God's demand, his restraint, his restriction, his claim. Christians are not free to take or leave this cross of self-sacrifice. We are free only to accept it if we choose to follow Christ. Yet the "law of liberty" also represents God's gift of freedom. In Christ, believers hold the keys of the kingdom. In him all windows are thrown open and all doors are unlocked. It was this insight of James about God's perfect law of liberty that moved Augustine to tell Christians to "love God and do what you please" or, as his thought is better translated, to "love God and then what you will, do."

The law of liberty speaks of the direction in which the Christian's river of life is to flow to find its true level in the ocean of God's perfect will. It speaks of the second mile of love, which presupposes the first mile of law. God's true law, perfectly revealed in Jesus Christ, leads to liberty, and liberty lives and grows in the necessary structures of law. The prophet Jeremiah spoke for God of this reality, "I will put my law within them, and I will write it upon their hearts; and I will be their God, and they shall be my people" (Jer. 31:33).

Any person who imagines himself to be religious while avoiding the discipline required to "bridle his tongue" is deceiving himself, and his "religion is vain" (v. 26). On the other hand, pure religion thrusts Christians out into the real world of blood, sweat, and tears, into the world of lost identities, of broken relationships, and raging animosities. In this work of pure religion involving practical care for "orphans and widows in their affliction," Christians must be vigilant to keep themselves from compromise with the world (v. 27).

Avoid Playing Favorites (2:1-13)

Prejudice and partiality are morally inexcusable in any form, but they are particularly objectionable among the people of God. This powerful passage comes directly to grips with the pressing moral issue of prejudice. With laser-beam intensity, James turned his moral indignation on the inexcusable class prejudice that has always represented one of the gravest threats to the spiritual life and health of the churches.

With characteristic conciseness, this passage presents a kind of parable about two church visitors and a morally-derelict usher (v. 2). The prejudiced usher bows and scrapes to the high-class visitor but contemptuously relegates the low-class stranger to a place of inferiority and humiliation (v. 3). It is not the prejudiced usher alone who is to blame for this sorry state of affairs, but the worldly and culture-compromised church which has developed a prideful spirit that not only tolerates but even requires such prejudiced actions. To become "judges with evil thoughts" (v. 4) is for Christians to forget that God has "chosen those who are poor in the world to be rich in faith and heirs of the kingdom which he has promised to those who love him" (v. 5). It is, James continued, "the rich who oppress you . . . who drag you into court" (v. 6) and who blaspheme the name of Christ, that honorable name by which believers are called (v. 7). Snobbery, worldly standards, servile regard for the rich and powerful, personal favoritism, and worship of rank have no proper place among the people of God anywhere at any time.

To love our neighbors as we love ourselves is to "fulfill the royal law" and to "do well" (v. 8), but to show prejudiced partiality is to "commit sin" (v. 9) against God and against persons made in God's image. Such rebellion leaves the sinner convicted as a transgressor of God's good and perfect law. It is not just that a rule has been broken but that a rebellious and wayward spirit has been invited in and then given lodging in the believer's life. Breaking the law is very serious business (vv. 10-11) which is to be avoided by those who give evidence by how they speak and act that they understand that they are to be judged under God's perfect "law of liberty" (v. 12). Judgment will be merciless to those who have shown no mercy, but the Christian is assured that in the grace of God "mercy triumphs over judgment" (v. 13).

Prejudice is carried, and it is caught. Prejudice is carefully taught, and it is studiously learned. Prejudice is intentionally accepted, and it is inadvertently absorbed. In no case, however, would prejudice find lodging in an individual's life or in the life of a church if it were not for self-centered sinners, each preferring himself over others, each trying pridefully to hold on to his own life instead of working sacrificially and joyfully in the Spirit of Christ to give life away to others. This first half of the second chapter of James presents a compelling case for Christians to avoid playing favorites. Prejudice strikes at the very heart of the Christian faith. It merits our open and vigorous opposition wherever it rears its ugly head. The Church should tolerate no class consciousness which would ape the world in ways guaranteed to alienate the poor, antagonize the spiritual, and offend the Almighty.

Cultivate Good Works (2:14-26)

The relationship of faith and work has been the cause of debate and division and rancor among Christians from the first century to the present. This passage, James 2:14-26, has been a battlefield of con-tinuing controversy for nearly two thousand years. It was because the great reformer Martin Luther found this portion of the letter so objec-tionable to his religious scheme of things that he actually discarded the entire letter from his approved canon of inspired books of the Bible. The immensely influential John Bunyan, whose *Pilgrim's Progress* has had untold influence among Christians for more than three hundred years (it is supposed that he wrote the book in 1675 while imprisoned in Bedford jail for his Baptist beliefs), wrote about allegorical characters who were practically void of outgoing ethical activism. Many of Chris-tendom's prominent theologians have focused their attention on faith to the essential exclusion of any concern for works. The unnecessary and unscriptural separation of faith and works has kept reappearing like a defective gene year after year, decade after decade, and century after century in the ongoing life of the church.

This inspired portion of the Bible, God's truth without any mixture of error, can deliver Christians from the false dichotomy which mistakenly assumes that there is a contradiction or conflict between faith and works in the lives of the people of God.

James himself was a man of profound faith. He trusted God su-premely. He acknowledged Jesus Christ as his Lord. He lived out his life beside the still waters of supreme confidence in God. As a practical man concerned about practicing pure religion and not just talking about it, however, James refused to be sidetracked to deal with philosophies and theories. He turned the focus of his prophetic passion to faith's expression through works of righteousness. As the Apostle of Good Works, James presented in this passage the Bible's clearest call for good works. Before the statement itself is considered, however, attention should be paid to the differences between James and Paul regarding faith and works.

James and Paul approached faith and works from different points of view. James's viewpoint was essentially pastoral, while that of Paul was essentially missionary. James saw faith and works in the light of what God requires of those who have already become Christians, while Paul saw faith and works in the light of what God requires for a person to become a Christian. James was concerned about the fruits of Christian experience, while Paul was concerned about the roots. As a pastor, James gave special attention to living the Christian life, while, as an evangelist, Paul gave special attention to beginning the Christian life. For James, the gospel of Christ was the consummation of the "law of liberty" (Jas. 1:25; 2:12), while for Paul the gospel of Christ was the antithesis of the "law of sin and death" (Rom. 8:2). James's focus was on the human factor in salvation, while Paul's focus was on the divine factor.

Also, James and Paul approached faith and works with different opponents in mind. The opponents of James were ethical relativists moral anarchists, antinomians, who thought moral conduct was inconsequential because they mistakenly imagined that inward faith was all that mattered. The opponents of Paul were legalists who believed that moral conduct could secure the favor of God without conversion to Christ. James directed his message primarily to those who gloried in their creed at the expense of their conduct, while Paul directed his message primarily to those who gloried in their conduct at the expense of accepting the creed's consummation in Christ.

Furthermore, James and Paul approached faith and works with significant differences in their usages of these two words. *Faith* was used by James to mean the giving of intellectual assent to the facts of Christianity, an assent that was barren of good works, inactive, and therefore useless. *Faith* was used by Paul, on the other hand, to mean saving faith in Jesus Christ, which faith issues normally and naturally in works of righteousness. *Works* is a word used by James to mean acts of ministry, mercy, love, and justice done in obedience to the demands of God's indwelling Spirit. Paul, on the other hand, used the word *works* to mean acts performed legalistically in obedience to the letter of the law in order to earn salvation. *Justification* was the term used by James to refer to the believer's final acceptance by God at the last judgment, while Paul used the word to mean God's immediate acceptance of any sinner who repented and believed in obedience to the call of the gospel.

The great faith and works passage of James 2:14-26 corrects an erroneous perception of the nature of saving faith. Dead faith mistakenly assumes that attention to good works is of no importance. In the early churches a special blessing was pronounced at the close of the observance of the Lord's Supper, "Depart in peace." A cheap charity that could find its fulfillment, however, in the mere pronouncement, "Go in peace, be warmed and filled" (v. 16) is useless, profitless, empty, dead.

Dead faith erroneously assumes that the acceptance of monotheism can make a person right with God. Such orthodoxy, apart from works of obedient submission to the heavenly Father's will, is utterly worthless. Faithful Jews for thousands of years have expressed their commitment to monotheism, in life and at death, in the great confession, "Hear, O Israel: The Lord our God is one Lord" (Deut. 6:4; see also Mark 12:29). This *Shema,* the Hebrew word for "hear," was thought to defend its user as a two-edged sword, keep demons at a distance, and cool the flames of hell. It was to be taught by a father to his son as soon as the child began to speak. Such belief that God is one is profoundly good, but it no more takes a person into a right relationship with God than mere belief that there is a moon transports astronauts to that distant heavenly body and back. The knowledge that God is one is even shared by the demons, who tremble in terror but who do not act on the basis of that knowledge. These devils are not atheists, but they are in trouble with God because they have not matched correct knowledge with right actions.

In this passage, James was shouting down the shoddy evangelism that would proclaim cheap grace which could be apprehended through shallow faith. For sinners to believe something about God is not enough. We must believe God, and believing him, choose, as our word *believe* originally made clear, to *be* in *life* committed without reservation to Jesus Christ as Lord.

To illustrate that a vital, living, relevant, working faith is intimately related to daily life, James called Abraham to mind. "Was not Abraham our father justified by works, when he offered his son Isaac upon the altar? You see that faith was active along with his works, and faith was completed by works, and the scripture was fulfilled which says, 'Abraham believed God, and it was reckoned to him as righteousness'; and he was called the friend of God. You see that a man is justified by works and not by faith alone" (vv. 21-24). God had originally chosen Abraham as the father of the faithful in the knowledge that he and his children after him would "keep the way of the Lord by doing righteousness and justice" (Gen. 18:19). In the full biblical tradition of a faith that works, James appropriately illustrated an immensely important point to believers of all times with this succinct but powerful reference to Abraham.

The same point is next illustrated with a reference to Rahab. Mentioned in Hebrews 11:31 as one who "by faith . . . did not perish with those who were disobedient, because she had given friendly welcome to the spies" from Israel, Rahab the harlot might be considered by many an unlikely heroine of the faith. Her inclusion here alongside Abraham is an important reminder that the marvelous grace of God is not bound, that it has been his purpose from the beginning to save sinners, and that anyone who acts obediently in true faith need not perish but may have everlasting life. That is shouting ground, and in that knowledge there is among the angels "joy in heaven over one sinner who repents" (Luke 15:7; see also 15:10).

Three times in this brief passage James used the phrase, "Justified by works" (vv. 21,24,25). This concept poses such a threat to so many carefully constructed theological systems that special attention must be paid to it. To be justified is to be made acceptable to God. It is to be made just or righteous in his sight. The Bible teaches that any trusting and obeying person is justified with God through his grace. When Paul wrote that Christians "are justified by his grace as a gift, through the redemption which is in Christ Jesus" (Rom. 3:24), he used the word *justified* to refer to the Christian's experience of conversion to Christ. When James wrote that "a man is justified by works" (v. 24), he used the word *justified* with reference to the righteousness experienced by a person of faith whose experience of grace is working itself out in deeds as well as in words. Justification from God comes to those who put faith to work and who perceive that faith and works are the two sides of the

coin of God's grace personally laid hold of by any believing and behaving person. Men of faith like Abraham and women of faith like
Rahab are, and in eternity will be, proven just by their obedient works.

God's grace-full gift of salvation and the Christian's sacrificial involvement in good works are a vital unity in the single fabric of authentic Christian experience. Faith and works are partners, not rivals. They
are complementary, not contradictory. They are two dimensions of
God's one great gift of salvation, not alternative gifts of the Spirit. They
are inseparably linked together. Faith does not exist apart from works,
and works cannot exist apart from faith. One without the other is a road
to nowhere.

Let Christians today then turn from all the old, tired talk about
which comes first or which is more important or which might possibly
be expendable, faith or works. Let us, rather, move forward with a living faith that issues in works of righteousness to the glory of God and
the furtherance of Christ's kingdom.

Pure religion requires that Christians cultivate good works, "For as
the body apart from the spirit is dead, so faith apart from works is
dead" (v. 26).

Warning and Counsel
3:1 to 5:6

Warning for Teachers to Take Their Work Seriously (3:1)

Among Christians, the teaching office is not to be selfishly sought for
any prominence or power that the position might provide. "We who
teach," James said, numbering himself among that important company
in the life of the Christian church, "shall be judged with greater strictness" (v. 1). Every bishop or pastor in a New Testament church was
expected to be "an apt teacher" (1 Tim. 3:2; 2 Tim. 2:24), rightly dividing the word of truth (2 Tim. 2:15), and carefully instructing church
members as to how they could and should grow in grace, in the knowledge of Christ, and in works of righteousness. When we all stand at the
final judgment to give an account to God of the deeds which we have
done in life, the teachers "shall be judged with greater strictness" than
the taught. Those to whom God has given special influence and special

responsibility must expect to stand finally before God to give special account. Of them, "will much be required" (Luke 12:48).

Counsel Concerning Control of the Tongue (3:2-12)

No subject dealt with in the letter of James, except that of poverty and wealth, receives as much emphasis as talk and the tongue. The major treatment of the topic is here in James 3:2-12, but significant statements on the subject are also made in 1:19; 1:26; 2:12; 4:11; 4:13; 5:9; and 5:12. Why? The tongue receives such major attention because it is inordinately influential in all human relationships. Its strength is out of all proportion to its size. Its power is out of all proportion to its form. Without a mind of its own or a bone in it, the tongue is possessed of an almost limitless potential for good or bad.

Human speech is the most godlike of human qualities. By our ability to make words we demonstrate a special relationship to God whom we understand to be, by his very nature, a communicator and of whom John said, "In the beginning was the Word, and the Word was with God, and the Word was God" (John 1:1). A word is reason expressed in a language that others can understand. The Bible in general and the letter of James in particular reveal a profound concern for clear communication and a deep understanding of the social dimensions of human life. Working both from his Hebrew heritage and from his special Christian experience, James engaged here in talk about the tongue which is immensely helpful to individual Christians of every age and to the church at large.

Acknowledging freely his human frailty, James was not too proud to admit that "we all make many mistakes" (v. 2). We all stumble. We all stutter. We all fail. We all fall. We all are frail and weak and inadequate. When such confession is honestly made, then there is hope for the sinner. God's strength is "made perfect" in such human weakness (2 Cor. 12:9). The point about to be made by James, however, is a more specific one, "If any one makes no mistakes in what he says he is a perfect man, able to bridle the whole body also" (v. 2). Of course just as we all sin, so we all make mistakes in what we say. Each of us daily and amply demonstrates that he is not "a perfect man" (v. 2).

Little bits are put in the mouths of big horses to direct them (v. 3), and small rudders are used by pilots to guide huge ships (v. 4). Similarly, "the tongue is a little member and boasts of great things" (v. 5). Following this line of thought, James then moved quickly to point out that "the tongue is a fire . . . an unrighteous world among our members . . . setting on fire the cycle of nature, and set on fire by hell" (v. 6). Human beings have tamed all kinds of creatures in the animal kingdom, "but no human being can tame the tongue" (v. 8). This does not mean that for Christians our talk is uncontrollable. It means that the tongue needs everlasting supervision, that it can never be trusted completely, that it can never be left alone without careful direction from the morally responsible and socially sensitive people of God. By the grace of God and with the continuing help of God, the tongue can be controlled; but we must be watchful without ceasing, for it cannot be perfectly and permanently tamed. It will break out of its cage like a roaring lion if we are not careful to keep it under the lordship of Jesus Christ.

Human hypocrisy is highlighted by our inclination to bless God with our tongues and then with the same tongues to curse humanity made in God's image. To fellow Christians, James simply said, "My brethren, this ought not to be so" (v. 10). In fact, he went on to write that God's people cannot talk in such a way as to bless the Lord on the one hand and curse humanity on the other. The illustrations following make it clear that such a mixture is impossible (vv. 11-12).

Talk affects the talker, who must control his talk or realize that his religion is vain (1:26), who must match his words with deeds or engage in an utterly profitless enterprise (2:16), and who must bridle his tongue or release in his own life a Pandora's box of evil and divisive forces (3:6).

Talk also affects others. A fist can reach only three feet, but the tongue is an intercontinental ballistic missile. Conversely, the helping hand holding a cup of cold water can extend only three feet, but the tongue, in this age of satellite-assisted, transistor-enabled communications, can preach the good news of God in Christ around the world. Evil talk is like a raging forest fire (v. 5); gossip is "a restless evil, full of deadly poison" (v. 8); and the cursing of other humans "made in the likeness of God" (v. 9) is intolerable.

More friendships are broken, more families are divided, and more churches are split by what is said than by what is done. It therefore behooves Christians to heed the counsel of James concerning the control of our tongues.

Counsel Concerning Wisdom and the Good Life (3:13-18)

James did not begin this section in a philosophical way by asking, "What is wisdom?" but in a practical way by asking, "Who is wise?" (v. 13). The wise person in the family of God will show his understanding "by his good life," by his good "works," and by his "meekness" (v. 13), or teachableness.

False wisdom, on the other hand, manifests itself in "bitter jealousy," in "selfish ambition," in strife, in boasting, and in false witness or infidelity to the truth (v. 14). This false wisdom is not the gift of God that "comes down from above, but is earthly, unspiritual, devilish" (v. 15). It is clear that where jealousy, selfishness, and inordinate ambition are unwisely allowed to "exist" or are tolerated, "there will be disorder and every vile practice" (v. 16). The devil is not said to make us do such things. These actions spring from personal rivalry, personal obstinance, personal pride, personal unscrupulousness, and personal ambition. For all of these, every individual is personally responsible and personally accountable.

Christians are to reject such false wisdom and cultivate true wisdom. Steeped in the tradition that "the fear of the Lord is the beginning of wisdom" (Ps. 111:10), James called Christians of his day to choose "the wisdom from above," or from God, and to walk the road that leads to life.

In strong preaching style, the distinguishing characteristics of true wisdom are here strung together to depict true wisdom. It is explained as being "first pure, then peaceable, gentle, open to reason, full of mercy and good fruits, without uncertainty or insincerity" (v. 17). This arrangement is alliterative. James began the list with a Greek word beginning with the letter a. It may have been a device for helping a preacher to remember his points, but the thrust of the message is powerful, and the message itself comes through loud and clear.

True wisdom is "pure." As God is pure, so he requires those who would stand before him to do so with clean hands and pure hearts (Ps. 24:4). Purity for the Christian is not ceremonial but practical. It is behavioral, physical, personal, sexual, and conversational, but it is more than that. It is a condition of being cleansed in the Spirit, in the mind, and in the will. Outer purity of life issues from inner purity of heart.

True wisdom is "peaceable." Peaceableness has to do with right relationships. It is the opposite of aggressive self-assertiveness. It speaks of
the timeless truth that "none of us lives to himself, and none of us dies to
himself" (Rom. 14:7). It speaks, too, of the ancient biblical revelation
that from the beginning humanity was intended for community, for
"the Lord God said, 'It is not good that the man should be alone' "
(Gen. 2:18). The peaceableness mentioned here effectively offsets the
strife associated with false wisdom in the passage immediately preceding.

True wisdom is "gentle." It is patient, considerate, moderate, re-
strained, respectful of the needs, and mindful of the feelings of others.
It listens and really hears. It leans towards forgiveness. It makes allow-
ances. It is always fair.

True wisdom is "open to reason." As the King James Version puts it, it
is "easy to be intreated." It is approachable. It is conciliatory. It is not
stubborn. It can be persuaded. It is not self-righteously rigid. It is not
extremist in its proud conviction that it has already apprehended all the
truth. Such wisdom today would help us to solve a multitude of serious
personal, family, social, national, and international problems which
have arisen because openness to reason is in such short supply.

True wisdom is "full of mercy." It is compassionate. It gives a cup of
cold water to the thirsty. It binds up the wounds of the injured. It provides things that others need. It is given to practical helpfulness.

True wisdom is also full of "good fruits." Its wholesome produce feeds
the hungry, strengthens the weak, heals the sick, nurtures the young,
and sustains the old. Unsatisfied with a fugitive and cloistered virtue,
such true wisdom rejects barrenness in favor of the self-sacrifice involved in bearing good fruit.

True wisdom is without "uncertainty." It is not fragmented. It is not
double-minded. It is not two-faced. It is not vacillating. It is not im-
mobilized by ambiguity. It is wholehearted. It knows its own mind. It is
principled. It has its bearings. It is oriented rather than disoriented.

Finally, true wisdom is without "insincerity." It is without hypocrisy.
It wears no mask. It puts on no airs. It plays no games. It tolerates no
pretense. It harbors no mental reservations. It is genuine. It is straightforward. It is honest.

Wisdom's "harvest of righteousness is sown in peace by those who
make peace" (v. 18). Righteousness and peace are frequently joined

together in the Bible. The fact that James joined them together at the conclusion of his profoundly important statement on wisdom is clear evidence that these qualities are properly perceived as evidences of the wisdom that is from above.

The true wisdom which God ever seeks to give to his people is not dependent on special intelligence or advanced education. God's gift of wisdom is made through grace to those who are teachable enough to take it.

Warning Against Moral Depravity (4:1 to 5:6)

Rome perished, according to Augustine, for want of order in the soul. Moderns, too, are close to perishing for want of order in the soul. They want to play tennis with the net down. They think that in order to breathe you have to break out all the windows. The fathomless moral depravity of our times is not really all that different, however, from the gross moral corruption of James's times. "Wars" and "fightings," possibly even among Christians of the first century but more likely commonplace in the culture and society of which they were a part, are the result of "your passions that are at war in your members" (v. 1).

James was accustomed to calling the recipients of this general epistle "beloved brethren," but in this passage we find them shockingly addressed, "Unfaithful creatures" (v. 4). Here James, using the literary form of diatribe, employed the style of a debater to issue stern warning against the moral depravity which always dogs the feet of humanity and of even the most earnest Christians. Those who "desire and do not have" and who "covet and cannot obtain" stumble tragically toward fighting, waging war, and killing (v. 2). This is no way for the redeemed of the Lord to behave. External conflict inevitably issues from evil lusts at war in the human spirit. Those internal conflicts soon escape to peddle their revolution abroad. That which is personal very quickly becomes social. When we sin, we sin against God and we sin against ourselves, but we also sin against our neighbors and against all humanity. Therefore, Christians are to pray for the things we really need (v. 2), not asking "wrongly, to spend it on" our own "passions" (v. 3).

Friendship with the world means enmity with God. "Whoever wishes to be a friend of the world makes himself an enemy of God" (v. 4). Like Lot's wife who looked back longingly and lovingly at the burning city of

Sodom and who thereby brought upon herself the wrath of the righteous God whom she had disobeyed, we simply cannot serve God and mammon. Indeed, God "yearns jealously over the spirit which he has made to dwell in us" (v. 5). That is, the Spirit who indwells us yearns tenderly over us, longing to make us wholly his and rejecting any and all divided allegiance. God is a jealous God in the sense that he can brook no rivals, tolerate no unfaithfulness, and permit no polytheism.

God sets his face like flint against the proud, but gives grace to the humble (v. 6). Those who resist the devil need not fear that he will conquer them. On the contrary, that wily coward "will flee from you" (v. 7) who resist him. When we "submit" ourselves to God and "draw near" to him, "he will draw near" to us (v. 8). Drawing near to God involves more than simply waiting for God to shower his blessings down on us. It involves a commitment of will for us to cleanse our hands and a submission of spirit for us to purify our hearts (v. 8). There is a questionable theology which has gained a considerable amount of influence in the world today. It says that human beings may just relax and simply realize what God has already done or else simply say the right words in order to receive what God has already given. James made it clear, however, that Christ's coming has not excused believers from moral responsibility. As free moral agents who are responsible to God for whatever mess we are in, we must cleanse our own hands and purify our own hearts by turning from sin and duplicity (v. 8) and repenting of our sin with mourning, tears, and true humility (v. 9). Such humble repentance before the Lord opens the way for him in grace not only to receive us but also to "exalt" us (v. 10).

Gossip, talebearing, harsh criticism, and evil speaking against one another are all forbidden, as is a spirit of critical denunciation of others (vv. 11-12). Judgment is in the hands of God, and his people do well to leave it there. He "who is able to save and to destroy" (v. 12) is mankind's only lawgiver and judge. It is therefore completely inappropriate for anyone to judge his neighbor. Such judgmentalism would reflect the moral depravity which Christians are obligated to shun.

Yet another evidence of moral depravity is the presumptuous planning projected by the arrogant "who say, 'Today or tomorrow we will go into such and such a town and spend a year there and trade and get gain' " (v. 13). James reminded such proud schemers of their finiteness: "You do not know about tomorrow" (v. 14). Life is in God's hands. Our tomorrows are known only to him. Our time on earth, like a morning mist which the sun soon burns away, appears for a little while and is then swallowed up in God's eternity. Haughtiness or evil boasting about the future is never appropriate. "Instead you ought to say, 'If the Lord wills, we shall live and we shall do this or that' " (v. 15).

Christians used to take James literally at this point, for when writing a letter which involved future appointments, they would add the initials D.V. for *Deo Valente,* Latin for "God willing." James, of course, did not propose a slogan or a formula or a smooth cliché for believers to use. Instead he stated an important principle for us to observe. We are finite in knowledge, limited in understanding, and totally dependent on God for every breath we breathe. We should project no plans and make no moves except in the knowledge that we are absolutely subject to the Lord.

Chapter 4 in the book of James is concluded with the Bible's best statement, negatively expressed, of the Christian ethic, "Whoever knows what is right to do and fails to do it, for him it is sin" (4:17). This sin is the missing of God's mark. It has always been at the negative point of good not done that Christians are most vulnerable to the judgment of God. The great shortcoming of a shallow moralism is that it interprets sin primarily as doing certain, specific, expressly forbidden things and righteousness as not doing those same things. Jesus explained that for the Pharisees sin was failing to give attention to "the weightier matters of the law, justice and mercy and faith" (Matt. 23:23). The recovery of this vital insight, clearly and plainly put here by James, is absolutely required for the spiritual vitality of the church in today's world.

Ill-gotten wealth is still another evidence of moral depravity. Without the slightest equivocation, James here again declared the word of the Lord about the rich and their riches (5:1-6). Although the dangers of wealth were dealt with briefly in James 1:9-11 and more fully in James 2:1-9, the tremendous importance of the topic seems to have compelled the pastor-prophet to return to it in this closing portion of the letter. "Come now, you rich, weep and howl for the miseries that are coming upon you" (v. 1). James said in effect that the present comforts of the rich will turn to hardships, their sumptuous and self-indulgent luxuries to painful loss, their pleasures to misery.

Looking ahead to the future judgment of God as if it had already come to pass, absolutely sure that the wages of sin not just *will be* but *is* death, James wrote, "Your riches have rotted and your garments are moth-eaten. Your gold and silver have rusted" (vv. 2-3). These strong words echo the insight of our Lord himself who warned, "Do not lay up for yourselves treasures on earth, where moth and rust consume and where thieves break in and steal, but lay up for yourselves treasures in heaven, where neither moth nor rust consumes and where thieves do not break in and steal. For where your treasure is, there will your heart be also" (Matt. 6:19-21). This is the reason James sounded such a stern note against riches and the greed which drives men to the accumulation of things: our hearts are inevitably where our treasure is. Those who trust in their "laid up treasure" of money may be sure that its corrosion "will be evidence against you and will eat your flesh like fire" in "the last days" (v. 3). The ill-gotten nature of the wealth here condemned is that it has been accumulated through fraud, and the anguished cries of the defrauded "have reached the ears of the Lord of hosts" (v. 4).

This name, Lord of hosts or Lord of Sabaoth, is one of the most majestic of all the names of God in the Bible. It is used to refer to God as the Lord of the armies of Israel, as the Lord of the hosts of heaven, and as the Lord of all might and power. James used this name of God here, as we might use the name, God Almighty, to refer to the omnipotence of God who, having heard the cries of the oppressed, can be trusted to show his power to right wrong, correct injustice, and bring to judgment the greedy rich who have defrauded the helpless poor.

In ancient times such fraud was perpetrated by rich landowners against poor day laborers or "hands." In today's complex, industrialized world, however, the fraud by the rich is perpetrated not just against manual laborers but against consumers, taxpayers, underdeveloped nations, and disorganized masses of common people without an earthly advocate. The fraud is perpetrated in the form of fixed prices, fixed taxes, fixed tariffs, and fixed programs designed to protect the vested interests of the very rich at the expense of the relatively poor. The word of the Lord through James is that God Almighty is patient but not asleep. He has not abdicated his throne. He will not forget. God is not dead. Though the ungodly rich live in luxury by grinding the life out of the righteous poor, their own "day of slaughter" and due punishment at the hands of the Lord of hosts is at hand (vv. 5-6). As Henry Wadsworth Longfellow said in his poem "Retribution":

Though the mills of God grind slowly,

> yet they grind exceeding small;
> Though with patience He stands waiting,
>   with exactness grinds he all.[3]

Exhortation to Discipline
5:7-20

Patience Advised (5:7-11)

As farmers wait for rain to bring their crops to maturity, as the prophets proclaimed their message and then waited for the will of God to be done, and as Job patiently endured the trials and sufferings that befell him, so Christians must "be patient" (vv. 7-8), must "not grumble . . . against one another" (v. 9), and must patiently and steadfastly endure until "the purpose of the Lord" is realized (vv. 10-11) and "the coming of the Lord is at hand" (v. 8).

The promise of the second coming of Christ is not a signal for Christians to withdraw from the world, or to sit down and wait, or to grow impatient and quarrelsome. Instead, it is a powerful stimulant to keep us working until "the Judge" who "is standing at the doors" (v. 9) brings down the final curtain on human history and "the kingdom of the world has become the kingdom of our Lord and of his Christ, and he shall reign for ever and ever" (Rev. 11:15).

The majestic moral earnestness that characterizes the letter of James is reflected in this passage about the second coming of Christ. For Christians, authentic morality uniformly and universally seems to thrive in an environment of spiritual urgency. Such a spirit of urgency has always characterized the church that clings to a clear vision of Christ's imminent return as Judge, "to judge the living and the dead" (1 Pet. 4:5). As James preached powerfully concerning the profound importance of moral issues, so he held unswervingly to a course where he constantly took his bearings by the important doctrine of Christ's imminent return.

Do Not Swear (5:12)

Returning to the grave concern about talk and the tongue which had already been frequently expressed in the letter, James sounded a final note on this subject: "But above all, my brethren, do not swear, either by heaven or by earth or with any other oath, but let your yes be yes and your no be no, that you may not fall under condemnation" (v. 12). The religious leaders with whom James was likely well-acquainted had worked out a formula for splitting the finest hairs with regard to oaths, staying barely within the letter of the law while still following the natural inclination to shore up weak arguments and provide props for questionable assertions (Matt. 23:16-21). Jesus spoke to these people when he said in the Sermon on the Mount, "Do not swear at all, either by heaven, for it is the throne of God, or by the earth, for it is his footstool, or by Jerusalem, for it is the city of the great King. And do not swear by your head, for you cannot make one hair white or black. Let what you say be simply 'Yes' or 'No'; anything more than this comes from evil" (Matt. 6:34-37). James here condemned both the subtle distinctions drawn by the scribes as to the binding force of this or that formula and the rash use of oaths in common talk. The casuistry or clever and cunning rationalization of the Pharisees is not an appropriate characteristic for the people of God. Simple honesty is enough. A man should be as good as his word. If he says yes he should mean yes. If he says no he should mean no. There should be no ifs, ands, and buts qualifying the word of a Christian. We are to cultivate a spirit of self-control, self-restraint, and self-discipline. We are to be dependable, straightforward, and trustworthy. The person who is honest has no need to prop up what he says with any oath. James knew, as Jesus had taught, that there is great value in simple truth communicated through ordinary speech.

Pray (5:13-18)

Here, almost at the very end of the letter of James, is a particularly passionate utterance about prayer. The subject is touched on very early in the letter (1:5-8), but it is dealt with more fully here in this final section. Those who are suffering are to pray, as those who are cheerful are to sing (v. 13). Anyone who is sick is to "call for the elders of the church," who are to come and "pray over him, anointing him with oil in the name of the Lord; and the prayer of faith will save the sick man, and the Lord will raise him up; and if he has committed sins, he will be forgiven" (vv. 14). Simple faith that trusts God in the context of a fellowship of believers is rewarded beyond any normal expectations that we might cherish. God both heals us of our sickness and forgives us of our sins. The confession of our sins to God opens our lives to God's grace. His mercy flows freely from the open windows of heaven into any life that will acknowledge, in true repentance, personal sins and personal need for him.

The early Christians often utilized anointment with oil together with united prayer by the elders of the church for the sick. It was not imagined that there was magic in the oil or healing in the hands of those who prayed. The early church cherished too robust a faith in the Lord God whom they had come to know in the power of Jesus' resurrection to let any substance or formula come between them and him. As salvation is from him, so healing is from him. Likewise, the confession of our sins to one another opens our lives to the forgiveness and acceptance and identification and affirmation of fellow Christians without which our own Christian lives would be infinitely poorer than they need be. A moving illustration from the prayer life of Elijah illustrates that "the prayer of a righteous man has great power in its effects" (vv. 16-18).

Rescue Sinners (5:19-20)

The disciplined Christian life involves not only patience and purity of speech and prayer but also persistence in rescuing the perishing. At the very heart of the life and work of the church is the restoration of the fallen, the finding of the lost, the saving of sinners. Again in this passage James used the only word for sin which he employed in any of his writing, or preaching, a word which means "to miss the mark." It is the way of human beings to err from God's way, to miss the moral targets which God has established, to turn from the ideals which God has ordained. To anyone willing, however, there is a way "back" to God, to light, and to life. It is the way of turning "from the error of his way" to "save his soul from death and . . . cover a multitude of sins" (v. 20).

Jesus Christ, the Lamb of God who takes away the sin of the world, is not specifically and in so many words pointed to throughout the letter of James. The whole letter, however, is baptized in a living hope through him as the Lord of life. Morally-stumbling men and women who are missing God's mark for their lives, who are sick unto death, can find grace and the good life when they trust and obey him.

The call of James to do the gospel has been often debated, often criticized, and often ignored. That call deserves to be heard. There may well be several keys to the lost radiance of the modern church, but one of those keys is in plain view in the gospel according to James. It is the key which unlocks the door between faith and works and once again joins together that which God never meant to be separated. The joys, victories, triumphs, affirmations, and ecstasies of pure religion are for those who, living under the conviction that Jesus Christ is Lord, are "doers of the word."

Notes

1. Martin Luther quoted in James Hardy Ropes, "A Critical and Exegetical Commentary on the Epistle of James," *The International Critical Commentary* (Edinburgh: T. & T. Clark, 1916), p. 64.

2. J. B. Mayor, quoted in William Barclay, "The Letters of James and Peter," *The Daily Study Bible* (Philadelphia: The Westminster Press, 1958), p. 39.

3. Henry Wadsworth Longfellow, "Retribution," quoted in John Bartlett, *Familiar Quotations* (Boston: Little, Brown and Company, 1940), p. 435.

1 PETER

Introduction

Martin Luther named 1 Peter, along with the Gospel of John, 1 John, Romans, Galatians, and Ephesians, as one of the New Testament books which shows us Christ and teaches us "everything that is needful"[1] for Christians to know. Of course, this letter by itself does not teach us everything Christians need to know; but it does show us Christ, and it does teach us many things we need to know about how Christians ought to live in the world.

The Occasion of the Letter

This letter was written straight from the heart of the apostle Peter, a great heart by then finely mature in Christian faith and fully seasoned in Christian service. Its purpose was to encourage Christians, to strengthen them for times of trouble which seemed to be approaching like a dark and ominous cloud, to provide them with pastoral counsel and practical instruction on how to live, and to support them in their Christian commitment in whatever time was to remain until Christ's second coming. The letter is warm and compassionate. Its message is as welcome and as helpful in the churches today as it obviously was when it was first written and first received by the early Christians.

Date and Place of Writing

This letter gives evidence of having been written in the sixties, possibly after Paul's death, which is thought by some to have taken place in AD 62, and before the Roman Emperor Nero's savage persecution of Christians based on his self-serving accusation that they had set fire to Rome (about AD 62 to AD 64). The date could be reckoned as shortly after AD 64, at a time when the Roman persecution of Christians had already begun in Rome but probably had not yet reached Asia Minor. Peter's death is thought by many to have taken place in the middle to late sixties, which would place the time of writing for this letter prob-

ably before AD 67. It is possible that the reference to Babylon in 1 Peter
5:13 should be taken as a reference to the ancient Mesopotamian city on
the Euphrates River in what is now Iraq, although there is practically
no tradition to support this view. The reference to Babylon is more
often taken to mean Rome, as it is in Revelation 14:8, and a conclusion
that 1 Peter was written in the middle sixties from Rome is defensible.
Precise fixing of the date and place of writing, however, is not possible.

Salutation
1:1-2

The author of the letter identifies himself as Peter, an apostle of Jesus
Christ. The apostles of the New Testament were disciples of Christ
especially called and especially responsible for carrying out the Lord's
work in the world. While Paul successfully laid claim to the title of an
apostle, and a number of other early Christians were also called apostles
in the New Testament, the term was most frequently applied to the
twelve. Peter, though one of the twelve apostles, did not here lay claim
to a special church office that was particularly restricted or exalted.
Instead, by calling himself an apostle, he identified himself as one commissioned by Christ to go into all the world and preach the gospel to
every creature, teaching believers to live and work as Christ had commanded. In that sense, all Christians of all the ages are obligated to be
involved in the apostolic mission.

The letter was addressed to Christian exiles, displaced persons who
were sojourning as pilgrims throughout much of Asia Minor, now Tur-
key. Peter referred to them as having been chosen by God the Father
and sanctified, or set apart, by God the Holy Spirit for a life of obedience through the cleansing work of God the Son (v. 2). The fact that
Peter mentioned obedience to Jesus Christ first and sprinkling with his
blood last in this reference is a helpful reminder that God has never
cleansed sinners as his first and most important work and then called
them to obedience as a secondary and merely optional matter which
they are free to take or leave. Obedience and cleansing go together.
Where there is no obedience there has been no cleansing, and where

there is cleansing there will be obedience.

Peter's especially expressed concern, a kind of invocation, was that "grace and peace" should overflow in the lives of his readers (v. 2). By grace, he meant God's unmerited favor. The basic idea in the grace to which Peter here referred is love; the idea encompasses God's planning love, his eager love, and his working love extended through Christ to all humanity. By peace, he meant to will for them not just the absence of hostility and violence but the positive presence of love and justice in their everyday relationships. If Peter could pray for us today, he could do no better than to petition God on our behalf for grace, grace to cover our sins and to permeate all our relationships, and for peace, peace to provide the practical evidence both within the church and to the world of our blood-bought, Spirit-sealed integrity, faithfulness, obedience, and good works.

A Survey of the Christian Life
1:3 to 2:10

Characteristics of God's Great Salvation (1:3-12)

This section begins with a burst of joyful enthusiasm. The apostle Peter followed his salutation with these fervent words, "Blessed be the God and Father of our Lord Jesus Christ!" (v. 3). It is by his abundant mercy that Christians are born again. Salvation begins with the living hope established by the resurrection of Christ from the dead. Immediately, in 1 Peter 1:3, the centrality of the resurrection of Christ is declared so that the first readers of the letter, and its current readers as well, are reminded of the resurrection as the first fact of Christianity. The resurrection, for Peter as for all the church through all Christian history, is the mightiest of the mighty acts of God. Though troubles and trials and even persecutions may overtake us, Christians have an inheritance in heaven which is "imperishable, undefiled, and unfading" (v. 4).

Believers are secure, guarded by the power of God for his great "salvation ready to be revealed in the last time" (v. 5). For Christians, salvation is not only past, in the sense that we have been saved from the

habit and dominion of sin, but salvation is also future, in the sense that
it is ready to be revealed in the last time when we shall no longer see
through a glass darkly, as Paul put it in 1 Corinthians 13:12, but face to
face, when we shall experience the fullness of God's grace which we can
only begin to know this side of eternity. Even though we "have to suffer
various trials" (v. 6) rejoicing is appropriate because victory is assured.
Peter had personally seen Jesus, but he honored those Christians who,
though they had not personally seen him, loved him and believed in
him. They, too, could "rejoice with unutterable and exalted joy" (v. 8)
in the Lord and the abundant life provided by him.

The salvation mentioned in verses 9 and 10 is the fullness of all that
God wills for his people to be and to experience and to have and to do.
It is both temporal and eternal. It is both physical and spiritual. It is
both earthly and heavenly. It is for the whole life or self or personality,
which is the meaning of "soul" in verse 9. The constantly persistent
church heresy that soul salvation can be experienced separate and apart
from life salvation misses the profound meaning of this Bible truth.
God's grace does not work through human faith just to provide security
for the shadowy substance that church people sometimes call the soul.
Salvation is for persons, whole persons. The Bible teaching about the
resurrection of the body ties directly to this insight about the fullness of
Christian salvation. Christ today is in the lifesaving business, and his
church must be everlastingly alert to maintain a compassionate and
vibrant concern not just for immaterial entities, as souls may be defined, but for persons.

The prophets of old and the preachers of the good news of God in
Christ both responded to the Spirit's leadership to bring believers to
salvation (vv. 10-12). That salvation which has begun by the grace of
God will continue by the grace of God and will be finally consummated
in heaven by the grace of God.

God's great salvation is therefore seen to be characterized by hope (v.
3), assurance (v. 4), faith (vv. 5,9), joy in spite of trials (vv. 6,8), praise
and honor and glory to Christ (v. 7), and the fulfillment in the lives of
believers of the deep searchings and yearnings of the faithful prophets
and preachers of God through the ages (vv. 10-12).

A Challenge to Obey the Gospel and Live the Christian Life (1:13-25)

After dealing with these fundamental, though lofty, introductory matters, the letter moves directly into its down-to-earth, primarily pastoral purpose.

"Gird up your minds" (v. 13) is a way of saying, "Collect your wits." Believers are forbidden to lapse into intellectual slothfulness. Ignorance is no virtue. Dullness of the mind is shameful. Careless mental habits are indefensible. Intellectual laziness is a disgrace. Taking note of Paul, Augustine, Martin Luther, John Wesley, and Jonathan Edwards, it may be observed that the Holy Spirit seems to have an affinity for a trained mind. Formal education can be immensely useful. It is not to be decried by responsible Christians. Academic training, however, is not what this reference is about. It is a call for Christians to sharpen our wits, concentrate our mental processes, and focus our intellectual perceptions so as, in all soberness, to set our hope upon the grace that is to encompass us fully at the revelation of Jesus Christ.

The "revelation of Jesus Christ" (v. 13) seems to have primary reference to the second coming. Both for the first recipients of this letter, however, and for us, there is a revelation of him which may come at death with our passing from this life into his immediate and personal presence. He has been revealed in history, and he will be even further revealed whenever and however we meet him face to face.

Here is a call to obedience and counsel to reject conformity to the former ignorance and passion characterizing unbelief (v. 14). It is an introduction to one of the apostle's most deeply moving pastoral pleas, "As he who called you is holy, be holy yourselves in all your conduct" (v. 15). Quoting Leviticus 11:44-45, "You shall be holy, for I am holy" (KJV), Peter pressed earnestly for Christians to keep striving for separation from sin and for genuine consecration to Christ. Holiness is not a stained-glass word referring to soft organ music, vaulted ceilings, and dimly lit church aisles. Holiness is a word that speaks to us of wholeness, integrity, and righteousness in daily conduct. Because our heavenly Father is holy, we are to be holy. Because our Elder Brother is holy, we are to be holy. Because the Spirit indwelling our lives is holy, we are to be holy. Because he is our God, we must *be* his people, and because he is our God we must *behave* as his people.

God judges not arbitrarily or with prejudice but "impartially," each "according to his deeds" (v. 17). Christians therefore are to be God-fearing in the sense that our conduct is to give evidence of our awareness of his never-failing presence. Our "ransom" has been accomplished with "the precious blood of Christ" (vv. 18-19). His sacrificial giving of himself made possible our deliverance from the futile strivings for salvation which once characterized the lives of our religious forebears. It is not silver or gold that brings us into right relationship with God and our fellowman, but God incarnate in Jesus Christ, "a lamb without blemish or spot" (v. 19) ordained "before the foundation of the world" (v. 20) to enable us to experience faith and hope in God (v. 21).

The importance of obedience in the Christian life is again emphasized when the readers of this letter are told to "love one another earnestly from the heart" (v. 22). Our entire lives are purified or cleansed by "obedience to the truth," which obedience is manifested through a sincere love for all believers united by God's grace in the redeemed family of the Father's divine intention. The new birth comes to believers "through the living and abiding word of God" (v. 23), which word Peter explained to be "the good news which was preached to you" (v. 25).

Although the preaching of the gospel has often fallen into disrepute or disfavor in Christian history, its recovery and prominence accompany all significant revivals of effective Christian experience and witness. The preaching of the Word of God is necessary for the church's successful missionary and evangelistic outreach. Buildings, music, teaching, stewardship, fellowship, and study all play significant parts in the ongoing life and work of the church; however, when Peter declared here that the living and abiding word of God "is the good news which was preached to you" (v. 25), he supported not only with pastoral care but also with prophetic force the church's everlasting responsibility for preaching the gospel.

Practical Advice for Living the Christian Life (2:1-8)

Christians have choices to make, responsibilities to discharge, and work to do in living the Christian life. To "put away all malice and all guile and insincerity and envy and all slander" (v. 1) is to assume personal and continuing responsibility for personal and continuing spiritual growth. It is not enough to have been converted and to have begun the Christian journey. We have trusted Christ in the past, and we will trust him in the future, but we are also trusting him here and now to enable us to keep turning away from sin to righteousness in daily living. It is in the present that Christians are responsible for the putting away of these sins which so easily beset us.

Peter here calls a spade a spade. "Malice" is hostility to others. "Guile" is deceitfulness in personal dealings. "Insincerity" is hypocrisy. "Envy" is resentful greed. "Slander" is vicious and destructive talk about individuals whom God loves. Not a single one of the sins in the list is physical. They are sins of the mind and spirit and heart. They are besetting sins not only of Christian men but also of Christian women, not only of Christian adults but also of Christian children, not only of the Christian rich but also of the Christian poor. Each of these sins is spiritually degrading, and all of them are personally ruinous. They are unworthy habits and customs which are all to be absolutely discarded. When they all have been put away, then believers are ready to move forward in the Christian pilgrimage.

Cultivating an appetite for pure nourishment from the divine parent, believers are "to grow up to salvation" (v. 2). Having initially "tasted the kindness" of God in Christ (v. 3), Christians are to keep on longing for sustenance that will provide support in the development of the new life in him. The recipients of this letter were already the recipients of God's saving grace. What then did Peter mean by telling them to "grow up to salvation"? He meant that the grace of God is not an excuse for laziness in the Christian life. He meant that God's great salvation had definitely begun in their lives but that it must not be perceived as having been fully accomplished in a conversion experience of the past. Peter meant that to the initial experience of the new birth Christians are to add a lifetime of disciplined devotion and faithful work. He meant that Christians as spiritual persons are never to stop growing spiritually.

When Peter said, "Come to him" (v. 4), he issued a call that may have been directly connected with Psalm 34:5. Christ is spiritual support, and he is living stone. Peter would have remembered that Jesus had personally pleaded, "Come to me, all who labor and are heavy-laden, and I will give you rest" (Matt. 11:28). The Master's call to come to him conveyed special authority. The word he used always intends the imperative. It is a pressing invitation. In spite of its eagerness and urgency, however, it does not deny personal freedom or reject personal responsibility. God's Spirit can call, but he will not compel. He pleads, but he will not overpower. He entreats, but he will not hijack. He invites, but he will not kidnap. Looking back to such a call from Christ himself, Peter sought to magnify Christ, to whom coming as to a living stone, the recipients of the letter were to be personally incorporated as themselves living stones in God's spiritual house, the church. Though Christ was rejected by men, he is "in God's sight chosen and precious" (v. 4). Further, Christians are "to be a holy priesthood" (v. 5) offering spiritual, and therefore, acceptable, sacrifice to God. These sacrifices are offerings of commitment, holiness, faithfulness, prayer, and service. Such gifts are the only sacrifices acceptable to God since the once-for-all sacrifice of Jesus Christ on the cross at Calvary.

Those "who believe" (v. 7), that is, those who not only give intellectual assent to the truth of prophesy concerning Christ, the promised deliverer (v. 6), but who actually become in daily life committed to him as Lord, will not be disappointed or confounded or "put to shame" (v. 6). On the other hand, those who will not believe, who will not be committed to him but whose daily lives are characterized by disobedience to God's word of good news, stumble and fall as Isaiah had prophesied that they would do (Isa. 8:14-15).

In this part of the letter, Peter's practical advice turned on some particularly powerful action words: "put away," "long for," "grow up," "come to him," "be yourselves built," "offer spiritual sacrifices," "believe." Every one of these action words is as appropriate for this generation of Christians as for the very first generation of Christians to whom the apostle originally addressed the letter.

God's Grace in the Calling to Live the Christian Life (2:9-10)

Peter wrote that by God's great grace, Christians are "a chosen race, a royal priesthood, a holy nation, God's own people" (v. 9). Peter was a Jew. So strongly had he believed in God's special covenant relationship with Israel that he vigorously resisted the idea that Gentiles might come to God without first becoming Jewish proselytes. Even after God taught him that what he had cleansed, Peter should not consider common or unclean (Acts 10:15), Peter resisted fellowship with non-Jewish Christians at Caesarea (Acts 10:44 to 11:18). He was a reluctant learner, but by the time he wrote this letter, Peter had learned the lesson thoroughly and was able to teach it with profound insight and great power. Like Paul, who clearly perceived the church as the true Israel chosen to carry on the redemptive work of God in the world (Rom. 9:6), Peter in this inspired utterance succinctly stated one of the great New Testament definitions of church.

The word *church*, of course, appears neither anywhere else in this letter nor in this particular passage. The idea of "church," however, permeates the letter and is especially evident in the reference here to "God's people" (v. 10), God's "kind of folks." The Jews were elected by God to be his people in preparation for Christ's coming, and God has never willed for them anything but full salvation through belief in his only begotten Son. In Christ, God has now broken down the middle wall of partition that once divided us and has elected Christians to be his "chosen race" (v. 9), to do the ongoing work of "a royal priesthood" (v. 9), to maintain the qualities and the characteristics of "a holy nation" (v. 9), and to be "God's own" or special "people" (v. 9). The church is not chosen just to be blessed but to be a blessing to all humanity. The work which God has cut out for the church is to "declare the wonderful deeds" (v. 9) of the Lord who has called his people out of darkness and who seeks to enlist all people everywhere to walk and live and spend eternity in God's "marvelous light" (v. 9). Hosea's prophetic vision was that God would "say to them which were not my people, 'Thou art my people'; and they shall say, 'Thou art my God' " (Hos. 2:23, KJV). Peter understood that in the church that vision had been gloriously, graciously, and completely fulfilled.

Practical Exhortations to Live the Christian Life
2:11 to 4:19

Abstain from Fleshly Lusts and Practice Good Works (2:11-12)

Peter began this part of the letter by addressing his readers with the characteristic term, "Beloved" (v. 11). This term was much used in the churches until very recent times. As one displaced person to other displaced persons, Peter reminded them they were "aliens and exiles" or, as the King James Version says, "strangers and pilgrims" (v. 11). The use of these terms in this connection could have meant that they were not Roman citizens, but more likely meant that as Christians they were citizens first of the kingdom of God and that as far as this world is concerned they were, as the old spiritual singers put it, "just a-passin' through." Their citizenship was in heaven. Their ways were not the world's ways, and their Lord was not Caesar but Jesus Christ.

Before Peter began his next major portion of his letter dealing with down-to-earth concerns of various kinds, it was appropriate to remind his readers that they, like the Jews in Egypt, were sojourners waiting for God's deliverance, an Exodus people moving out to the ultimate Promised Land. Because the people of God are planted on earth, however, they are everlastingly tempted to cozy up too much to the world, thereby losing their orientation to God and to the things of God. Because they are pointed toward heaven, however, they are tempted to pull so far away from the world in pious introspection and irresponsible escapism that they lose any opportunity to witness effectively to the world's needy multitudes, hungry for good news, for some redemptive and understandable word from the Lord.

Christians today can profit from this reminder. We, too, are strangers here, pilgrims passing through on our way to the city of God, "aliens and exiles" who must not sink our roots too deeply into the soil of this world. The temptation to settle down and be conformed to this world is to be resisted no matter what the cost.

Having dealt with this reminder that this world is not our final home, however, Peter then proceeded to give a refreshingly frank and detailed body of practical advice on how to live the Christian life in this world, here and now.

"Maintain good conduct among the Gentiles," he counseled, so that "they may see your good deeds and glorify God" (v. 12). The words of Jesus from the Sermon on the Mount come readily to mind, "Let your light so shine before men, that they may see your good works and give glory to your Father who is in heaven" (Matt. 5:16).

Peter was not introducing new teaching here. It was the very thing he and his brother, Andrew, heard Jesus saying very soon after they first responded to the Master's call, "Follow me, and I will make you fishers of men" (Matt. 4:19). The "good conduct" of verse 23 means morally commendable conduct. The "good deeds" of verse 12 are a sign to the Gentiles that God's Holy Spirit is dwelling productively in the lives of believers. They are likewise a sign to unbelievers that it makes a difference to have been with Jesus.

When Christians do good works they are not working for grace but from grace; they are not working for victory but from victory; they are not working for salvation but from salvation. Good works done faithfully and consistently by the people of God can do more to extend evangelism, further missions, and undergird the total witness of the church than all the church's great buildings, aggressive programs, and special offerings combined.

"The day of visitation" (v. 12) could have meant the time of the second coming of Christ but more likely referred to a time of trial when the Christians would be brought into court by those who would persecute them.

Practice Responsible Citizenship (2:13-17)

The admonition to "be subject for the Lord's sake to every human institution, whether . . . to the emperor . . . or to governors" (v. 13) is a clear acknowledgement that government as such is ordained by God. Particular emperors or particular governors may do the work of the devil and may not deserve the support of faithful Christians, as Adolf Hitler did not. Government as such, however, is better than anarchy, and this passage is a reminder that our citizenship is to be discharged responsibly "for the Lord's sake." "By doing right," Christians "put to silence the ignorance of foolish men" (v. 15), whereas by doing wrong, occasion would be made for others to criticize and to stumble.

Picking up the great theme of freedom, Peter then offered strong support for liberty, the most precious and noble of all social values: "Live as free men" (v. 16). The Christian's freedom, however, is not "a pretext for evil." It is not the freedom of lawlessness but a freedom of careful discipline to Jesus Christ as Lord. The libertine is not free but is rather the slave of his appetites. The anarchist is not free but is rather the captive of his violent defiance of all authority. The moral nihilist is not free but is rather the servant of his rebellious confusion. Christians are responsibly free to honor everybody, love the brotherhood, fear God, and respect the political leaders (v. 17).

Endure Even the Mistreatment of Evil Masters (2:18-20)

In an era when slavery was an accepted part of the social system, Peter counseled servants to be submissive to their masters, not only to those who were kind but even to those who were cruel (vv. 18-20). Christ suffered for us all, and Christians may well be required to suffer even for doing right.

Follow Christ's Steps and Live in Righteousness (2:21-25)

Jesus has left Christians "an example" that we "should follow in his steps" (v. 21). His saving work was done "that we might die to sin and live to righteousness" (v. 24). Negatively, Christians are to abandon rebellion and mark-missing as a way of life, dying to sin; and positively, we are to adopt God's right way of justice and truth and goodness as we "live to righteousness" each day of our lives (v. 24). Righteous living in all the difficult arenas of daily existence is possible because by his sacrifice, we have been made healthy and whole. Though we all once strayed like witless sheep, by God's mercy we now are at one with our "Shepherd and Guardian" who perfectly cares for us in every area and relationship of life (v. 25).

In today's world where slavery has been almost universally abolished and where the actual terms "servants" and "masters" have been dropped from most vocabularies, what does this passage mean? How does God's Spirit here speak to our own generation? Christians, no matter whose human authority we work under and no matter whom we are accountable to, are obligated to do our work responsibly. We are obligated to maintain the kind of relationship to those to whom we are accountable and to those who may be accountable to us that will conform to the example set by Christ. Paul stated this same point, "Whatever your task, work heartily, as serving the Lord" (Col. 3:23).

Live Together as Wives and Husbands Who Are Joint Heirs of the Grace of Life (3:1-7)

The subject of relationships between husbands and wives is treated next, in one of the most intensely practical parts of this very practical letter. Paul had a good deal to say about this subject in his letters (Eph. 5:22 to 6:4; Col. 3:18-21; 1 Tim. 2:8-15; 1 Cor. 7:1-17), although he was himself unmarried (1 Cor. 7:7-9)—a fact that has been often noticed by both husbands and wives. Peter, however, was married. Matthew 8:14-15 refers to his wife's mother, who when she was sick with a fever in Peter's house was miraculously healed by Jesus. What he says about marriage is therefore of special interest to the married.

As Peter counseled servants to be submissive to their masters, so he said wives are to "be submissive" to their husbands "so that some, though they do not obey the word, may be won without a word by the behavior of their wives, when they see your reverent and chaste behavior" (vv. 1-2). The submission which Peter counseled wives to observe in relationship to their husbands reflects the acceptance of the existing order in husband-wife relationships which, like the acceptance of human slavery, prevailed throughout the then known world. To "be submissive to" is to be subject to, to be subordinate to. Duly constituted authority regarding husband-wife relationships was to be accepted, as was "every human institution," including slavery and the totalitarian authority of Caesar (2:13) in the political realm. Both in the Jewish culture and throughout the Greco-Roman world of the first century, wives were uniformly subordinate to their husbands. The Christian gospel in all of its power had just begun to work on behalf of both slaves, government, and women. At the time of the writing of 1 Peter, however, there had been little time for the good news significantly to transform the structured institutions of society. That work of gospel penetration and permeation of individual lives and of social institutions continues today and will be perfectly completed only with God's consummation of human history. Peter was directly concerned at this point "so that" unbelieving husbands might be won to Christian faith "without a word" when they observed the "reverent and chaste behavior" (v. 2) of their Christian wives. Christian women are not to be preoccupied with outward adornment and decoration but are to give primary attention to the development of "the hidden person of the heart" (vv. 3-5). The advice to "do right and let nothing terrify you" (v. 6) is superb advice. No matter what the Christian woman's social position or personal limitations may be in our still imperfect society, it is well to remember that by trusting God and doing right any believer has the best possible reason not to be terrified by anything that the world may throw at him or that the devil may devise to ensnare him.

And what does the apostle have to say to husbands? "Likewise you husbands, live considerately with your wives, bestowing honor on the woman as the weaker sex" (v. 7). Christian husbands are to recognize their wives as "joint heirs of the grace of life" and are to maintain a spirit of considerateness and kindness and honor toward their wives "in order that your prayers may not be hindered" (v. 7) or blocked or made of no effect.

Do Right, Seek Peace, and Follow Righteousness (3:8-13)

Calling Christians to "unity of spirit, sympathy, love of the brethren, a tender heart and a humble mind" (v. 8), Peter here emphasized some of the qualities that are vital, not optional, for the Christian life. Unity of spirit is oneness in Christ resulting in oneness of life, oneness of hopes and prayers and aims. In the early days of the church, Christians gathered together of one accord with "one heart and soul" giving testimony to the resurrection of Christ, "and great grace was upon them all" (Acts 4:32-33). Mindful of Jesus' prayer, "I do not pray for these only, but also for those who believe in me through their word, that they may all be one" (John 17:20-21), Peter affirmed the importance of avoiding divisions and of maintaining supreme loyalty to Christ. Such an attitude helps keep his people together to do his work in the world. "Sympathy" speaks of selflessness in concern for the hurts of others. "Love of the brethren" speaks of a love for God's people which is evidence of genuine love for God. (See also 1 John 3:14 which specifically says, "We know that we have passed out of death into life, because we love the brethren.") "A tender heart" speaks of the compassionate pity which, because it is at the heart of God, must be also at the heart of the Christian life. "A humble mind" speaks of the Christian's knowledge of his own creatureliness or limitations in the presence of the Creator, of his need never to count himself to have apprehended, and of the need to maintain before God and the church a continuing spirit of teachableness.

Next, Peter mentioned the importance of forgiveness and clearly said something which Christians today need to be very careful to hear, "Do not return evil for evil or reviling for reviling" (v. 9). Peter summed up this section of powerful ethical preaching by quoting Psalm 34:12-16, which is one of the great Bible passages calling us to be "zealous for what is right" (v. 13).

Endure Suffering for Righteousness' Sake (3:14-17)

Faithful Christians can expect suffering to come into their lives. When it does come, Peter said, "If you do suffer for righteousness' sake, you will be blessed" (v. 14). Persecutors are not to be feared, and believers are not to be troubled by detractors (v. 14). Reverencing Christ as Lord, we are always to be prepared to defend our faith, to give an account of the hope we hold because of him who holds us, and to maintain a spirit of "gentleness and reverence" in the process (v. 15). By maintaining tenacious commitment to Christ resulting in uncompromising righteousness in daily life, the Christian will keep his "conscience clear" so that when abused, the abusers will "be put to shame" by the believer's "good behavior in Christ" (v. 16). If it is God's will for Christians to suffer, then we should be careful that the pain comes from doing right and not from doing wrong (v. 17).

Paul said that all who live godly lives in Christ Jesus will suffer persecution (2 Tim. 3:12); James said that the friendship of the world is enmity with God (Jas. 4:4); and Peter here wrote about what Christians should do when, not if, abuse and suffering come. There is a message here for our generation. It is that we are to prepare ourselves for such trials and tribulations as may come to us from a hostile world, not by hardening our minds and steeling our wills but by immersing ourselves in righteousness. It is that unqualified and uncompromised righteousness before God and humanity which is the Christian soldier's finest armor.

Maintain a Clear Conscience in View of Christ's Life and Work (3:18-22)

Christ is the Christian's best example of how to bear suffering for righteousness' sake. He "died for sins once for all, the righteous for the unrighteous" to bring us to God (v. 18). Although Jesus was "put to death in the flesh," crucified by sinful men, he has been "made alive in the spirit," resurrected to become the pioneer for all the faithful who will all also be made alive in the resurrection (v. 18). The translators of the King James Version of the Bible took "spirit" in the Greek manuscripts to refer to the Holy Spirit, but the translators of the Revised Standard Version took the word to mean the ongoing life of Jesus Christ even after his physical death by crucifixion. Both views are, in fact, defensible, and both are instructive and helpful. Christians believe that after Christ died, he was resurrected and that the spirit of his life continued and will continue forever, as the Revised Standard Version renders this passage; and Christians also believe that the Holy Spirit especially serves to lead us to light and life through the gospel, as the King James Version renders it.

It was not in the Lord's flesh but after his physical death that Peter appears to have meant that Jesus "went and preached to the spirits in prison" (vv. 19-20). This is the most difficult part of 1 Peter and is actually one of the most obscure passages in all of the New Testament. It has been subject to much debate and serious division in the churches for nearly two thousand years. Scholars have disagreed about how to interpret every word in the passage. What are we to understand that Peter meant to say to the recipients of this letter long ago, and what does God's Spirit mean for this passage to say to us in our own generation?

Peter seems to have been saying that between his death and resurrection Jesus somehow went in spirit to "the spirits in prison" and there preached to the formerly disobedient the deep meaning of salvation by grace through faith. That deep meaning had been preached by Noah to his generation. Moreover, through the Bible account of the flood, and Noah and the ark, God has proclaimed that deep meaning to all generations.

Moving on immediately Peter then wrote, "Baptism, which corresponds to this, now saves you, not as a removal of dirt from the body but as an appeal to God for a clear conscience through the resurrection of Jesus Christ" (v. 21). Noah and his wife and their three sons, Shem, Ham, and Japheth, and their wives were saved by God's grace through their trusting obedience. Similarly, believers now are saved by the grace of God laid hold of through our trusting obedience, of which baptism is a profoundly significant symbol. Was it the ark that saved Noah? Or was it Noah's faithful obedience that saved him? Or was it God? Or was it God working through Noah's trusting obedience that led him to follow God's way that resulted in his salvation? It was clearly the latter. As the ark by itself did not save Noah, so baptism by itself saves no one. Yet the ark was not an optional matter for Noah to take or leave, and baptism is not an optional matter for believers to take or leave. It is the Christian convert's appeal to God "for a clear conscience" (v. 21) for having obeyed God. Even our Lord came, at the very beginning of his public ministry, to John the Baptist and submitted himself for baptism in the Jordan River saying, "Thus it is fitting for us to fulfil all righteousness" (Matt. 3:15), after which there came "a voice from heaven, saying, 'This is my beloved Son, with whom I am well pleased' " (v. 17).

At the very beginning of the Christian's life, baptism beautifully, graphically, and powerfully demonstrates both the death and "the resurrection of Jesus Christ" (v. 21) and the Christian's death to the old life of sin and resurrection to "walk in newness of life" (Rom. 6:4). It is the Christian's commitment to God resulting in faithful obedience that produces "a clear conscience" (v. 21) and honors Christ "who has gone into heaven and is at the right hand of God, with angels, authorities, and powers subject to him" (v. 22). This moving note of victory concludes the line of thought which has been pursued. It was not only an encouraging, victorious note for the early Christians of Asia Minor, but it is also an encouraging, victorious note to our own generation. Wherever people are, Christ can and will save those who trust and obey.

Shun Sin and Live in the Will of God (4:1-6)

Christ's suffering is a challenge for Christians to arm themselves with the same mind (v. 1), or thought, attitude, and conviction, that characterized Jesus who said, "He who finds his life will lose it, and he who loses his life for my sake will find it" (Matt. 10:39). Though Christians committed to living the Christian life are engaged in a tremendous struggle against the world, the flesh, and the devil, we are fully ready for the fight when armed with the mind of Christ. His attitudes and approaches to life's challenges and responsibilities are the Christian's ideal example.

For Christians, suffering is not a dead-end street. Suffering is a means to an end. God's purpose is to bring us through it purer and stronger and finer than we were before it came. When Peter said that "whoever has suffered in the flesh has ceased from sin" (v. 1), he was not teaching a doctrine of sinless perfection for those who have experienced trials and tribulations, or even for those who have experienced persecution for Christ's sake. Rather, he seems to be making the point that sin no longer has dominion over Christians, that a break with sin as a way of life characterizes the life of every believer. Rebellion, disobedience, and mark-missing do not characterize the lives of believers. By God's grace we are finished with that way of life. He may also have meant to say that patient endurance of whatever vicissitudes life may bring has substantial moral value for Christians.

The commitment of ourselves to God in the initial experience of personal faith is in some sense sealed in the symbolic act of baptism. After that, Christians are to live out the rest of life controlled "no longer by human passions but by the will of God" (v. 2). The "will of God" is his entire and perfect intention for the Christian's ongoing daily life. Human lusts are spelled out as being "licentiousness, passions, drunkenness, revels, carousing, and lawless idolatry" (v. 3).

"Licentiousness" is self-serving sensuality, and the reference here is to shameless conduct that indecently gratifies the senses and paralyzes the

Spirit. "Passions" refer in this instance to sexual lust, the sin of perceiving another person as a means to selfish, personal, sexual gratification rather than as a person of infinite value in God's sight. "Drunkenness" is the subjection of body and mind to ethyl alcohol's evil effects and to the risk of its ruinous enslavement through addiction. The word which Peter actually used here may properly be translated "wine-drinkings" or "excess of wine." For Christians, a strong case can be made to avoid alcohol altogether in the knowledge that drinking may cause others to stumble, that those who totally abstain never become addicted, and that in our culture in these times all drinking of ethyl alcohol in any form is irresponsible and anti-social. "Revels" or revellings are orgies—wild parties where animal instincts are shamelessly called forth and irresponsibly turned loose. "Carousing" is wanton violence, the senseless abandon of concern for life and property, actions commonly associated with the release of the inhibitions of civilized human beings who have numbed their higher senses with alcohol. In every age humanity's most abused and most deadly drug is alcohol. "Lawless idolatry" is abominable substitution of strange and perverse gods of man's own making for the living God who has shown us himself in Jesus Christ. As the first two of the Ten Commandments clearly stated, the Lord God was fundamentally and unequivocally opposed to idolatry in ancient times; this reference here clearly states that he is unalterably opposed to the abomination of idolatry now.

The primary concern of this passage, however, is not the rejection of these pagan passions. The primary focus is on living the rest of our lives "by the will of God" (v. 2). Christians rightly rejoice because the rule of pleasure and passion and pride has ended and because, by his grace, life by the will of God is in progress.

Few ideas in Christianity have been as powerful, as pervasive, and as important through the centuries as the idea of the will of God. The will of God for Christians in modern times is like the law of the Lord for God's people in ancient times, spoken of by the Psalmist: "The law of the Lord is perfect, converting the soul: the testimony of the Lord is sure, making wise the simple. The statutes of the Lord are right, rejoicing the heart: the commandment of the Lord is pure, enlightening the eyes. The fear of the Lord is clean, enduring for ever: the judgments of the Lord are true and righteous altogether" (Ps. 19:7-9, KJV). As the law represented the whole character of God and his purpose for Israel, so the will of God speaks of his nature and of his purpose for his people, the church, in these times. God's will for us requires a clean break with immorality, but far more importantly, it requires a life of disciplined commitment to Jesus Christ as Lord, a life of obedient subjection to God the Father, a life of intelligent communication with God the Holy Spirit, and a life of faithful service through the church to the world. This "world," we remember, God so loved "that he gave his only begotten Son, that whosoever believeth in him should not perish, but have everlasting life" (John 3:16, KJV). For the Christian, life's deepest concern is not what human appetites desire but what God's will dictates. This important counsel from Peter is in complete accord with Paul's advice to the Thessalonians: "This is the will of God, your sanctification . . . " (1 Thess. 4:3).

Unbelievers "are surprised" that believers will not join them in that "same wild profligacy" (v. 4), and in perverse vindictiveness the unbelievers sometimes abuse faithful disciples of Christ intent on walking in the way of righteousness. They, Christians are to remember, will have to give an account of themselves to God who will "judge the living and the dead" (v. 5).

There comes next a statement that is particularly hard to interpret, "For this is why the gospel was preached even to the dead, that though judged in the flesh like men, they might live in the spirit like God" (v. 6). The idea that unbelievers who now die in their sins will have an opportunity to hear and respond to the gospel after death is held by some. This interpretation, however, is neither required by what Peter actually said here nor supported in the context of what he wrote, or by the witness of the rest of the New Testament. If between his death and resurrection Christ did actually go to the realm of the dead and preach to those from the days of Noah who had died in their sins, then that was a once-for-all event which we are not to assume is to be repeated for those who now turn away from the gospel. Another view, more scripturally defensible and more theologically acceptable, has been held by such eminent churchmen as Augustine, Erasmus, and Luther to the effect that the statement refers to the spiritually dead to whom the gospel was preached in order for them to come to life through faith in Christ. Some feel that a still more satisfactory view of what the passage actually means is that the dead mentioned here were dead believers, Christians from the Asia Minor communities named in the introduction of the letter who believed but subsequently died. They would give account to God of their lives "in the flesh" (v. 6) as all people must, but would live eternally "in the spirit like God" (v. 6). Whatever the full, true, and complete meaning of this difficult passage, Jesus Christ is Lord of time and eternity, of this world and the next, of the living and the dead. Every Christian does well to love him and serve him with the whole heart and soul and mind and life.

Practice Christian Ethics and Thereby Glorify God (4:7-11)

Peter began this section with a declaration about the imminence of the second coming of Christ. The early church firmly expected his return in their generation. "The end of all things is at hand" (v. 7) means the end of history, the end of the present age, the end of the world. This strong emphasis on the expected consummation of the age is especially prominent in Peter, James, Hebrews, Mark, Matthew, Paul's letters, and Revelation. This expectation of the early return of Christ was generally viewed by New Testament writers and New Testament Christians as a special challenge to the most rigorous kind of morality in everyday living. This ought to be the case for Christians today. Our anticipation of Christ's imminent return is no excuse for irresponsible withdrawal from the great personal challenges and social issues that affect humanity. It is, rather, a pressing reason for us to pray faithfully and work tirelessly until " 'the kingdom of the world has become the kingdom of our Lord and of his Christ' " (Rev. 11:15).

Because "the end of all things is at hand" Christians are to "keep sane and sober" for effective prayers (v. 7). To "keep sane" means to maintain self-control. Both a cool head and a clear mind are necessary for power in prayer. The advice to "hold unfailing your love for one another" (v. 8) is advice for Christians not to go off the deep end in preoccupation with their own personal preparations for the second coming, but rather for them to keep their love for each other at full strength; and the primacy of such love requires the introductory words, "Above all" (v. 8). Such love, as James said of the ministry of restoration and reconciliation "covers a multitude of sins" (v. 8; Jas. 5:20). Ungrudging hospitality is to be practiced among Christians (v. 9).

The gifts of God to individual Christians, whether speaking or serving, are to be employed on behalf of others that God may be glorified through Jesus Christ to whom "glory and dominion" belong for ever and ever (v. 11). It is such a moving thought that Peter must have been compelled to say "Amen" not to the way he had said this but to the truth which he had proclaimed.

Continue Steadfast in Trials That Come for Obeying the Gospel (4:12-19)

Christians are not to "be surprised at the fiery ordeal" of persecution which is destined to come and test, or prove, the faithful (v. 12). Persecution is not to be perceived as though something unexpected, unusual, or strange were happening. It is very often part of the given situation and the given relationships prevailing in this kind of world. Peter told them to rejoice when they came to share Christ's sufferings that they might all the more rejoice at the revelation of Christ's glory when he returns (v. 13). Reproach for Christ's sake brings special blessing, for upon such believers rests "the spirit of glory and of God" (v. 14). Then Peter hastened to say, "But let none of you suffer as a murderer, or a thief, or a wrongdoer, or a mischief-maker" (v. 15).

It might seem that the apostle Peter would have had more confidence in the recipients of this letter than to issue such a possibly insulting warning to them. It was evident from Peter's own wretched denial of Christ at the time of the Lord's arrest and trial that the flesh is weak, and that the devil is active. In this life we can never count ourselves to have apprehended. Suffering as a Christian is not something to be ashamed of but is to be seized as an occasion to give special glory to God (v. 16).

Although the time had apparently come "for judgment to begin with the household of God" (v. 17), for persecution to fall on the church, the final outcome for the people of God will be victory. The final judgment of unbelievers, however, is here left fearfully hanging: "What will be the end of those who do not obey the gospel?" (v. 17). It is hard to imagine how Peter might better have closed this moving part of the letter than with these words, "Therefore let those who suffer according to God's will do right and entrust their souls to a faithful Creator" (v. 19). There is still no better life insurance for time and eternity than to do right and trust God.

Special Exhortations Related to the Christian Life

5:1-11

To Elders (5:1-4)

The first part of this last chapter of 1 Peter is given to a special exhortation to elders in the churches. The advice came from one who identified himself as "a fellow elder" as well as one who, as an apostle, was "a witness of the sufferings of Christ" (v. 1). Peter's reference to his having witnessed the Lord's sufferings was not made to bolster the authority of his person but the authenticity of his counsel. The reference makes no claim to a superior position or special authority for the writer. On the contrary, he identified himself as sharing with them the same office and, once again, as one who knew enough about trials and tribulations and even the laying down of life itself. Such identification merited a careful hearing from those particular elders.

Their responsibility would include a compassionate concern for suffering believers in their spiritual care. Harsh persecutions appeared to be about to break over them. The further indication that the writer was himself "a partaker in the glory that is to be revealed" (v. 1) could refer to Peter's having been with Christ in his great and memorable transfiguration experience (Mark 9:2-8). It could refer to the fact that Peter understood himself to be included among the faithful people of God of whom he had previously written that "the spirit of glory and of God rests upon you" (4:14). It could refer to Peter's absolute assurance that final victory in Jesus was so perfectly assured that it could be perceived as having been already actually accomplished. None of these interpretations does violence to the reference, and there may be validity in all of them.

The focus of this passage, however, is not on Peter but on the duties of the elders of the church, as the people of God. The primary meaning of the word *elder* is simply "older." Christians at a very early time, however, began to use the term as a title for a person providing pastoral care and leadership in a church. The term "bishop" was commonly used with reference to the pastor's overseeing responsibility, while "elder" seems to carry the connotation of special honor and respect which church members held for the leader or leaders of their family of faith. Elders in the churches had special responsibility as overseers (Acts 20:17,28), so it is not proper to draw too precise a line between the terms *elder* and *bishop.* On the first missionary journey of Paul and Barnabas, elders were appointed in every church (Acts 14:23). The original word for *elder* was Jewish in origin, while the original word for *bishop* was Greek in origin. By the time the New Testament was being written, the terms were essentially interchangeable.

To these leaders in the churches, Peter wrote, "Tend the flock of God that is in your charge, not by constraint but willingly, not for shameful gain but eagerly, not as domineering over those in your charge but being examples to the flock" (vv. 2-3). The tending of the flock of God which elders are exhorted to do is the work of leading and feeding, caring and sharing, protecting and directing. That work is not to be done by elders because of any outside pressure but "willingly"; not for any personal profit but "eagerly"; not out of any desire for superiority or personal power but as "examples." Faithfulness in carrying out these duties as elders will bring certain reward, for "when the chief Shepherd is manifested you will obtain the unfading crown of glory" (v. 4).

Nowhere else in the New Testament is the term "chief Shepherd" used for the Lord. It is a richly expressive concept with special meaning for all responsible undershepherds, elders, or pastors who know and love Psalm 23. These cherish the special references made by Jesus to himself as the "good shepherd" (John 10:11) and to his people as the sheep of his pasture (John 10:11-18; Luke 12:32; 15:3-6; 19:10; Matt. 10:16; 25:32) who are to be loved, cared for, and fed (John 21:15-17).

To Younger Christians (5:5)

As elders have special responsibilities, so do the "younger" who are charged to "be subject to the elders" (v. 5). The younger church members are not meant to be actual servants of the elders. They are not expected to cower or cringe before them or to be servile to them. What is called for here is the recognition that the younger have something important to learn from the older, that the inexperience of the young people in the church should profit from the experience of the old people in the church, and that the exuberance and enthusiasm of young Christians are properly directed and channeled by the experience and wisdom of older Christians. Peter's advice here is comparable to Paul's advice to the youthful Timothy, "Do not rebuke an older man but exhort him as you would a father" (1 Tim. 5:1) or "Rebuke not an elder" (1 Tim. 5:1, KJV).

Instead of selfishness and prideful protection of prerogatives, Christians are told, "Clothe yourselves, all of you, with humility toward one another" (v. 5). The reason for this wise counsel for believers to clothe themselves with humility is that "God opposes the proud but gives grace to the humble" (v. 5). The quotation is from Proverbs 3:34 and is a good example of how the word of God, hidden in Peter's heart, came readily to his mind to illustrate an important point being made. Few exercises can be more lastingly helpful to Christians today than the faithful memorization of special Bible passages so that unfailingly helpful, relevant, and powerful truths will leap from the heart when needed in everyday life.

To the Faithful Who Are Encouraged to Persevere (5:6-11)

In moving to the close of the letter, Peter again offered a practical exhortation for all Christians to cultivate with care some special qualities of the Christian life. Those qualities would stand them in especially good stead in the suffering that was likely to come to them. Not quite ready to leave the subject of humility about which he had just written in a different context, Peter urged them not just to be humble toward each other but to humble themselves "under the mighty hand of God" (v. 6). Humility is teachableness, meekness, lowliness of mind, modesty of heart. Humility's opposite is pride, pretension, and pomposity. It is completely inappropriate for Christians ever to assume a spirit of arrogance, insolence, or haughtiness. In recognition of God's sovereign power, Christians properly bow the knee of the spirit to him, acknowledging that we live and move and have our being only under the mighty hand of God. Pride is one of the most deadly of the seven deadly sins—pride, envy, anger, lust, avarice, gluttony, and sloth. So humility, corresponding to the repentance with which the Christian life begins, is appropriately listed here as the first of the virtues to be cultivated in preparation for the ultimate victory that God will give to all believers (v. 10). As God scorns the scorners, so he gives grace to the lowly (Prov. 3:34, KJV). As he rejects the arrogant, so he accepts the teachable. As he cuts off the grasping, so God provides for the generous. As he judges the judgmental, so he embraces the meek. Those who humble themselves under God's mighty hand are to do so in the assurance "that in due time he may exalt you" (v. 6).

Christians are not to wait until God takes all the initiative to pluck from our hands and pull from our hearts the anxieties which would ulcerate us. We have major responsibility at this point ourselves. Jesus emphasized our personal responsibility when he said, "Do not be anxious about tomorrow" (Matt. 6:34), and Peter was highlighting our personal responsibility when he urged, "Cast all your anxieties on him, for he cares about you" (v. 7). True believers are to throw away the debilitating worries that would rob us of the assurance of God's complete trustworthiness in caring for us. We are intentionally and positively to reject the doubts and apprehensions, the misgivings and forebodings with which people who hold no living faith in Almighty God must necessarily live. "Take your burden to the Lord and leave it there"[2] is both a phrase from a song to be sung and a deed to be done.

"Be sober, be watchful," the admonition continues, for our "adversary the devil prowls around like a roaring lion, seeking some one to devour" (v. 8). The sobriety and watchfulness here called for have to do with mental alertness, with spiritual discernment, with a vigilant testing of the impressions and inclinations that come to us: "Do not believe every spirit, but test the spirits to see whether they are of God" (1 John 4:1). It is often observed that eternal vigilance is the price of liberty. Eternal vigilance is also the price of escape from the devil's claws and clutches. Like a roaring lion enraged by hunger, the devil's insatiable appetite is well known. He will pounce on the unwary whenever and wherever he is given an opening. Christians who are truly "sober" will avoid the ignominy of falling prey to the enemy which came to Peter when he cursed and denied Christ (Matt. 26:69-75). Those who are truly "watchful" are assured that with every temptation God makes a way to escape that we may be able to endure, avoiding the fate of being compromised, entrapped, or devoured.

Christians tempted or threatened by the devil's evil presence are told, "Resist him, firm in your faith" (v. 9), knowing that when God's people resist the devil, he will flee from them. Peter's connection of this talk about the devil with the words "knowing that the same experience of suffering is required of your brotherhood throughout the world" (v. 9) would seem to indicate that the devil's work of persecuting Christians was reaching out to Christians wherever they lived throughout the

Roman empire. Although no single malicious and ruthless Caesar is now personally directing such a persecution of Christians throughout the world, the devil is nevertheless active in tempting, discouraging, oppressing, and even persecuting Christians wherever he can find personal or national or social or institutional opportunities to do his evil work.

In spite of all that the world, the flesh, and the devil can throw at Christians, however, God will see his people safely through: "And after you have suffered a little while, the God of all grace, who has called you to his eternal glory in Christ, will himself restore, establish, and strengthen you" (v. 10).

The cross is for a little while, but the crown is forever. Persecution may destroy us, but God will "restore" us. Suffering may shake us, but God will "establish" us. Troubles may shatter us, but God will "strengthen" us. Triumphantly, God's persevering people shout together, "To him be the dominion for ever and ever. Amen" (v. 11).

Conclusion
5:12-14

Final Greetings (5:12-14a)

The actual letter of Peter to the Christians in Pontus, Galatia, Cappadocia, Asia, and Bithynia was written or carried or both written and carried by "Sylvanus, a faithful brother" (v. 12). This Sylvanus, a Latin name which is probably the same as the Greek "Silas," may have been the same person mentioned in Acts 15:22,27,32,37-40; 16:19,25,29; 17:4; 18:5; 2 Corinthians 1:19; 1 Thessalonians 1:1; and 2 Thessalonians 1:1. Peter's own moving summary of his purpose was, "I have written briefly to you, exhorting and declaring that this is the true grace of God; stand fast in it" (v. 12). Even when finishing the communication, he could not refrain from a final admonition to "stand fast" in the Christian life.

Peter then added, "She who is at Babylon, who is likewise chosen, sends you greetings" (v. 13). Who was "she" and where was "Babylon"? Most of the evidence is generally believed to identify the "Babylon" mentioned here as Rome. The use of this code name for Rome was widespread among early Christians, particularly after the waves of persecution began to emanate from the city of the Caesars. Churches were commonly referred to among Christians, even as they have been down through the centuries, in the feminine gender. The plainest, and perhaps the most satisfactory, interpretation to put on this passage is that Peter meant to say that the church at Rome, "likewise chosen" by the Lord, sent greetings as did his "son Mark" (v. 13). It may be assumed that this son, Mark, was the John Mark of Acts 12:12,25; 13:5,13; 15:37; Colossians 4:10; 2 Timothy 4:11; and Philemon 24, though such an assumption cannot be proved and therefore should not be pressed. Christian tradition later connects John Mark to Peter and identifies him as Peter's interpreter.

"Greet one another with the kiss of love" (v. 14) was the apostle's way of encouraging the early Christians to whom he wrote to renew their devotion to one another and to seal their bond of fellowship with one another. Such a kiss of love, or holy kiss, was commonly practiced at the observance of the Lord's Supper until about the thirteenth century and is retained by some church groups even until the present. As a token of true Christian love, such a kiss of love was a sign to Christians of all ages that all believers are members of God's great church, included as accepted persons in the family of the Father's divine intention.

Benediction (5:14*b*)

Finally, and with a simplicity and power that make comment inappropriate, Peter concluded the letter, "Peace to all of you that are in Christ" (v. 14).

Notes

1. James Hardy Ropes, "A Critical and Exegetical Commentary on the Epistle of James," *The International Critical Commentary* (Edinburgh: T & T Clark, 1916), p. 106.

2. C. Albert Tindley, "Leave It There," Copyright by C. Albert Tindley, *The Modern Hymnal* (Dallas: Robert Coleman, 1926), pp. 318-19.

2 PETER

Introduction

Second Peter is a brief message that is more like a short sermon or an essay than an actual letter. It is more similar to the letter of James than it is to 1 Peter. Differing a good deal from 1 Peter in style of language and method of composition, 2 Peter could easily have been read aloud, as was the letter of James, in the early churches. It can be so read in about ten minutes. Eusebius, writing about AD 325, observed that 2 Peter actually was read in public in most churches. Several of its passages show such remarkable spiritual power and insight that they are still widely read in public in the churches today, being used as texts for preaching and as resources for special instruction and study.

The message of 2 Peter is one of pastoral encouragement, support for living the Christian life, prophetic warning against false doctrine, and concerned attention to proper preparation for the day of judgment. This message is timeless. It is as important for our generation as it was for the earliest Christians. As 2 Peter was a tract for the times in which it was first written, so it is a special tract for our own special times.

Together with Jude, James, 2 John, and 3 John, 2 Peter stood apart from the rest of the New Testament writings almost from the beginning of the Christian era as a letter whose authorship was disputed and whose authenticity was therefore in question. Second Peter was a general epistle, however, which was more and more deemed to be useful in the ongoing life and work of the churches. This usefulness to the churches is one of the characteristics of all the books of the Bible and was one of the elements carefully considered when 2 Peter was finally accepted as a part of the Bible in its present form. In AD 367, the twenty-seven books of our present New Testament were named by Athanasius of Alexandria as being generally accepted by Christians as inspired, and the Council of Carthage in AD 397 approved the same twenty-seven books, including 2 Peter.

The author identified himself as "Simon Peter, a servant and apostle of Jesus Christ" (1:1).

The Occasion of the Letter

A careful reading of 2 Peter can keep students of the Bible from arriving at wrong conclusions about the occasion or purpose of this letter. In the first chapter, the focus is primarily on how to live the Christian life. The second chapter turns the spotlight of attention on false teachers and destructive heresies. The third and last chapter provides support and assurance for believers who continue to wait for Christ's return. The tone of the letter is supportive. The purpose is to provide general admonition to the people of God. The original occasion of the letter was the pastoral need being experienced by Christians of that especially turbulent era when the letter was first sent out. Essentially the same needs are still being experienced by Christians of this day and age. Second Peter is therefore particularly profitable to believers today.

The Date and Place of Writing

There are some indications that 2 Peter may have been the latest or at least among the latest of the New Testament books to be written. There are several signs in the letter pointing to a relatively late date of writing. Persecution had come. Paul's letters were well known and had come to be viewed as Scripture. Christians had grown weary of waiting for the second coming. Heresies had crept in. Early church leaders had died.

It was in vogue among some scholars a few decades ago to date 2 Peter as late as the middle of the second century. Some evidence in the Dead Sea Scrolls of the Qumran community, however, now points to an earlier date for many New Testament writings than had formerly been supposed. It seems possible that the letter could have been written as early as AD 64 or possibly AD 70. On the other hand, many responsible scholars still think it more likely to have been written in the second century. Since the place and date of death for the apostle Peter are not known, no help can be derived from speculating at that point.

There is no clear evidence, either internally in 2 Peter itself or externally in history, as to the place of writing of this letter. It has been surmised that 2 Peter may have been written in Egypt, but most scholars assume Rome to have been the more likely place of writing. All such surmising, with our present knowledge, is guesswork.

Salutation
1:1-2

The letter begins like an office memo, with the writer's name, "Simon Peter." The Jewish name Simon is used first. It appears here in some, though not all, of the New Testament manuscripts in the same form or spelling, Simeon, which is found in Acts 15:14, where James explains how God had used Simeon to open the doors of the church to the Gentiles. The name Peter is employed too. That is the name Jesus assigned to him to signify his character as a rock in the life and work of the early church. The use of both names in this greeting may have been intended to convey special apostolic authority to the original readers of the letter. At any rate, the use of both names reminds readers of all time that the Jewish fisherman Simon had been touched by the Master's hand and changed to become Peter, the powerful Christian preacher and mighty Christian missionary.

Simon Peter identified himself as "a servant and apostle of Jesus Christ" (v. 1). The writer is first a slave and then an apostle of Jesus Christ. Faithful saints of God throughout Old Testament times were identified as servants, or slaves, of God: Abraham, Isaac, Jacob (Deut. 9:27), Moses (Deut. 34:5), Samuel (1 Sam. 3:9-10), David (2 Sam. 7:5; Ps. 78:70), Solomon (1 Kings 1:26), Job (Job 1:8), Isaiah (Isa. 20:3), and Daniel (Dan. 9:17). Israel as a whole was perceived to be God's servant (Isa. 49:3). With the coming of Christ, the work of all these servants of God had been faithfully shouldered by Simon Peter and those like him who accepted Jesus as the promised Redeemer and gave their very lives to work for him. It is true, Simon Peter was an apostle of Jesus Christ. First and foremost, however, he was a servant of the Lord.

The recipients of the letter are not identified with regard to place or time. They are addressed simply as "those who have obtained a faith of equal standing with ours in the righteousness of our God and Savior Jesus Christ" (v. 1). The disciples who were with Jesus Christ in his earthly ministry, and particularly the apostles who were especially chosen and trained by him and who were eyewitnesses of the resurrected Christ, were evidently held in very special respect by the early churches. Without church buildings, without formal organization, and without the Bible as such, the early Christians had particular need to

look to those who had personally been transformed and taught and
trained by Jesus Christ. Nevertheless, all who later believed "obtained
a faith of equal standing" (v. 1) with that of the apostles themselves.

The faith of the apostles, the faith of the early Christians to whom
this letter was originally addressed, and our faith today is the same
faith. It is laid hold of "in the righteousness of our God and Savior Jesus
Christ" (v. 1). That is, faith is the gift of God. It is the righteousness of
God, "not of blood nor of the will of the flesh nor of the will of man, but
of God" (John 1:13), that brings those who receive him as Lord and
believe in him as Savior into right relationship with him and with
others.

Righteousness here is the fair and totally impartial justice of God in
all his dealings. It is the ethical dependability and righteous activity of
God. It represents his just and right way of providing for us and of dealing with us. With the exception of Thomas' cry, "My Lord and my
God" (John 20:18), when he saw the resurrected Christ, this is the only
place in the New Testament where Jesus is directly and specifically
called God, even though the thrust of the entire New Testament affirms the deity of the Lord Jesus.

The actual greeting is, "May grace and peace be multiplied to you in
the knowledge of God and of Jesus our Lord" (v. 2). Grace and peace
are wonderfully present in the believer's life at conversion. These qualities are *multiplied* in the ongoing Christian life, however, so that what
began as a marvelous spring is enlarged in the course of the Christian's
life until, like a mighty river, it is at last ready to empty into the ocean
of God's eternity. God's way of blessing his people is not the way of
simple addition but of multiplication. *Grace* has been called the greatest word in the Christian vocabulary. It is almost a synonym for Christianity. It is a word for love and mercy and kindness, a word which was
uniquely filled full by Jesus Christ. Grace is here called down from
heaven to be multiplied and fulfilled in the lives of God's people.

Peace is a natural outgrowth of grace. As God's people today have no
greater word than *grace,* so God's people in Old Testament times had
no greater word than *peace.* That intense concern of Israel for peace did
not cease with the coming of the Messiah. Jesus did not come to destroy
the law but to fulfill it. The ancient concern for peace was not only not
destroyed by his coming but was in fact marvelously fulfilled and multiplied through Jesus Christ.

Grace and peace are multiplied for believers "in the knowledge" (v. 2) of the Lord. That "knowledge" is not knowledge of the facts of Christianity. It is, rather, the Christian's full, complete, experiential, and continuing encounter with God. It is knowing God. It involves appropriation of the grace and truth of God and total submission to the will and purpose of God. This knowledge is not abstract perception of data. It is concrete discernment of God in Christ. Such knowledge represents experience that is deeper and more profound than that which human intelligence alone could ever achieve.

Counsel on Living the Christian Life
1:3-21

Sources and Resources of the Christian Life (1:3-4)

God's "divine power" is the source of the Christian's "life and godliness" (v. 3). Both eternal life and practical godliness in daily life are laid hold of by believers "through the knowledge of him who called us to his own glory and excellence" (v. 3). There is some evidence that 2 Peter was written in part to combat the heresy of gnosticism. The Gnostics defied God, denied Christ, and divided the spiritual from the physical so radically that they actually taught that salvation was totally spiritual without any application to, or concern for, the physical life. Gnostics believed that since only spiritual things are important, people were free to do whatever they pleased with their bodies and their appetites since God has no interest in physical things anyway. The Gnostics got their name from the Greek word for knowledge, and their central doctrine was that salvation came through knowledge which delivered them from the clutches of matter.

Against such a perverted perception of knowledge, Christians must realize that they are given true salvation through true knowledge, "the knowledge of him who called us to his own glory and excellence" (v. 3). God has granted the faithful "precious and very great promises, that through these" we "may escape from the corruption that is in the world because of passion, and become partakers of the divine nature" (v. 4). To partake of the divine nature is not to escape from the world but, through Christ, to experience salvation as the door to authentic humanity.

A Call to Diligence in Moral and Spiritual Development (1:5-11)

The best known passage in 2 Peter is found here. "For this very reason make every effort to supplement your faith with virtue, and virtue with knowledge, and knowledge with self-control, and self-control with steadfastness, and steadfastness with godliness, and godliness with brotherly affection, and brotherly affection with love" (vv. 5-7). Because Christians have become "partakers of the divine nature," we are, "for this very reason" to "make every effort" to equip ourselves adequately, even lavishly, so as to climb this ladder of moral achievement.

It did not seem right to the writer of this letter, or to the Holy Spirit who moved him, that the Greek Stoics alone should be concerned about moral development. Christians, of all people, should give attention to moral progress and not just settle for a thrilling conversion which would then trail off into a lifetime of spiritual lukewarmness, ethical neutrality, and moral stagnation.

"Faith" is the first rung of the ladder. By faith we begin the rewarding but demanding ascent of the Christian life. The faith here referred to is saving faith in God laid hold of through personal repentance for sin and personal commitment to Jesus Christ as Lord. The most debilitating sin of most modern Christians is the failure to exert our wills and expend our energies so as to "supplement" or add to our saving faith.

"Virtue" is the second rung on the ladder. Faith leads directly to it. The basic meaning of virtue is moral excellence, although it may also have reference to work, vigor, energy, and endurance in the attainment of moral excellence. The word here translated as "virtue" is sometimes translated as courage, excellence, goodness, resolution, or fortitude. This virtue is the firm resolve to shun corruption and to embrace righteousness. When the leap of faith has been made, then the next step to virtue comes, if not easily, then at least appropriately.

"Knowledge" is the third rung on this ladder of moral achievement. It is not the accumulation of facts but the gaining of practical understanding. The reference is not to data memorized but to wisdom apprehended. It is the personal perception that Jesus Christ is the way, the truth, and the life and that anyone who comes to him will find the way, know the truth, and have everlasting life.

"Self-control," the fourth rung on the ladder, is mastery of appetite, mastery of impulse, mastery of temper, mastery of self. It is responsible constraint as opposed to irresponsible passion. It is the harnessing of your ego as opposed to letting yourself go. "Get hold of yourself," we say to someone whose emotions have flown out of control. This self-control is keeping control of your self in daily life so that you are master rather than servant of your whims, appetites, and drives.

"Steadfastness" is the fifth rung on the ladder, and it refers to the calm, determined, resolute, unflinching resolve to go with God. The Christian goes with God not only into eternity but also into all the challenges and opportunities of daily life. Steadfastness speaks of endurance, perseverance, and courageous patience. It is not passive but active. It is not blind resignation to the fates and the confluence of the stars that might be thought to affect life. It is rather the brave and hopeful certainty that all things are working together for good for those who love God and are called according to his purpose (see Rom. 8:28).

"Godliness" is the sixth rung on the ladder of moral achievement. It is the quality of being like God in daily life. It is genuine piety. Such godliness is not other-worldly. It takes its cue from Jesus Christ, God come to earth in human form. It is incarnational. It is being involved redemptively in the world. It is being helpful. It is loving and lifting and serving. This godliness is looking up to God in heaven and therefore caring about what is going on among people on earth. When a person has met God in the great experience of grace called conversion, the normal result is not godless withdrawal from the world but godly involvement in meeting the needs of the human family in the world around us. That practical involvement is true godliness.

"Brotherly affection," the seventh rung on the ladder, is a word that has been transliterated, literally carried over letter by letter from Greek to English to make our word, "Philadelphia." It means love of the brothers and sisters, in Christ. It calls for kindness within the Christian family. The experience of grace does not draw Christians out of the world. Instead, it thrusts us into a life of involvement and sacrificial crossbearing. "We know that we have passed out of death into life," John said, "because we love the brethren" (1 John 3:14).

"Love" is the top rung of the ladder of moral achievement. It is the greatest of the ethical qualities for which Christians are to strive. It is self-giving for the good of others. It goes beyond the Christian brotherhood to embrace all of humanity. Love is faith's finished product. Since "God is love" (1 John 4:16) and Christians are to "be like him" (1 John 3:2), we can never pause in the upward climb until we have supplemented our faith with virtue, our virtue with knowledge, our knowledge with self-control, our self-control with steadfastness, our steadfastness with godliness, our godliness with brotherly affection, and our brotherly affection with love.

This is a hard but immensely rewarding climb, "For if these things are yours and abound, they keep you from being ineffective or unfruitful in the knowledge of our Lord Jesus Christ" (v. 8). Moreover, any believer who neglects to climb this ladder of moral achievement "is blind and shortsighted and has forgotten that he was cleansed from his old sins" (v. 9). To avoid such a shameful and tragic circumstance, Christians are to "be the more zealous to confirm your call and election, for if you do this you will never fall" (v. 10). The basic teaching here is not that Christians can fall from grace but that Christians must not lag in the faith and fail to be zealous in giving attention to the development of their Christian lives. God's call and election are confirmed by the believer's continuing commitment and growth. That commitment is to Christ, and that growth is development both in grace and the knowledge of Christ and in progress up the ladder of moral achievement. "If you do this you will never fail" (v. 10) is assurance for the faithful. If, at the same time, it is a warning against backsliding, then that warning ought to be carefully heeded.

The assurance of God's great provision is then offered, "so there will be richly provided for you an entrance into the eternal kingdom of our Lord and Savior Jesus Christ" (v. 11).

Authority for the Counsel Given (1:12-21)

The writer then declared, "I intend always to remind you of these things" (v. 12). The recipients of the letter already knew those things, even as Christians today have a basic knowledge of them. Nevertheless they needed reminding, and we need reminding. It is our nature to forget. Yesterday's experience of grace tends to be obscured by today's confrontations with evil and temptations to sin. Our knowledge of the truth of God in Christ and of his requirements of us with regard to development in the morally responsible Christian life have "established" us or made us stable. Still, it is right for us to be aroused "by way of reminder" (v. 13) from this divinely inspired writer who was convinced when he wrote that his own death was near at hand (v. 14). By saying that he would "see to it that after" his "departure" they might be able at any time "to recall these things" (v. 15), the writer seems to have meant to share with his readers his intention that this letter should continue to be generally circulated. It was to become known as one of the New Testament's general epistles.

By identifying himself as one of those who "were eyewitnesses of his majesty," the writer emphasized his special right to be heard when he declared "the power and coming of our Lord Jesus Christ" (v. 16). In the realm of religion, "cleverly devised myths" were the stock-in-trade of the ancient world. The apostles and disciples and early missionaries allowed no such falsehoods or imaginative embroidering of the truth but were steadfast in testifying to what their eyes had seen, their ears had heard, their hands had touched, and their hearts had felt.

Calling to mind the dramatic experience of Jesus' transfiguration when God the Father, "the Majestic Glory," had affirmed Jesus by saying, "This is my beloved Son, with whom I am well pleased" (vv. 17-18; Matt. 17:1-8; Mark 9:2-8; Luke 9:28-36), the writer declared that "we have the prophetic word made more sure" (v. 19). This means that the ancient prophecies of Christ's coming were sure when they were first uttered, and it means that those prophecies, in the light of Jesus' power and glory experienced in his actual coming, were even more certain than the prophets of old had any way of knowing. On the high mountain the transfiguration of Jesus had been witnessed and the affirmation of the Father had been heard by Peter and James and John. Concerning this affirmation of Jesus as the Son of God, the writer said, "You will do well to pay attention to this as to a lamp shining in a dark place, until the day dawns and the morning star rises in your hearts" (v. 19). The affirmation that Jesus Christ is God's beloved Son whom all the world is to hear, to trust, to love, and to obey is an affirmation that drives away darkness and ushers in light whenever and wherever it is accepted.

"No prophecy of scripture" (v. 20) is to be interpreted according to private whims. Rather, every such prophecy is to be accepted faithfully, studied carefully, and interpreted responsibly because those prophetic writers "moved by the Holy Spirit spoke from God" (v. 21). As they spoke from God to their own day and generation, so the Holy Spirit uses

the Bible to show God's will and clarify his way for our own day and
generation.

Warnings Against Deceivers
(2:1-22)

The Agenda of the False Teachers (2:1-3)

Christianity has never been free from false teachers and false teachings. The false prophets of Old Testament times found their successors
in the false teachers of New Testament times. These deceivers did not
operate from some great distance but were said actually to be "among
you" (v. 1). Not working openly but "secretly" to "bring in destructive
heresies," they denied "the Master who bought them" (v. 1). That
denial may have consisted of clever arguments against the true deity of
Christ or persuasive contention against the true humanity of Christ.
Both heresies sprang quickly to life among the early Christians. The
Arians denied that Jesus was God, and the Gnostics denied that he was
man. Their modern counterparts are alive and active among Christians
today, working tirelessly to confound the faith, confuse the faithful,
and comfort the faithless. Their denial of the Master, however, was not
as likely to have been communicated through intellectual arguments
against the deity or the humanity of Jesus Christ as through lives and
teachings that denied Jesus Christ as Lord. By confessing Christ with
their mouths while denying him with their daily lives, they would have
pushed the most damnable and destructive of all heresies. Such false
professors of the faith bring "upon themselves swift destruction" (v. 1).
God is sovereign and perfectly capable of personally pouring out his
wrath of judgment on evildoers. He never judges capriciously or arbitrarily, however. The destruction which was said to be coming was
something they were bringing on themselves. Sin invites devastation.
Sin earns death. The false teaching that the Master can be honored with
our mouths while being denied with our lives is teaching that guarantees ruin.

"Many will follow their licentiousness" (v. 2), it is said. That is, many
will be enticed into their blatant immoralities. The denial of Christ

leads to immorality. Both sins have a common source in the rejection of God's will. Doctrinal heresy and sexual promiscuity often go together, for where lust and sensuality abound it is clear that Christ has already been driven out.

Because of the false teachers who deny the Master and practice sexual corruption and depravity, "the way of truth" is "reviled" (v. 2). Followers of Christ are especially called to walk in "the way of truth." Since Jesus is "the way, the truth, and the life" (John 14:6), denial of him leads to denial of his way of truth and his way of moral uprightness. Blasphemous thoughts lead to blasphemous actions and, as a consequence, Christian witness is shamefully compromised and Christian witnesses are sadly ineffective.

It is in a spirit of self-serving "greed" that these false teachers move in to "exploit" the weak (v. 3). These exploiters are deceivers, not disciples; they are money-grubbers, not ministers; they are peddlers, not prophets; they are seducers, not supporters. Using "false words" they lure the unwary away from the Lord and into lust. There is enormous power in words. Words can be used to bless or to curse. They can be employed to serve God or to support greed. Christians today are able to transmit words almost instantaneously around the world, and it is more important than ever before that we speak God's truth in love, share the truth of the gospel with all people everywhere, and avoid using "false words" in any shape, form, or fashion.

Yet, "from of old their condemnation has not been idle, and their destruction has not been asleep" (v. 3). This is a way of saying that the doom of the false teachers is sure. God is not asleep. They will not escape the hound of heaven. The mills of God grind slowly, but they are grinding all the time. "The wages of sin is death" (Rom. 6:23, KJV). You reap what you sow. As false prophets of old sealed their doom with unbelief and unbridled profligacy, so these today sow for themselves sure condemnation. It is not a pretty picture. It is nevertheless a picture that humanity must everlastingly have set before us in clear perspective. God will not, he cannot, treat error and truth as if they were the same. He will not, he cannot, deal with evil and good as if there were no difference between them. He will not, he cannot, deal with the unrighteous and the righteous as if they were indistinguishable. God knows. God sees. God will judge.

The Destiny of the Disobedient (2:4-10a)

The next passage in this letter is a section of powerful illustrations showing how God's judgment is earned by disobedience. The passage begins with the words, "For if God did not spare . . . " (v. 4) and ends with the words, "Then the Lord knows how . . . " (v. 9). Since God's judgment has worked inexorably in the past, it is certain that it will continue to work inexorably in the future. This whole paragraph is one long and complex sentence which should be read and studied as a single unit. It deals with the destiny of the disobedient as illustrated in the Fall, the Flood, and the Fire.

The first illustration has to do with the fallen angels (v. 4). In spite of the false teachers who were apparently uncontrolled, unchecked, and unjudged, the sobering reminder is given that "God did not spare the angels when they sinned, but cast them into hell and committed them to pits of nether gloom to be kept until the judgment" (v. 4). In this reference, in Jude 6, and in Revelation 12:7-12 there is indication that rebellious angels long ago had been cast out of their special place of special service to God. Even though they were angels, their disobedience earned God's disapproval. Therefore he "did not spare" (v. 4) them. Instead, he "cast them into hell" (v. 4). The word for hell here is not the Old Testament word for the unseen state of the dead nor its New Testament equivalent used most frequently for the unseen world of death. Nor is it the other New Testament word which took its name from the Valley of Hinnom where Jerusalem's refuse was constantly burning. In this passage, "hell" is a translation of the place in Greek mythology, Tartarus, where the wicked dead were thought to be cast down, in contrast to the Elysian Fields where the virtuous dead were thought to dwell. When it is said that these rebellious angels were "committed to pits of nether gloom" (v. 4), the picture is one of banishment to abysmal darkness where they must "be kept until the judgment" (v. 4). The disobedient earn such a fate.

The second illustration has to do with the Flood (v. 5). Once again the reminder is given that today's false teachers must not imagine that their sins are undetected in view of the fact that God "did not spare the ancient world . . . when he brought a flood upon the world of the ungodly" (v. 5). That was a great and awful judgment. Its prominence and familiarity were especially powerful instruments in communicating the certainty of God's wrath against evil. The first illustration about the fallen angels spoke of judgment that was being partly reserved until the end of time, but this one speaks of God's judgment that was poured out in time on the occasion of profound provocation by people who had rebelled against God and who would not hear God's call through Noah to repent and be saved.

Even in this illustration of God's judgment, however, his grace is interjected. It is said that God "preserved Noah, a herald of righteousness, with seven other persons" (v. 5). Without the interjection of God's grace, no one could stand. Without God's mercy, none could escape destruction. God's grace, however, does not indiscriminately preserve the willing and the unwilling. Noah was a righteous man, submissive to God's will and obedient to his voice. Noah believed God. His wife and their three sons and their wives trusted their lives to the ark of God's design. Genesis 6:8-9 says that Noah found grace in the eyes of the Lord and that he was a just man who walked with God. The author of Hebrews called him a man of faith (Heb. 11:7). The King James Version has Peter calling him a "preacher of righteousness" (v. 5). This translation refers to him as "a herald of righteousness" (v. 5). Noah's commitment to righteousness was a commitment to the right ways of God, ways of truth, justice, integrity, and love. If the ancient world, called to repentance by Noah, had been willing to turn from their wicked ways, then God would have gladly heard from heaven, forgiven their sins, spared their lives, and healed their land (2 Chron. 7:14). Instead, those "ungodly" people perished as the unrighteous and unrepentant false teachers of the early Christian era, and of all eras, are bound to perish.

The third illustration in this passage deals with Sodom and Gomorrah. Readers are reminded that God "by turning the cities of Sodom and Gomorrah to ashes . . . condemned them to extinction and made them an example to those who were to be ungodly" (v. 6). It is a fearful and terrible thing for rebellious and unrepentant sinners to fall into the hands of the living God (see Heb. 10:31). Modern Christians who have sought to remove the judgment of the Almighty from his redemptive love have done sinners no favor. Only when sinners come to God in repentance and faith with a commitment to obedient discipleship will his judgment be escaped. God "rescued righteous Lot" (v. 7), we are told. It was an act of grace. That just man was "greatly distressed by the licentiousness of the wicked" and "was vexed in his righteous soul day after day with their lawless deeds" (v. 8). Lot's comparative decency caused him to feel great consternation, torment, and even torture in the presence of their abominable immorality. Even today that abomination derives its name, sodomy, from the name of one of those wicked cities. Perhaps there is no better way to avoid sin than to be always sensitive to it, always shocked by it. If Christians ever become comfortable in its presence, we would be in grave danger of accepting it in others and of embracing it for ourselves.

Since God cast out the rebellious angels, destroyed the unbelievers in the Flood while delivering Noah in the ark, and condemned Sodom and Gomorrah to extinction while providing Lot with deliverance, "then the Lord knows how to rescue the godly from trial" today "and to keep the unrighteous under punishment until the day of judgment" (v. 9).

Singled out for special punishment at the judgment will be "those who indulge in the lust of defiling passion and despise authority" (v. 10). The former are lewd, and the latter are lawless. The former engage in sordid sexual abuses and wallow in foul sexual perversions, while the latter engage in lawless conduct and rebel against God-ordained authority. The former fancy themselves above moral rules as they hanker for corruption, while the latter imagine themselves above any authority, human or divine, and do whatever is right in their own eyes. Their destiny is destruction.

Characteristics of These Deceivers (2:10*b*-22)

The false teachers are denounced in this passage in such scathing, scalding terms as are seldom found elsewhere in the Bible. These malicious heretics are "bold and wilful" (v. 20*b*), brazen and self-willed, presumptuously arrogant and determined to have their own way, daring and not hesitant to scoff and to scorn. "They are not afraid to revile the glorious ones" (v. 10*b*); that is, they impudently blaspheme the unseen powers and audaciously defame the dignitaries. It is not possible to be certain whether the reference here is to "the glorious ones" in heaven or on earth. The reference actually could encompass both. Even the "angels, though greater in might and power, do not pronounce a reviling judgment upon them before the Lord" (v. 11) since God alone is judge. These deceivers, however, are "like irrational animals, creatures of instinct, born to be caught and killed, reviling in matters of which they are ignorant" and "will be destroyed" (v. 12). The King James Version says here that these who speak evil of the things they do not understand "shall utterly perish in their own corruption" (v.

12). They must expect to receive the reward of their own unrighteousness, "suffering wrong for their wrongdoing" (v. 13).

The letter moves forward now with a further characterization of the ravening wolves who have been bloodthirstily at work among the flock of God. "They count it pleasure to revel in the daytime" (v. 13). That is, they live day and night for luxury and sensuality. "They are blots and blemishes" (v. 13) besmirching the name of the church and compromising the witness of the people of God. They revel "in their dissipation, carousing" not just among themselves, but, unfortunately, with the Christians who ought not to have any dealings at all with these deceivers (v. 13). "They have eyes full of adultery" (v. 14), hungry for sin. They tempt and ensnare "unsteady souls" (v. 14) not adequately rooted in the faith. They "have hearts trained in greed" and are "accursed children" (v. 14). "Forsaking the right way they have gone astray" (v. 15), following the way of Balaam who prophesied falsely for money (Num. 22:5-31) and to whom the dumb ass spoke to restrain him from his madness. These deceivers "are waterless springs and mists driven by a storm" (v. 17). Their punishment will be "the nether gloom of darkness" (v. 17). They entice with "passions of the flesh" (v. 18) those who have only recently been delivered from the perils of paganism. They offer mirages, not real water, to thirsty travelers in the desert of life. They traffic in fine phrases that are actually senseless. They bait their hook with lust (v. 18) and promise freedom while "they themselves are slaves of corruption" (v. 19). These deceivers are unbelieving and immoral, and it is clear that they are the slaves of their own unbelief and the victims of their own immorality.

The last three verses of chapter 2 deal with backsliding. This has been a matter of special interest to the churches throughout Christian history, and it should be of special interest to Christians today. Emphasis on the security of the believer should not result in too little concern for development in the Christian life. Emphasis on obedience and growth in the Christian life should not result in too little emphasis on the security of the believer. It is a tightrope to walk. The counsel contained in this important passage is enlightening. "If, after they have escaped the defilements of the world through the knowledge of our Lord and Savior Jesus Christ, they are again entangled in them and overpowered, the last state has become worse for them than the first" (v. 20). The writer of the letter is not the judge, God is. The "if" here introduces a concessive clause, a statement that tends to concede a point for the sake of argument. The false teachers were free. They were not helpless. The tempted Christians of the early churches were not obliged to yield to temptation. Believers today are free moral agents. The grace of God that brought us to light and life through the gospel can fully and completely keep those who are committed to him.

The emphasis, however, has to be not on just a past knowledge of him and commitment to him. The emphasis must be also on a present knowledge of him and a continuing commitment to him so that entanglement with, and a possible overpowering by, the defilements of this world will be avoided. It would be better not to begin learning about the Christian way than, having begun, to turn back from God's "holy commandment" (v. 21), the faith once for all delivered to the world through Jesus Christ. The reference to the dog's returning to its vomit and the washed sow's returning to the mud wallow are included to show that those who would exercise their precious freedom so as to become again entangled and then overpowered by the defilements of sin would be, in fact, like the dog and the hog, never genuinely changed. Reformation without regeneration is futile.

To know Christ and experience his saving grace so as to begin to walk in "the way of righteousness" (v. 21) is to enter into salvation which has no stopping place. This is a solemn warning about the false teachers who had heard Christian truth and lived for a while in that high knowledge but whose commitment was too shallow to allow God to bring about radical, permanent change in their lives. Christian readers of this passage today may perceive it as the Holy Spirit's pleading for us to maintain never-failing commitment to Christ and his way of righteousness in daily living.

Assurances Related to Christ's Return
3:1-18a

The last chapter of 2 Peter gives some final warnings against the false teachers and provides assurance and encouragement for the faithful. The recipients of the letter are three times called "beloved" in a warmly pastoral tone. The major concern is that believers should not grow impatient and doubtful concerning the second coming, but that all should continue to grow in grace and the knowledge of Christ.

God's Judgment on the Unrighteous and His Deliverance
for the Faithful (3:1-10)

Reminding the readers, "This is now the second letter that I have written to you," Peter wrote that in both letters he was calling them to "remember the predictions of the holy prophets and the commandment of the Lord and Savior through your apostles" (vv. 1-2). They must understand "that scoffers will come in the last days . . . saying, 'Where is the promise of his coming?' " (vv. 3-4). One of the ways the false teachers deliberately sought to undermine the faith was by raising questions about the Lord's return. Rightly understanding that the second coming was imminent, many of the early Christians made the mistake of setting the date as being during their lifetime. For nearly two thousand years, such date setting has exposed some Christians to disappointment, ridicule, and shame. Peter reminded them that God's schedule is much more patiently worked out than ours. In creation (v. 5), in the Flood (v. 6), and in the final judgment (v. 7), God shows that time is not the big thing with him, for with him "one day is a thousand years, and a thousand years as one day" (v. 8).

Yet God is not slack concerning this promise of Christ's return as some might count slackness, "but is forbearing" or patient "toward you, not wishing that any should perish, but that all should reach repentance" (v. 9). If the consummation of history had already taken place, then those alive now who are not yet right with God would have perished in their sins. As it is, there is still time for all who are willing to come to a change of mind and heart and will and life. Here the word *repentance* is practically synonymous with conversion. It is a powerful reminder that faith does not stand apart from repentance, that hope cannot endure without repentance, and that love can have no substance without repentance. This repentance is not just godly sorrow for sin but a profound turning from sin to the Savior. It represents the reorientation of the Christian's whole personality and entire life to Christ and to the righteousness for which he stands.

Have no doubt about it, "the day of the Lord will come like a thief" (v. 10), that is, at a time no one knows, in a way not to be fully comprehended by even the most faithful of Christians. When he comes, "then the heavens will pass away with a loud noise, and the elements will be dissolved with fire, and the earth and the works that are upon it will be burned up" (v. 10).

It is the tendency of Christians to speculate not only about *when* this will happen but about *how* it will happen. Some propose that it will be precipitated by nuclear war. Others imagine that the sun's incredible fire will rage out of control. Still others fear that some celestial body will come hurtling in from outer space to a mighty and cataclysmic collision with the earth. All such speculations are unprofitable. They are positively presumptuous. They miss the point made by Peter, that Christians ought to live "lives of holiness and godliness" (v. 11). In view of approaching judgment, sure and final, Christians ought to be morally and spiritually careful to live daily in holiness and godliness.

Holiness speaks of separation from sin and separation to Christ. Godliness speaks of love and justice, mercy and truth, goodness and light, righteousness and peace, and kindness toward others and sacrifice of self. While Christians are to cultivate practical holiness and godliness in daily life, "according to his promise we wait for new heavens and a new earth in which righteousness dwells" (v. 13). When God has finished clearing out the old, fallen, sinful order, he will provide a new order characterized not by sin but by righteousness. There is no reference here to streets of gold or angels' harps or mansions or celestial choirs. The focus is on righteousness. Righteousness is the main characteristic of God's new order.

Moral and Spiritual Advice Related to the Coming Judgment (3:11-18a)

While waiting for new heavens and a new earth, Christians are not to be lazy or asleep but "zealous to be found by him without spot or blemish, and at peace" (v. 14). While Christians do not and cannot achieve sinless perfection, we are striving zealously to be found by Jesus, when he comes, with purity of life and at peace. That is, we want to present him lives which are clean, living sacrifices, holy and acceptable to him, lives that demonstrate that we are at peace with God, at peace with others, and at peace with ourselves.

"Count the forbearance of our Lord as salvation" (v. 15), Peter said. God is patiently waiting, tenderly calling for all to come to repentance. The delay in his judgment has already enabled us to come to salvation. Moreover, the opportunity of salvation is extended so that Christians may redeem the time in winning others to Christ while it is day, before the night of judgment comes.

The reference in verse 15 to Paul's "speaking of this *as* he does in all his letters" may have meant to call to their minds Paul's concern with God's forbearance and our salvation in such passages as Romans 3:25 and 9:22-24. The observation that "there are some things" in Paul's letters which are "hard to understand, which the ignorant and unstable twist to their own destruction, as they do the other scriptures" (v. 16) could have pointed to a persistent and pervasive problem in the early churches. That problem related to the relationship between law and grace. Christians understood that they were saved by grace and freed from bondage to the law. Some, however, imagined that they were free not only from the Mosaic law but also from God's moral law. These moved quickly into ruinous antinomianism, the denial of all law and the rejection of all authority together with the acceptance of licentiousness and gross immoralities of all kinds. Paul had dealt at length with this problem. Since it was of major concern to Peter in this letter, the reference to Paul's writings would have been readily understood by the original recipients of the letter, even as it is today.

A final warning against being "carried away with the error of lawless men" is issued lest they lose their "own stability" (v. 17). God establishes his people in the faith. They must then maintain everlasting vigilance against false teachers, false doctrines, and false ethics lest they stumble pitifully and fall painfully.

"But grow," Peter concluded, "in the grace and knowledge of our Lord and Savior Jesus Christ" (v. 18a). There is hardly any admonition in the New Testament better known or more widely quoted than this one. Christians are to keep on growing in grace and knowledge of Christ. God's grace and the knowledge of Christ are the roots which support growth into Christian stability and maturity. It is advice by which Christians of every age should live daily.

Conclusion
3:18b

Having finished what he had to say about living the Christian life, rejecting the temptation to follow false teachers, and preparing properly for Christ's return, Peter pronounced a simple, beautiful benediction,

"To him be the glory both now and to the day of eternity. Amen" (v. 18*b*). This powerful affirmation of faith focuses on "our Lord and Savior Jesus Christ" as worthy of glory both now and forever. It is still the shout of triumphant faith for Christians today, and it will be till the day breaks and all the shadows have fled away for God's believing and behaving people.